Praise for "D[...]

"Once again Professor Woods has brought forward the remarkable story of a little-known event in the history of the Mormon migration to its Rocky Mountain "Zion" in the nineteenth century, while at the same time he tells a miraculous story of shipwreck and survival on a remote uninhabited Pacific island. . . . Woods finds documentation from [not only] the survivors themselves but also from the very capable captain in the form of first person narratives. . . . We also learn about the immigrants themselves and what happened to them as well as the legacy of the event from descendants and scholars. It is an amazing true story of faith, struggle, and perseverance in the face of overwhelming odds."

—Riley M. Moffat, senior librarian and head of reference at the Joseph F. Smith Library, Brigham Young University–Hawaii

"Of all the stories of Mormon transoceanic emigration, few are as compelling as that of the *Julia Ann*. Its shortened voyage contains elements of faith, tragedy, and heroics, and both Mormons and non-Mormons alike saw the divine hand of providence in the rescue of the survivors.

"In *Divine Providence*, Fred Woods recounts the unique story of the only vessel carrying Mormon emigrants that did not complete its journey and puts it in the broader context of the LDS concept of gathering, the history of the LDS Church in Australia, and Pacific maritime history. Additionally, Woods provides a new look at the lives of those who were on the *Julia Ann* and a glimpse into the impact that the story of the *Julia Ann* continues to have upon individuals today. As a result, *Divine Providence* is a valuable addition to the historical literature."

—Chad M. Orton, editor, *The Journals of George Q. Cannon: Hawaiian Mission, 1850–1854.*

"Fred Woods has again shown why he is the go-to scholar in regards to Mormon emigration. His new book, *Divine Providence: The Wreck and Rescue of the* Julia Ann, fills a void in regards to early Mormon migration from Australia to Zion. This well-researched, enjoyable book is a must-read for anyone interested in the early history of the LDS

Church in Australia and the trials experienced and lives lived by those who emigrated from Down Under to America."

—**Tom Farmer**, coauthor of *When the Saints Came Marching In: A History of the Latter-day Saints in St. Louis*

"As an Australian convert to the LDS faith in the mid 1960s, I have gained great inspiration from reading of the trials and sacrifices of early Mormon pioneers. In particular, those from Europe who crossed the Atlantic and then the expansive American wilderness to settle the Salt Lake Valley.

"Until fairly recently, I had never heard much of similar voyages of faithful Australian Latter-day Saints who answered the call from a prophet of God and journeyed thousands of miles from the antipodes, across the Pacific, to help establish and strengthen Zion.

"From the very beginning of Fred's book, I was enthralled. I could feel the spirit of gathering and could imagine the excitement of those early pioneers from various parts of Australia who set out for Zion and a new life. I reflected on the faith of these good people, from all strata's of society, who united in the cause of the gathering.

"My own spirit was both uplifted and inspired as I read of some of the miraculous interventions, which are the theme of the book. Even the secular ship's captain and other crew members are quoted as acknowledging that the hand of God intervened on their behalf, on not just one, but on numerous occasions, to assist them on their perilous journey. My special thanks to Dr. Fred Woods who has articulated so powerfully, reflecting the spirit of those early Church pioneers, whom we owe so much."

—**Philip Baker**, Perth, Western Australia, *Meridian Magazine*

"*Divine Providence* captures so well the historical atmosphere in Australia at the time of the early Mormon emigration to America and combines it in such a personal credible way with excerpts from the original accounts of those who were involved in the perilous sea journey. Their convictions and traumatic experiences offer testimony to the far-reaching consequences the indomitable human spirit can have when faith is unwavering. I loved the book. It's an informative and inspirational read."

—**Marie Cray**, Melbourne, Victoria, Australia

DIVINE PROVIDENCE

THE WRECK AND RESCUE OF
— THE *JULIA ANN* —

FRED E. WOODS

CFI
An Imprint of Cedar Fort, Inc.
Springville, Utah

ISBN 13: 978-1-4621-1365-1

Published by CFI, an imprint of Cedar Fort, Inc.
2373 W. 700 S., Springville, UT, 84663
Distributed by Cedar Fort, Inc., www.cedarfort.com

LIBRARY OF CONGRESS CATALOGING-IN-PUBLICATION DATA

Woods, Fred E., author.
Divine providence / Fred E. Woods.
   pages cm
Includes bibliographical references and index.
  ISBN 978-1-4621-1365-1
1. Shipwrecks--Religious aspects--Church of Jesus Christ of Latter-day Saints. 2. Church of Jesus Christ of Latter-day Saints--Australia--History. 3. Mormon Church--Australia--History. 4. Australia--Emigration and immigration. 5. Emigration and immigration--Religious aspects--Church of Jesus Christ of Latter-day Saints. I. Title.
BX8617.A8W66 2014
289.309'034--dc23

                             2013045969

Cover design by Shawnda T. Craig
Cover design © 2014 Lyle Mortimer
Edited and typeset by Jessica Ellingson and Emily Chambers

Printed in the United States of America

10 9 8 7 6 5 4 3 2 1

Contents

ACKNOWLEDGMENTS

THIS COMBINED BOOK AND DOCUMENTARY DVD were made possible through the assistance of a number of individuals and institutions. (See the credits in the documentary, which list those who assisted with making the film possible.) For support of this manuscript, gratitude is expressed to the College of Religious Education at Brigham Young University (BYU) for its services rendered via transcriptions made from oral history interviews transcribed by student employees in the Religious Education Faculty Support Center and research funding for travel. I am also grateful for the competent staff employed at BYU in the L. Tom Perry Special Collections, Harold B. Lee Library; BYU Family History Library; the Church History Library of The Church of Jesus Christ of Latter-day Saints (Salt Lake City); the Utah State Historical Society; the Daughters of the Utah Pioneers (Salt Lake City); LDS Family History Library (Salt Lake City); Beaver DUP Museum; Bergen County Historical Society (New Jersey); the Mitchell Library as well as the Australian National Maritime Museum (ANMM), both based in Sydney, Australia; and the Library of Congress.

Within these institutions, special thanks are extended to Patty Smith, director of the Religious Education Faculty Support Center, and Sarah Porter, one of Smith's staff, for assistance with the bibliography and index. Gratitude is also expressed to William W. Slaughter and Anya Bybee for their help with images; Brittany A. Chapman for research assistance (CHL); Mark Jackson for providing a map showing the route of the *Julia Ann* (BYU); Russ Taylor and staff for expediting research materials (BYU Special Collections); and Kieran Hosty, ANMM curator, for his bibliographic research suggestions and aid with images.

Thanks also to Glade Nelson and Shauna Johnson, descendants of *Julia Ann* passengers, who provided valuable assistance with research for the biographical register. I also want to extend heartfelt gratitude to my competent and reliable research assistant, Olivia Tess Swenson, for her significant contribution in producing this work, as well as the editorial expertise of Don Norton, emeritus BYU professor of the Department of Linguistics and English Language. Thanks also to Emily Chambers and Jessica Ellingson for editorial assistance as well as Catherine Christensen for managing the publication of this work on behalf of Cedar Fort Publishing and Media. I wish to thank all the interviewees who gave of their time for the production of this joint work. Gratitude is also expressed to all those who carefully reviewed this manuscript: Riley M. Moffat, former senior librarian at BYU–Hawaii and Mormon Pacific specialist; Chad M. Orton, CHL archivist; John Devitry-Smith, author of *Australian Mormon History*; and especially Paul Hundley, former senior curator at the Australian National Maritime Museum, who shared an abundance of file materials, footage of the underwater expedition, and expertise from many years of studying the *Julia Ann* story.

I am also very thankful to Meg Rasmussen and Frank Pond for providing images and access to the original artifacts and papers of their great-grandfather, Captain Benjamin F. Pond. I am particularly grateful to my friend and colleague Martin L. Andersen, with whom I had the pleasure of coproducing our fourth documentary. We enjoyed several trips to California as well as excursions to Australia and French Polynesia to capture oral history interviews and gather research materials. Martin also carefully read the manuscript and provided useful feedback as well as images used with each of the interviewees. Finally, I express my appreciation for my wife, JoAnna, and our family, who have been a continual support to all my diverse projects at home and abroad.

PREFACE

"They that go down to the sea . . . these see the works of the Lord, and his wonders in the deep. . . . Oh that men would praise the Lord for his goodness, and for his wonderful works to the children of men!"
—Psalm 107:23–24, 31

WELL-KNOWN MORMON HISTORIAN RICHARD L. Bushman has encouraged authors "to write more frankly from their own perspectives."[1] This statement resonates with me, and therefore I felt it best to commence with a personal account of why I wrote this book and from what perspective it is written.

I spent the first two decades of my life living in southern California less than an hour from of the Pacific Ocean. I spent many days of those years riding the waves, listening to their crash on the shoreline, or simply gazing at them, especially as the sun rose in the early morning or disappeared in a glorious sunset. Though I am now landlocked due to my employment at Brigham Young University in Provo, Utah, suffice it to say that the sounds of the sea prompt myriad memories that still beckon me to return to the Pacific.

In my earlier years, I was captivated by the tales of Robinson Crusoe and the Swiss Family Robinson, both of which provided riveting accounts of shipwrecks and survival. When it came time for my dissertation, I decided to write about water miracles in the Hebrew Bible. From this undertaking, I experienced in a deeper manner the words of the Psalmist, who declared, "They that go down to the sea . . . these see the works of the Lord, and his wonders in the deep" (Psalm 107:23–24). Following the completion of my doctoral degree,[2] I began to ask myself the question of why

Mormon historians spent so much time focusing on the pioneer trail to Utah and so little on the "sail before the trail." In other words, I wondered, "Have we missed the boat?"[3]

This question led to my serious study of Mormon maritime migration, which I commenced in 1995. At that time I planned to write a book about the maritime segment of the Mormon immigration to Utah in anticipation of the sesquicentennial commemoration of Brigham Young's vanguard company entering the Salt Lake Valley in 1847—the sail before the trail. However, when I was doing research on the East Coast, I felt I should first compile a database that contained vessel names, passenger lists, and Latter-day Saint (hereafter cited as LDS) immigrant accounts for the years 1840–1890. This research resulted in the Mormon Immigration Index CD-ROM, which was published by The Church of Jesus Christ of Latter-day Saints (hereafter cited as LDS Church) in 2000. This database contained records of over 90,000 passengers on hundreds of voyages, laced with over one thousand first-person accounts. Since that time I have continued my research and expanded the database to include the years 1891–1932, now available online at a website titled "*Mormon Migration*."[4]

The Mormon immigrant accounts I encountered were captivating, but what I found most fascinating were the stories that told of deliverance at sea. It is remarkable that out of thousands of voyages transporting Mormon immigrants across the Atlantic and Pacific oceans between 1840 and 1932, only one wrecked resulting in the loss of human life.[5] This statistic is truly notable. The fateful voyage of the Mormon maritime migrants across the Pacific was steered by the vessel called the *Julia Ann*, which wrecked in 1855. Although the story has been related by several authors in short studies, it has yet to receive a book-length treatment—thus, the reason for this work.[6] Though the work focuses primarily on LDS history—the doctrine of the gathering and Australian converts—there is still significant research presented on all crew members and passengers of varied backgrounds and faiths on the second LDS voyage of the *Julia Ann*.

Divine Providence: The Wreck and Rescue of the Julia Ann builds on the shoulders of those who have gone before and presents a comprehensive narrative of the *Julia Ann* story, weaving together all known primary sources on the topic (which have been preserved with their original spelling, punctuation, and so on). Such sources include Mormon journals and diaries and Church records; Captain Pond's full account of the voyage; and a collage of contemporary newspapers from Australia and America published by the LDS Church and others. Also included is a biographical register on each passenger, crew member, and officer of the *Julia Ann*; some of the original missionaries to Australia and indispensable early converts Down Under; and highlights of interviews and vivid illustrations of people and places to create a portrait of an amazing story.

The book is deliberately designed with a wide scope of historical and doctrinal information and background to supply readers with the proper context and circumstances to best understand this singular event in Mormon maritime history. Chapter one provides a sweeping panorama of the doctrine of the gathering and the establishment of the LDS Church during its first decade (1830–1840). Chapter two presents a historical overview of the first fifteen years of LDS Church history in Australia from the first time that Mormon missionaries entered the country until the embarkation of the *Julia Ann* in 1855. Chapter three offers a look at the first LDS voyage of the *Julia Ann* in 1854, which lays the groundwork for a thorough recounting of the wreck of the *Julia Ann* the following year and the rescue of the passengers and crew members in chapter four. Finally, chapter five examines the aftermath of what happened to the survivors following their rescue and the meaning behind this extraordinary narrative.

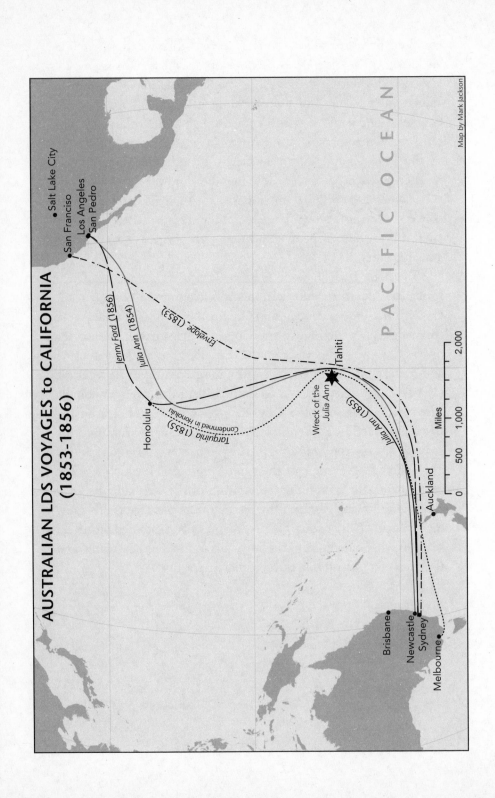

AUSTRALIAN LDS VOYAGES to CALIFORNIA (1853-1856)

Salt Lake City
San Francisco
Los Angeles
San Pedro

Jenny Ford (1856)
Julia Ann (1854)
Envelope (1853)

Honolulu

Tarquinia (1855)
Condemned in Honolulu

Wreck of the
Julia Ann

Tahiti

Julia Ann (1855)

Auckland

Miles

0   500   1,000   2,000

Brisbane
Newcastle
Sydney
Melbourne

PACIFIC OCEAN

Map by Mark Jackson

CHAPTER ONE

The Call to Gather

"Ye are called to bring to pass the gathering of my elect. . . . The decree hath gone forth from the Father that they shall be gathered in unto one place upon the face of this land."
—Doctrine and Covenants 29:7–8

THE CALL TO GATHER TO ZION IS A DOCTRINE that has echoed for millennia from the portals of both heaven and earth. For Jews, Zion was the ancient land of Israel, with its core in the holy city of Jerusalem. For members of The Church of Jesus Christ of Latter-day Saints in the nineteenth century, it was to an American Zion they would go. Latter-day Saints consider themselves descendants of the ancient house of Israel and part of "the literal gathering of Israel."[7] But why the need to physically gather somewhere? Wasn't it enough to travel the crossroads of conversion? Why the call to leave the comforts of one's family and homeland? Why did the ancient Israelites have to leave the fertile soil of Egypt's Goshen and pass through the waters of the Red Sea and the deserts of Sinai? Why did Abraham need to leave Ur and cross over the Mesopotamian midlands to Canaan? Why the ongoing commandment to leave Babylon and come to Zion? We must find the trailhead beyond the plains of man's limited reasoning to determine why this doctrine has been continually emphasized by the Lord's chosen servants throughout the ages and kept in sacred records since the earliest times.

Following the establishment of the LDS Church in 1830, its principles included adherence to the doctrine of the gathering, which resulted in dramatic life changes; many converts made an arduous journey to a new homeland. The many migrant miles traversed by tens of thousands of Mormon converts in the nineteenth century begs the question, Where does the Mormon Trail really begin? One observer queried, "How many branches does it have, and how shall we compute its duration?"[8]

For North American converts in the East, it meant only a trip west to the Mormon gathering places of Kirtland, Ohio; Jackson County, Missouri; or Nauvoo, Illinois, all nestled within the boundaries of Zion's American borders—such journeys did not require an ocean crossing. For many others abroad, there was the "sail before the trail," and the winds did not always blow toward the promised land. It was a voyage of faith, and it meant not only crossing the borders of belief but crossing over into another culture, which required tremendous fortitude and patience in a sea of change.

Kirtland Temple, ca. 1880–1920
George Edward Anderson collection, courtesy of BYU, L. Tom Perry Special Collections

And yet, despite the diverse waves, Saints who traveled via sail and trail knew the purpose of the voyage: to gather as a people and build a temple to the Lord in order to receive special blessings. The Prophet Joseph Smith once asked rhetorically, "What was the object of gathering the Jews, or the people of God in any age of the world?" His answer: "The main object was to build unto the Lord a house whereby He could reveal unto His people the ordinances of His house and the glories of His kingdom, and teach the people the way of salvation."[9]

In the preface to a book of LDS scripture known as the Doctrine and Covenants, reference is made to people who were choosing to follow the ways of the world rather than gathering in righteousness: "They seek not the Lord to establish his righteousness, but every man walketh in his own way, and after the image of his own god, whose image is in the likeness of the world, and whose substance is that of an idol, which waxeth old and shall perish in Babylon, even Babylon the great, which shall fall" (D&C 1:16).[10] The appendix to this same book contains an invitation to flee Babylon and return to Zion: "Go ye out of Babylon; gather ye out from among the nations, from the four winds, from one end of heaven to the other. Send forth the elders of my church unto the nations which are afar off. . . . And behold, and lo, this shall be their cry. . . . Go ye forth unto the land of Zion" (D&C 133:7–9). And again, "Go ye out from among the nations, even from Babylon, from the midst of wickedness, which is spiritual Babylon" (D&C 133:14). This theme of leaving Babylon and gathering to Zion became a prominent subject in LDS scripture during the nineteenth century and is still addressed in modern times, though now with reference to a spiritual condition rather than a physical journey.[11]

Plymouth Dock, 1863
Courtesy of Church History Library (CHL)

A universal call to gather was received by the Prophet Joseph Smith Jr. during the second Church conference of the Latter-day Saints, less than six months after its organization in 1830:

> And ye are called to bring to pass the gathering of mine elect; for mine elect hear my voice and harden not their hearts; wherefore the decree hath gone forth from the Father that they shall be gathered in unto one place upon the face of this land, to prepare their hearts and be prepared in all things against the day when tribulation and desolation are sent forth upon the wicked.[12]

Yet missionary work and gathering were limited to the boundaries of North America during the first decade of the Church's existence; new converts did not need to cross international borders to suffer stiff opposition from those who tried to thwart the work of the Latter-day Saints. The Saints first assembled in the region of upstate New York, where the Church was established in Fayette on April 6, 1830. As the year 1831 dawned, they were instructed to gather to the Kirtland, Ohio, region and were given specific reasons for so doing: "And that ye might escape the power of the enemy, and be gathered unto me a righteous people, without spot and blameless—Wherefore, for this cause I gave unto you the commandment that ye should go to the Ohio; and there I will give my law; and there you shall be endowed with power from on high" (D&C 38:31–32).

From Kirtland, missionary work expanded during the 1830s to various places in the United States and Canada. Converts from pockets of North America were encouraged to gather to Kirtland, where the temple was being constructed during 1833–1836. Once the temple was complete, Church members were inspired by ordinances performed in this sacred edifice. However, social prejudice soon followed, which forced the Saints to leave the Kirtland region. It was not intended that Kirtland be a permanent Mormon gathering place; in the fall of 1831, the Latter-day Saints were told, "I, the Lord, will to retain a stronghold in the land of Kirtland, for the space of five years" (D&C 64:21).

During the decade of the 1830s, some Church members also gathered to western Missouri; in 1831, Joseph Smith told Church members that Jackson County, Missouri, was the heart of Zion. LDS scripture noted that "the place which is now called Independence is the center place; and a spot for the temple is lying westward" (D&C 57:3).[13] Yet the Missouri temple was not built at this time, partly because the Saints were driven out by Jackson County mobs at the close of 1833.[14] Five years later, the Missouri Saints who had generally migrated north to Caldwell and Davies Counties, as well as hundreds of Kirtland Saints who had fled to this region, were exiled from the state of Missouri as a result of the extermination order issued by Governor Lilburn W. Boggs on October 27, 1838.[15]

Therefore, a new gathering place for these displaced Ohio and Missouri Saints was chosen the following year: Nauvoo, Illinois. Here, Saints from Canada and the eastern United States, and soon thousands of British converts from abroad, combined their faith and works to build a beautiful city and temple on a mosquito-infested swampland on the eastern bank of the Mississippi River.[16]

Nauvoo Temple
Courtesy of CHL

The assembling of these foreign Saints from abroad did not commence until the necessary priesthood authority for the gathering of Israel was restored to the earth. The designated time and place for such a restoration occurred April 3, 1836, just one week after the dedication of the Kirtland Temple. In this sacred edifice, LDS scripture records that the ancient prophet Moses appeared and restored to Joseph Smith Jr. and Oliver Cowdery "the keys of the gathering of Israel from the four parts of the earth" (D&C 110:11).[17]

The following year, Joseph Smith charged his trusted associate Apostle Heber C. Kimball with the assignment to open up missionary work in Great Britain. Elder Kimball was joined by fellow Apostle Orson Hyde and five other missionaries.[18] These elders were instructed to teach the message of the restoration of the primitive Church of Jesus Christ and were also warned by Joseph Smith before their departure to "remain silent concerning the gathering . . . until such time as the work [is] fully established, and it should be clearly made manifest by the Spirit to do otherwise."[19]

After a concerted effort by the missionaries in England, the doctrine of Mormonism penetrated the hearts of many English people, and soon several desired baptism. However, this did not come without much opposition. Shortly after plans were made to baptize the first converts in the River Ribble, Elder Heber C. Kimball noted, "By this time the adversary of souls began to rage, and he felt determined to destroy us before we had fully established the kingdom of God in that land, and the next morning I witnessed a scene of satanic power and influence which I shall never forget." Among other things, Elder Kimball also recounted the following:

> I was struck with great force by some invisible power, and fell senseless on the floor. The first thing I recollected was being supported by Elders Hyde and Richards, who were praying for me; Elder Richards having followed Russell up to my room. Elders Hyde and Richards then assisted me to get on the bed, but my agony was so great I could not endure it, and I arose, bowed my knees and prayed. I then arose and sat up on the bed, when a vision was opened to our minds, and we could distinctly see the evil spirits, who foamed and gnashed their teeth at us. We gazed upon them about an hour and a half (by Willard's watch). We were not looking towards the window, but towards the wall. Space appeared before us, and we saw the devils coming in legions, with their leaders, who came within a few feet of us. They came towards us like armies rushing

to battle. They appeared to be men of full stature, possessing every form and feature of men in the flesh, who were angry and desperate; and I shall never forget the vindictive malignity depicted on their countenances as they looked me in the eye; and any attempt to paint the scene which then presented itself, or portray their malice and enmity, would be vain.[20]

Despite the fierce opposition from both the seen and unseen world, during the space of just nine months (July 1837–April 1838), these missionaries obtained over fifteen hundred converts,[21] most of whom eventually immigrated to America. Mission success was augmented less than two years later when other members of the Twelve launched another mission in Great Britain at the dawn of 1840. They came not only to expand the work but also to revive a lethargic spirit that had crept in among some of the British converts.[22] The Mormon Apostles reaped great success in the British Isles, and by the spring of 1840, the Church was firmly established in the land. It was in this season that the Quorum of the Twelve Apostles decided it was time to commence the gathering of the British converts to America. About five thousand heeded the call and journeyed to Nauvoo, Illinois, to build and enjoy the blessings of another temple.[23]

CHAPTER TWO

Early Mormon History in Australia (1840–1855)

While on these distant Isles I roam
To Preach the gospel far from home
It's there I look with wishful eye
To see my wife and family

. . . .

And when I call upon his name
My wife and children to see again
His spirit answer to me is
We shall be satisfied with bliss
—John Murdock [24]

ROM THE TIME THE LDS CHURCH WAS ORGA-
nized (1830) until the end of the nineteenth century (1899),
LDS leaders sent more than twelve thousand full-time missionaries into the field. Historians have specifically noted that
these Church leaders "assigned 6,444 (53 percent) of church
members to evangelize throughout the United States and Canada
and designated 4,798 (40 percent) of the laity to missionize in
Europe, especially in Great Britain and Scandinavia." Historians
also noted that "Mormon authorities sent the remaining 803 (7
percent) elders and sisters to the peoples of the Pacific. In short,
they allocated not even a tithe of their missionaries to the Pacific
world during the nineteenth century."[25] Of this 7 percent, there
were only two known part-time LDS missionaries sent to Australia in the 1840s, and only a dozen other American elders were

called to serve in Australia between 1851 and March 1854, when the *Julia Ann* embarked on its first voyage carrying Australian Saints.[26]

William James Barrett, ca.1880
Courtesy of John Devitry-Smith

During the same year that British converts began to immigrate to America (1840), Elder William James Barratt became the first Mormon missionary sent to Australia.[27] On July 11, 1840, LDS Church Apostle George A. Smith recorded that he had ordained Barratt "to the office of Elder, furnished him with what books I could, and gave him instructions preparatory to his mission to Australia; he was 17 ½ years old."[28] Leaving London in the summer of 1840, the teenage Barratt traveled 16,000 miles and finally disembarked in Adelaide in the late fall of the year. The *History of the Church* officially noted that after a "rough passage" Barratt arrived safely in Adelaide but by spring "had not baptized any persons."[29] On April 9, 1841, he wrote to Alfred Cordon, noting, "I never saw so much Prostitution, Drunkeness and Extortion in England [as] is practised here."[30]

Although it appears Barratt baptized few converts and apparently became uninvolved after a couple of years, evidence reveals that his brief harvest indirectly yielded an increase. One that he reaped who produced good fruit (the only known person he baptized) was Robert Beauchamp, who brought many into the fold and later presided over the Australasian Mission for several years.[31]

Other converts reached Australia a year after Barratt, like the Andersons from Scotland. A Scottish bricklayer, Andrew Anderson and his wife, Elizabeth, were baptized by Elder Orson Pratt in Edinburgh. Pratt ordained Andrew to the office of elder and gave him a license to preach before the Andersons left their homeland for Sydney, where they arrived in the fall of 1841 with their three children. By 1844, Andrew had apparently baptized nearly a dozen people and had organized the very first branch in Australia in the Wellington district.[32] Concerning his missionary labors, Anderson wrote;

> I have gone many miles to preach the gospel, and by so doing pulled down censure upon my own head, for I was told that one of the magistrates of the district of Wellington was to banish me out of this, however, they have never tried as yet. The last two winters I put out hand bills the same as put up in Edinburgh at the first announcing by O. [Orson] Pratt in that city. I preached on the subjects therein contained every Sunday evening; the last winter I preached in the town of Montpelier, where the first night the room was full and some standing out, and most of them Catholics.[33]

John Murdock
Courtesy of CHL

However, it would not be until the decade of the 1850s that official missionaries from Utah would embark from California to be sent Down Under to reap where Barratt and Anderson had sown. The first during this period were John Murdock and Charles Wesley Wandell. Wandell told of the contact made between him and Anderson in the spring of 1852 through a convert named Henry Gale, who had been baptized by Elder Anderson eight years earlier. Anderson, at the time living in the country, wrote the following letter to Wandell (May 17, 1852), who had sent Anderson an invitation to attend an upcoming conference.

> My Dear Brother:—It gives much joy to see from your hand, that you and another of my dear, brethren has come to this wide extended field.
>
> I received your much-welcomed letter on the evening of the 16th; I cannot easily express my feelings when I opened your letter and saw that it was from one I had not seen yet loved on account of the new and everlasting covenant.

I then formed an idea of starting the next day for Sydney and could have wished myself there in the midst of my dear brethren and sisters, but I found this morning that the idea I had forever last wisht, was not in wisdom; because I could not easily get away at present, and besides it might deprive me of attending the conference that is to be held on the 6th day of July, which I would not on any account absent myself. God willing, I will be in Sydney a few days before the 6th of July.

My beloved brethren, I rejoice to see that the Lord has blessed your labors so much: pray for me your weak and unworthy brother, that I may be strengthened and that a way may be prepared that I may soon enter into the field with you; from your loving brother in the gospel. Elder Andrew Anderson.[34]

Charles W. Wandell
"Hero or traitor: a biographical study of Charles Wesley Wandell" by Marjorie Newton

Yet at this time most Australians were not as welcoming as Anderson and seemed quite distant from the peculiar message of American Mormonism, although there were distinct similarities between the two countries. For example, the *San Francisco Whig* in 1852 described a resemblance in the landscape between the American West and Australia: "Vast plains, entirely naked, or presenting an orchard-like prospect of scattered trees— river channels that at one season are washed and worn by impetuous torrents, and at another dry, or basins or stagnant ponds— ranges of grass-covered knolls and lofty hills—a floral profusion— a bright sky and a balmy and health-conservative atmosphere, are characteristic of both."[35]

Beyond the landscape, there was also the more obvious connection between the gold rushes that were going on with great luster in both regions. California was booming with activity in the mid-nineteenth century, and, during the decade of the 1850s alone, more than one-third of the global gold output came from the Australian colony of Victoria. This rush would transform the Australian colonies as gold seekers rushed in. In just two years (1851–1853) the number of newly arrived immigrants was greater than the number of convicts who had been placed on Australian soil during the preceding seventy-year period.[36]

San Francisco Harbor, 1851
Murdock and Wandell left this port for Australia the year this image was taken.
SanFranciscoharbor1851c_sharp.wikipedia

Despite the overwhelming number of new arrivals, rippling effects from the convict era were certainly manifest, and evidence reveals that spiritual conditions "down under," particularly during the decade of the 1850s—the Australian gold-rush period—were a bit challenging; in general, gold became God for many.[37] In a letter to the Mormon leadership recorded in his journal, John Murdock, the first mission president in Australia, noted, "The people in this country are very shy of strangers; for they are jealous of each other, from the circumstances of so many convicts being the first settlers of this country."[38]

Murdock and his companion, Charles Wandell, were the first full-time LDS missionaries to go Australia, as well as the first American missionaries to go to Australia.[39] Just getting to Australia proved a bit challenging for this companionship. Before disembarking at Sydney in late October 1851, they had already endured a lengthy seven-week, eight-thousand-mile voyage across the Pacific, accompanied by passengers who were initially unreceptive to their teachings. In fact, according to Wandell, a group of disgruntled ruffians being sent back to Sydney from San Francisco threatened to hang these two Americans on the yardarm during the early stages of the voyage.[40] Yet Murdock optimistically recalled, "Altho there was much prejudice by the 70 passengers on board against our religion, yet we preached each Sunday on the passage and got friends and assendency over their prejudice."[41]

On Sunday morning, November 2, soon after arriving in Sydney, Murdock went to Hyde Park, popularly known as the "race course,"[42] in an attempt to give a sermon, but the opportunity did not present itself. He returned in the afternoon and requested to preach after a Methodist minister concluded his remarks. Murdock, then nearly sixty years old, notes;

> I then requested the attention of the people a few minutes, they gave it. I informed them who I was, where I came from, and what I had cum fore; that it was to preach the gospel. One man wanted to know, who sent me? I told him the God of Heaven sent me. They agreed the[y] would hear me. I spoke on the first principals of the Gospel a short time. . . . They were attentive, but manifested a great deal of curiosity that so old a man should come so far to preach to them; it was to some of them as novel as if I had come from some other planate.[43]

Recounting the early entrance of Mormonism into Sydney, Wandell further explained;

> On the first Sunday, brother Murdock preached a discourse on the public grounds called the Race-Course. On the next Sunday he preached again at the same place, and I bore testimony. I preached in the evening in a school room. We found it impossible to get at the people, except on Sundays on the Race-course. The people are very shy and suspicious of Strangers, and of one another: . . . a great majority of the male inhabitants have gone to the gold diggings; and those that are left are too much excited by it to think of the true riches of Christ: and it is worthy of remark that those who professed to love Christ the most and lucre the least, were the first

to be off to the diggings for a little gold, which, in the end, will be worth nothing to them.[44]

Yet in some instances the elders' tenacity paid off, and after nine weeks of hard work, Murdock reported in his journal on January 22, 1852, that after he had returned from laboring in two villages nearby Sydney, he had witnessed three baptisms; Brother Wandell, during Murdock's absence, "had baptized ten; and organized a branch of the Church [in Sydney], himself President."[45] About two weeks later, Murdock wrote to the Church leadership about the missionary labors in Australia and requested qualified elders to assist with the vast harvest: "There is labor for many after the way is opened, and it requires experienced hands to do that. Bro. W. and I, would be glad to leave as soon as you can supply the mission. . . . And brethren I wish you would attend to this matter, for bro. Pratt has but little idea of the multitude of inhabitance on these Isles. And they [are] continually increasing from Europe."[46]

Regarding other denominations and religion among the Aussies during this mid-nineteenth-century era, one historian noted, "It was already established that there was no established religion in Australia, and that all were entitled to worship as they chose. This was in part a recognition of ethnic diversity: the overwhelming majority of Catholics were Irish, most Presbyterians Scottish, and they demanded equality of status with the Church of England."[47] Two historians reasoned that such diversity resulted generally in a measure of forbearance:

> In religious matters, distant Australia delivered a relatively large degree of tolerance, if more by muddled uncertainty than deliberate intention. While ardent advocates tried their best to spark disputes between and within denominations, there was little appetite for the importing [of] Britain's battles over establishment and disestablishment. If the baggage of faith was carried to Australia, not all of it was unpacked. Adherents of the Church of England might have hoped for an established church, and British authorities tended to act and speak as if it was, but growing demands for rights of political representation were accompanied by calls for religious toleration.[48]

Notwithstanding, Mormons appear in large part to be one exception to such a tolerant view. For example, John Murdock observed in traveling to proclaim the gospel that he "had no chance to preach, because of the incredulity of the people."[49] Murdock also noted with apparent frustration, "It was with the greatest difficulty I could stay over night . . . and could get no public meeting: for it is verry rair [rare] to attend meeting here only on Sunday, except in the Chapels to read preyrs, and we cannot get there to preach. It is a common thing when I travel in City, Village or country, tho I should talk an hour at the door in the heat of the Sun they would not ask me in."[50]

When they did have a chance to preach, they also faced obstacles as described by Murdock when Wandell tried to speak in a meeting: "But a number of young men, stood round the door, to oppose and accuse bro Wandell of lieing [and] a multitude of boys were in the street pleying, hollowing, yelling, squalling, and one at the door whistling, and they disturbed the meeting all they could."[51]

Concerning the continual antagonism, Wandell explained that there was "a constant influx of Australio-Californians, who are sure to be more or less prejudiced against us by California newspaper stories; and those who are professors of religion are the ones that take the utmost pains to influence the people against us."[52] Less than two years later, it was noted by the Australian Saints that the local clergy was particularly responsible for stirring up the most opposition against them: "In Sydney the bitterness of their feeling is peculiarly manifested in their counsel to their flock, whose fleece they are in fear of losing. Tracts are circulated mis-representing the principles of truth; visitors go abroad impunging the moral standing of the Saints. Priests rise up and lecture against the revelations of God."[53] It was later observed by another LDS missionary in Australia, "Mostly in entering new places, there is great opposition manifested."[54]

In spite of such resistance, the Mormon missionaries found ways to get the word out, and sometimes the word got out regardless. Therefore, Wandell wrote articles in defense of Mormonism that were later published by the Australian press.[55] In reporting missionary work from Down Under to the First Presidency,

Wandell noted, "The work continues to increase in interest, and our congregations are large and attentive. The press and the pulpit are actively engaged against us . . . but they only assist in spreading the work, by bringing it into notice. We complacently smile at their holy anger, and their mad efforts recoil upon themselves."[56]

Though costly, printed LDS literature proved to be an effective tool with a positive impact on spreading Mormonism through such a vast country, equal to the size of the continental United States.[57] Geoffrey Blainey, in his catalytic work *The Tyranny of Distance: How Distance Shaped Australia's History*, observed that "distance is as characteristic of Australia as mountains are of Switzerland."[58] The effort required to harvest was great, and the laborers were few. Augustus Farnham, who followed Wandell as mission president of the Australasian Mission, wrote, "We want Elders . . . of good physical strength; for it is hard to travel in this land. To preach and travel here, soon wears a man out. The cause of so much travelling being necessary is, that the settlements are scattered. . . . It costs on an average about £3 per day to visit the different Conferences."[59]

The following comment by Josiah W. Fleming about the scarcity of men in Australia also echoed a reverberation that would last the duration of the nineteenth century: "If we had a few more good, faithful Elders in this land, they would make many a poor honest heart rejoice, for we cannot supply half the calls."[60]

Though the first American missionaries may not have fully recognized this fact when first arriving in Sydney, Elder Murdock felt it wise to print a proclamation penned by Elder Parley P. Pratt of the Quorum of the Twelve Apostles, who supervised the entire Pacific region.[61] Soon thereafter, Murdock evidences that he was also using Elder Pratt's

Parley P. Pratt, President of the Pacific Mission, and his wife, Belinda ca. 1851
Courtesy of CHL

well-known tract "Voice of Warning," adding, "We had 2000 copies of P. P. Pratt's Proclimation printed for £9. 2000 [copies of] O. [Orson] Pratts remarcable visions £9. [And] 500 pamphlet form of Hymns £6. And now printing 2000, *History of the persecution of the Saints* in America £32. In all £56."[62]

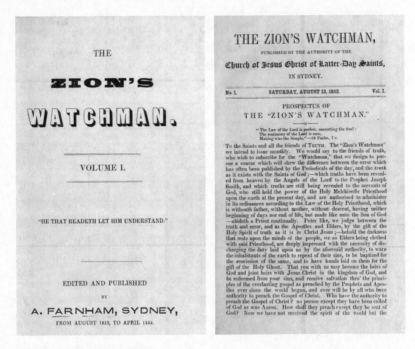

Front Cover of the *Zion's Watchman* (left) and Prospectus to *Zion's Watchman* (right) *Courtesy of BYU Harold B. Lee Library, L. Tom Perry Special Collections*

These tracts proved useful in spreading the word about the Mormons to various regions of Australia. An Australian LDS periodical titled *Zion's Watchman* was used to strengthen local Church members, attract investigators, and defend the Mormon faith. Launched in the late summer of 1853, its presence caught the attention of the British Saints. The English periodical of the Church, published in Liverpool, the *Millennial Star*, noted, "We hail the first tidings from our fellow-watchman of the Antipodes with gladness, and we trust his warnings may be attended to by those who may be located near his tower of observation. We have no doubt that the Saints in Australia rejoice that they have a watchman now in their midst, to tell them of the night."[63]

Zion's Watchman was a monthly periodical published in Sydney by Augustus Farnham and was similar in general content to the *Millennial Star*, though the *Watchman* generally had only eight pages per issue, and the *Star* sixteen. The first edition went to press on August 13, 1853, shortly after Farnham arrived in Australia, and ran somewhat regularly until the second group of American missionaries began to travel home about two years later. Augustus A. Farnham served as the paper's editor while also serving as the president of the mission.[64]

The prospectus of *Zion's Watchman* released the following announcement in its first issue: "To all the Saints and all the friends of truth. . . . We would say to the friends of truth, who wish to subscribe for the 'Watchman,' that we design to pursue a course which will shew the difference between the error which has often been published by the Periodicals of the day, and the *truth* as it exists with the Saints of God."[65] The preface also emphasized the need to defend the LDS faith and calm the apparent troubles with local Australian newspaper firms:

> We would assure the reader, that we did not take upon us the duties and responsibilities of conducting the Watchman, because that we were secularly educated, or practically qualified for the duties of an editor, neither was it to gratify our own personal ambition, but we were actually forced into our present position by the press in these colonies, who were continually inserting articles against the character and doctrines of the saints, and uniformly refused to insert a reply except as an advertisement, for which they charged an exorbitant fee.[66]

This LDS Australian periodical was especially timely: plural marriage had been announced the previous year, and the doctrine of polygamy was bombarded with continuous slander and stood in need of constant defense. After plural marriage became public, the *Sydney Morning Herald* and other Australian papers spread the word, usually in an unfavorable light.[67]

In the earliest issues that followed, the *Watchman* printed a defense of plural marriage: "A Sermon of Plurality of Wives, Delivered in the Tabernacle at Great Salt Lake, August 29th, 1852, at 10:00 a.m., by Orson Pratt, one of the twelve Apostels of the Church of Jesus Christ of Latter-day Saints."[68] In additional issues, a lead article appeared that refuted false claims by a local Sydney Christian newspaper titled "A Reply to the 'Christian Herald' on the Plurality of Wives," immediately followed by an article titled "Celestial Marriage in Deseret," extracted from *The Seer*, authored and published by Elder Orson Pratt.[69] By the end of the following year, evidence suggests that polygamy was still an issue, and the *Watchman* continued to provide ammunition to defend the doctrine.[70]

Salt Lake City Tabernacle, 1855
Courtesy of the Utah State Historical Society

Right before the issue of polygamy became public, Elder John Murdock returned to Utah due to poor health (mid-1852), and Charles Wandell, the only full-time LDS missionary left, carried on the work for another ten months with forty-seven members to shepherd. However, he was assisted by a number of local brethren who served as part-time missionaries.[71] In the early spring of 1853, an additional ten missionaries came to Australia aboard the *Pacific*, and this very ship carried the newspapers that publicly announced the practice of polygamy by the Mormons as reported by the *Sydney Morning Herald*.[72] Coincidentally, Wandell was just leaving Sydney aboard the *Envelope*[73] at the time the new missionaries arrived in port with the news.[74]

Not only did the missionaries have to deal with polygamy in a metropolis such as Sydney, but this doctrine also became a challenge to the elders laboring in rural regions as the word spread to the Australian countryside. For example, Elder Burr Frost, one of the ten missionaries who came from America aboard the *Pacific*, recorded in his journal on November 19, 1853, that he had met a man who "saw something about the celestial marriage and taking a second wife which he felt to reject and us with it."[75] However, fervent testimonies by the missionaries and printed literature in the *Zion's Watchman* and other LDS publications helped to address the issue throughout this period.

Another topic that received frequent attention in the *Watchman* was the doctrine of the gathering. Conversion and the importance of gathering to Zion went hand in hand. New converts were continually encouraged to emigrate to Utah as soon as occasion would permit. In an article penned by a Utah elder who accompanied Frost, the urgency of the gathering to Utah in order to receive sacred ordinances was laid out: "We have many ordinances to attend to which pertain to our own salvation, and also to the salvation of our dead, which we cannot attend to in our scattered condition."[76] Letters from Brigham Young to Australasian Mission president Augustus Farnham were also published to encourage the Saints on the topic of the gathering, telling the Saints to take every opportunity to gather as quickly as possible.[77] In one epistle of Young to Farnham on the gathering, Brigham wrote, "You will . . . organise and regulate matters in the most judicious manner for the continuance of the work; but gather out the Saints and bring them with you as far as you shall be able to do so."[78]

Brigham Young, ca. 1851–1852
Courtesy of CHL

The gathering from Down Under was a different story than the European harvest. Instead of reaping tens of thousands of converts in the mid-nineteenth century, as in Scandinavia and Great

Britain, the Australian soil would yield only hundreds of converts. The difference can be somewhat understood when the number of missionaries per square mile is considered, as well as the demographics; most of the work in Australia was done by about a dozen missionaries covering a vast continent, compared to the thousands with sickles in their hands in far larger cities in the British Isles.[79] Less than 1 percent of the total gleanings from the foreign mission field came from Australia.

Burr Frost
Pioneers and Prominent Men of Utah, 59

Further, Australian Saints were required to travel twice the distance at three times the cost.[80] While there was the doctrine of the gathering, there was also the immediate need to take care of local Church members. They struggled to obtain needed funds to care for their families and prepare for the expensive journey to Zion. The needs of members in the Sydney Branch, near Church headquarters for the Australasian Mission, varied from the needs of members in the gold fields hundreds of miles away. Nevertheless, members from various regions were dedicated to the gospel. For example, soon after Burr Frost arrived in the mission field, he headed for the gold fields to proselytize; less than six months later, Frost organized a small branch in the Bendigo gold fields named the Gold Diggers Branch. He also collected a large sum of gold from the miners who wanted to pay their tithing.[81]

The everyday operations of the Church, as well as a glimpse of the lives of Australian Church members in the Sydney region, are illuminated in the 1854–187 journal of John Perkins, a "college bred man." After reading the Book of Mormon day by day, as well as other LDS literature, John Perkins was baptized in February 1854.[82] Concerning this life-changing event, Perkins wrote, "I felt quite light and revived after coming up out of the water."[83] The following day, when he was confirmed a member of The Church of Jesus Christ of Latter-day Saints and received the gift of the Holy Ghost through the administration of the laying on of hands, he wrote, "While being confirmed today I felt (at the time that the Ministers of God had their Hands on my head[)] . . . as tho there was a stream of fire running through my body. I may thank God['s] Son [for] bringing me into the only true Church on this earth founded as it is on direct revelation from Heaven."[84]

Endowment House, Salt Lake City, used to perform sacred
ordinances before completion of the Salt Lake Temple
Courtesy of Utah State Historical Society

Journal entries reveal that the Australian Saints in the Sydney region, although a small group, held Church meetings several times during the regular work week as well as on Sunday. The first week of Perkins's church membership was very active. Three days after his baptism, Perkins describes gathering in President Farnham's room with a small congregation of Saints for a testimony meeting held on a Wednesday.[85] It was here that he made his first attempt at speaking publicly. The following day (Thursday) Perkins attended what he describes as a "Singing Meeting at the President's Room."[86] On Friday, another singing meeting was held at the President's Room.[87] On Sunday, he noted, "Attended divine service at the rooms in King Street three times today. Very much edified by the several discourses."[88] Such a regular series of meetings continues throughout his journal. Perkins's written record also provides evidence of individual needs being met via visits to local Sydney Branch members in his priesthood capacity of a teacher.[89]

Yet during the nineteenth century, the ministry of the local Saints in Australia was meant to be temporary until they could flee Babylon (the world) and travel permanently to Zion. This counsel to immigrate to America (Zion) as soon as possible was repeated frequently to Church members worldwide by local Australian Church leaders and LDS General Authorities throughout the century. The directive was particularly clear in letters written by President Brigham Young to the Australasian Mission president, Augustus Farnham. In 1853, President Young wrote, "On the subject of the gathering, you are aware that the spirit and word to scattered Israel is, 'come home to the vallies of the mountains, as fast as circumstances will permit.'"[90] Less than two years later, this same counsel came from Young to Farnham again.[91] In the same month the directive was repeated, a sermon appeared in the *Zion's Watchman* stating that the foundation stones had been laid for the Salt Lake Temple, echoing the invitation to "let Zion complete this Temple."[92] This communication no doubt influenced the Australian Saints in their decision to travel to America.

During this same time, the Australasian Mission Presidency issued a second general epistle to the Australian Saints that strongly advocated the critical need to gather to the Salt Lake Valley to receive temple blessings through apostolic authority:

> We would again entreat the saints to use every possible effort in their power to flee the confines of Babylon, ere the way becomes more closed than it is at present; cease to spend your money on that, that neither benefits body or mind, remember that all will be required for securing your temporal, yea, and your eternal salvation, for if you gather not with the saints, and are not administered to in the holy ordinances of the house of God, by those who hold the keys of the Holy Apostleship, and who have power to bind on earth, that which will be bound in heaven, you cannot attain unto the blessing, honour, glory, and exaltation that await such as are thus privileged.
>
> Beloved saints, the very end of this dispensation, which is "the dispensation of the fulness of times," is to "gather [together] in one"

dispensation, all the dispensations ever sent to the earth; to gather in one authority all the keys and powers of the previous dispensation, so that the power and authority of the saints on the earth may be one with power and authority of those behind the veil, for the purpose of accomplishing the design and purpose of God in relation to man and this earth, this design and purpose is, "the restoration of all things spoken by the mouth of all the holy prophets since the world began." It is in this dispensation that the Lord hath said, that, He will bring His saints together unto him; those that have made a covenant with Him by sacrifice, these will be gathered in one on the earth. This dispensation is *preeminently a gathering dispensation.* The peculiar influence of the spirit given in this dispensation is a spirit to gather, therefore none, whatever their profession may be, can enjoy the spirit of the Lord, and possess the blessings of the gospel, who neglect or disregard the important commandment to gather. Then let the saints arouse themselves with deeper interest than ever on this important matter. . . . Prepare to gather with us to a place of safety . . . gather to where the prophet of God is, where his temple is being built, where his angels will minister, where his power will protect and deliver. Gather before the desolating scourges overtake these lands, for the Lord has decreed a consumption of the whole earth.[93]

During the nineteenth century, about half of the Australian converts followed this counsel to gather to Zion; the peak decade for immigration to America was the 1850s, when 62 percent of foreign converts immigrated. Between 1853 and 1859, a total of 440 Australian Latter-day Saints immigrated to California on eight voyages. Of this number, 96 percent had been born in the British Isles and had therefore immigrated to Australia prior to their departure for America.[94]

Immigration to America could have been motivated by secular reasons as well as spiritual ones. Augustus Farnham, writing in the fall of 1854, stated, "The desire to leave the confines of Babylon pervades the mass of the Saints here, and they are striving with all their power to gather."[95] A few months later, as the new year dawned, Farnham again wrote, "The Saints here are generally very anxious to gather out—the extremely high rate of living here, united with the prospect everywhere felt of an approaching commercial crisis, increases that desire."[96]

Farnham's comment about the cost of living suggests that a secondary factor for immigration to America was economic, but his additional mention of leaving Babylon, coupled with an abundance of other LDS first-person immigrant accounts, reveals that the primary motive for both Australian and British converts was spiritual.[97]

In a letter sent from Salt Lake City on October 28, 1853, to LDS convert Captain Thomas C. Stayner[98] written by his children who were recent passengers on the *Envelope*, the first voyage of Australian Mormons to America, we find strong evidence of a spiritual call to a father from his offspring:

> When do you think of leaving Babylon and come to Zion, let the time not be far distant, I feel that if you do not take the first opportunity that offers, you will either not come, or it will be in much sorrow and mourning. I am glad, Tom and Arthur are glad, that we are in Zion, in the city where the Prophet of God dwells, here is manifested the power of God. I feel thankful that we have the privilege of hearing Brigham tell us the mind and will of God, we now cannot feel sorrow that we did not live in the days when the Prophets of old revealed the will of God, no, for we are favoured as much as they were.[99]

Jane C. Robinson Hindley and child
Courtesy of CHL

This spiritual call to gather is also evident in a riveting journal entry by British convert Jane C. Robinson Hindley, who immigrated to Zion the same year the ill-fated *Julia Ann* left the Sydney docks in 1855. It no doubt reflects the views of Australian Latter-day Saints, like the Stayners, who were bound for Utah during this same time period: "I believed in the principle of the gathering and felt it my duty to go although it was a severe trial to me and my feelings to leave my native land and the pleasing associations that I had formed there. But my heart was fixed, I knew in whom I had trusted and with the fire of Israel's God burning in my bosom I forsook my home but not to gather wealth or the perishable things of this world."[100]

CHAPTER THREE

First Mormon Voyage of the Julia Ann and Settlement in San Bernardino

"All nature is in commotion, and the elements seem to have waged war, and to be coming in furious contact. . . . But . . . the Spirit of the Lord . . . seems to say all is well. Fear not, for the lives of all are in my hands, and my people will I preserve." —From the journal of William Hyde

AN ARTICLE IN AN EARLY MARCH 1854 ISSUE OF *Zion's Watchman* announced the upcoming voyage of the *Julia Ann*, a 372-ton bark that measured 119 x 27 x 13 feet and was built in 1851 at Robbinston, Maine.[101] The article stated, "The time is close at hand when another company of saints will leave this land, in the fine new barque *Julia Ann*, Captain Davis. Mr. Bond [Pond], of California, owner of the vessel, will accompany them.[102] They will sail from Newcastle, bound for San Pedro." The article also noted that "the company is under the charge of Elder William Hyde, who during the past year has labored faithfully, diligently, and perseveringly, in the Hunter River district.[103] His labours have been blessed; many have obeyed the Gospel, and are gathering with him. He goes hence with the full confidence and approbation of all true saints."[104] This was the second vessel to sail with a load of Australian Saints to Zion in the nineteenth century.[105]

The previous month, Hyde, one of the ten missionaries who had come to Australia aboard the *Pacific* in the spring of 1853, went to inspect and secure the *Julia Ann*.[106] His journal notes, "February 13th [1854]. I started for Sydney, having with me 400 pounds passage money, which was to secure the vessel.[107] . . . The 15th. Paid £425 on our passage, the amount for each passenger being £24 stirling," which was costly, especially for the poor Saints.[108] Hyde further notes on March 9, after arriving in Newcastle, he "met with Elder Farnham, also the barque '*Julia Ann.*' . . . Took my trunk on board the vessel and took possession of my state room. The 10th. The company was received on board with their luggage, etc."[109] He further notes, "Wednesday, the 22nd, at half past 3 p.m. the vessel having completed her landing, and all things being in readiness, we weighed anchor and set to sea. At 4 p.m. took the last shake of the hand with Elder Farnham and he returned in the pilot boat to Newcastle."[110] Several days later (March 26th), Hyde preached to both Church members and the vessel's leadership. Hyde then records, "The 27th. Made arrangements for a school for the benefit of the children, to be kept on the deck house, under the care of Richard Allen, Jr."[111]

"The *Julia Ann* Entering San Francisco, 1852,"
1999; Oil on canvas by David Thimgan (1955–2003)
Courtesy of ANMM, purchased with USA Bicentennial Gift funds

Zion's Watchman also explained that this company was composed of sixty-three Saints, who were from the Hunter River district and were mostly farmers. They were "respectable . . . possessing firm, good, and obedient spirits." [112] The announcement in the *Watchman* was followed by this charge, which emphasized the need to gather for both spiritual and physical security:

To all the faithful Saints who remain we say, Brethren, as much as you can, prepare to follow in the next company, which will start about twelve months hence. Brethren and sisters, our first duty is to obey the Gospel; then to gather with the saints to the land which, by the counsels of eternity and the power of the Holy Priesthood, has been dedicated for the upbuilding of the kingdom of God in the last days, on which Zion on the sides of the north is to be erected, from whence will proceed the law of the Lord, by which law the saints will have to regulate their lives, in order to attain unto their blessings and privileges. On Zion the glory of the Lord shall rest. His Spirit shall make her sons mighty. Within her precincts shall be safety; and those who will not flee to Zion will have to take up sword against their brother. It is expressly written that in Zion shall be deliverance. We are determined to the utmost of our power to push the saints to Zion. Our counsel to one and all is to flee to the home of the saints before the destroyer is let loose upon this land, for there is a day of darkness, distress, and perplexity awaiting this people. Our prayer is, that the Lord may stay his hand until the honest in heart are gathered out.[113]

Such was the millennial fervor of the times for the gathering, and such was the knowledge of the Saints who were about to embark from Newcastle, about seventy miles northeast of Sydney. For example, in the latter part of March 1854, John Perkins noted, "there [h]as been a company of saints embarked on board the Barque *Julia Ann* lying at Maitland[114] to go to Zion under the guidance of Elder W. Hyde for which purpose he is gone to Maitland. President Farnham is also gone to Maitland . . . to see the Saints of[f]. The vessell is to sail some time this week."[115]

Captain Benjamin F. Pond (L) and Henry Wetherbee (R), owners of the *Julia Ann Courtesy of Meg Rasmussen*

The sendoff of the *Julia Ann* was officially recorded in the Australasian Mission[116] History: "March 22 [1854]. The bargue '*Julia Ann*', Commander Davis, sailed from Newcastle, with a company of Saints (numbering 63 souls) on board, under the direction of

Wm. Hyde. Mr. Pond, the owner of the vessel, was also on board, and the destination of the ship was San Pedro, Cal."[117] Less than two weeks into the voyage Hyde wrote with apparent pleasure;

> The wind is blowing a gale, and the seas are rolling mountains high, and are bursting over the bullwork so that all is rendered disagreeable. . . . All nature is in commotion, and the elements seem to have waged war, and to be coming in furious contact. But as to our barque, thank the Lord, she rides triumphantly along, as it were, over hills and valleys, and each officer is seen at his post, and appears to understand his business. But while the furious wind is whistling through the rigging, and the lightenings are chaining their way through the heavens, and the seas are rolling to mountain heights, all is calm within my bosom, for there is a measure of the Spirit of the Lord there which seems to say all is well. Fear not, for the lives of all are in my hands, and my people will I preserve.[118]

William Hyde
Courtesy of DUP, Salt Lake City

Hyde, an experienced traveler and former member of the Mormon Battalion,[119] presided over the company along with counselors Charles Stapley and Richard Allen. Although overall the company had a favorable passage, there were a few challenges—occasions of seasickness, an outburst of measles, and the passing of a "Sister Allen,"[120] who died soon after giving birth. Along the way, the *Julia Ann* replenished supplies at Huahine (an island northwest of Tahiti), Tahiti, and Honolulu.[121] Throughout the voyage, meetings were held each Sunday and occasionally during the week. Daily prayers were attended with vigilance. Several crew members also became converted en route, including the first mate.[122] The officers and crew were generally kind and respectful to this company of Australian Saints. After a long voyage across the Pacific, the *Julia Ann* landed at San Pedro,

California, on the 12th of June.[123] Apparently the port wasn't much to speak of; one Saint who gathered to San Pedro two years later noted: "Arrived at San Pedro. All in good health. Many of the Saints feel to appreciate their Safe Arrival whilst others owing to the bleak appearance of the Port wished themselves back to Sydney's 'flesh pots.'"[124] However, the firm of Alexander and Banning were on hand as agents to assist the incoming Saints and proved to be gentlemen "in every respect."[125]

Phineas Banning
Courtesy of Friends of Banning Museum

Upon the day of arrival in San Pedro, Hyde provided a report of the voyage to Augustus Farnham, who was still presiding over the Australasian Mission in Sydney. Because of its rich detail, it is provided here in its entirety:

San Pedro Harbor 1850 daguerreotype
Courtesy of Los Angeles Public Library and waterandpower.org

Original Correspondence — San Pedro, June 12th, 1854.

Beloved President Farnham,

I improve the first opportunity of informing you of our passage and safe arrival in this place, on board the barque " *Julia Ann.*"

35

We sailed from Newcastle, as you are aware, on the 22nd of March; the breeze on our setting off was excellent, and for several days our speed was at the rate of ten knots per hour; at first there was considerable sickness among the passengers, as was to be expected; but this, as also the measles, which were with us when we started, soon wore away. On the 29th Sister Allen gave birth to a son, and all got along well. We had then a strong breeze which continued to increase, and by the 5th, 6th and 7th augmented to a gale, and our way was on the mountain wave, but our gallant barque bore us proudly and safely over it. Sister Allen, who had taken a slight cold, was by my advice taken into the cabin, where she was faithfully watched over for a week, when she thought herself able to return to her own room, and was permitted to do so. On the 16th of April we put into Huaniea, an Island of the Society group, about thirty leagues westward of Otahita, our object was to take in a fresh supply of water. The heat of the sun was intense, and had great effect upon Sister Allen. On the 17th, at twelve o'clock, she was found running very low, and so sudden was her relapse, that at sunset her life was despaired off, on the 18th, at nine o'clock, she died, or rather fell asleep, as it appeared to those who were watching over her. She was buried in a respectable manner, at twelve o'clock, the 19th, I delivered a short discourse on the occasion, the scene was truly impressive, and every possible respect was shown by the officers and all on board, as soon as the funeral service was over, we again hoisted sail and put to sea, all in as good spirits as could be expected under existing circumstances. We had preaching every sabbath, and prayers every night and morning, and felt that the Lord was with us. On the 9th of May we came in view of two or three of the Sandwich Islands, and on the 10th were alongside Owhyhee, and sent a boat to the shore for a supply of fresh provisions, while there, I learned that Brothers Cannon and Snider were on the Island, but I had no opportunity of getting any particular news, I left a letter for them, and a few numbers of the "*Zion's Watchman*," after a detention at that place of about twenty-four hours, we again pursued our course to the best advantage the wind would permit. The north-east trades continued up to their highest latitude, at which point we came in contact with adverse winds, which drove us to the north and west, to Latitude 43, Longtitude 164, our place of destination being in Latitude 33, Longtitude 118, after reaching the above named point, the wind turned in our favour, and we again began to near our anxiously wished for port of destination. You will see by dates that the first part of our passage was performed in excellent time, and the last half does not change my views of the sailing qualities of the vessel, as no vessel can make a speedy passage with the winds dead a head, as before stated, our meetings were kept up every sabbath, and generally once or twice during the week, and what is gratifying to me, some three or four who never before heard the gospel, have become fully convinced of its truth, amongst whom is the first mate. The officers generally, have shown us every kindness I could reasonably look for. The saints as a general thing have been quick to listen to my instructions, for which my soul feels to bless them. Sisters Staply and Bryant have lately remarked to me, they were told before leaving Australia, they would not be able to endure the fatigues of the journey, but they could not see but they enjoyed as good health, and were just as happy on the vessel as when at home, and much more so in anticipation of soon bein[g] numbered with the saints in Zion.

Relative to the return of the vessel to Sydney, Mr. Pond is still of opinion, he will perform the trip in seven months from the time we sailed, and should there be a company of saints in readiness, I do not think the chances will be very frequent for finding a vessel on this trade, where the same number of passengers can be accommodated. I have written this on board the vessel, and have no particular news, save such as relates to our voyage, my health has been improving during the entire passage, and if ever a person was truly grateful, I think I am. Mr. Pond will be either the bearer of this, or forward it to you, from San Francisco. The saints all unite with me in love to you, and all those they have left behind; Sisters Lilly and, Geordge who sailed from Sydney, are well. Don't forget my kind regard to all the brethren of the Mission, and may the Lord whose servant you are, bless you and all the saints, with much of his spirit, and with every desirable favour, is the sincerest desire of your ever faithful friend and brother in the cause of truth,

William Hyde.

P.S.—I have just been on shore and find by a letter left for me that Elder C. [Charles] C. Rich has just left here on his way from San Francisco for San Bernadino, that he had got the news in San Francisco of this company's being on the way, and has left directions for our course of proceedings, all of which is truly satisfactory to us. All is well in San Bernadino, heavy crops coming in, saints gathering from the upper country, &c.[126]

According to the Australasian Mission Manuscript History, the following day Hyde left his company at San Pedro and started on the back of a mule for San Bernardino, where he arrived June 14. Two days later, teams were started for San Pedro in order to pick up the incoming converts, and soon they were safely gathered to San Bernardino. Upon arrival, "rooms were immediately rented, in which the Australian emigrants were comfortably quartered and most of them were soon busily engaged in assisting the saints to secure their grain. Soon afterwards Wm. Hyde started for G. S. L. [Great Salt Lake] Valley with the mail company and arrived in Great Salt Lake City, Aug. 14 1854." His company from the *Julia Ann* stayed in San Bernardino and waited for additional instructions.[127]

"Fort San Bernardino," drawing by William R. Hutton, 1852
Reproduced by the Henry E. Huntington Library

San Bernardino, at the southern end of the road from Salt Lake City to Southern California, lay seventy miles from the port of San Pedro, thirty miles closer than San Diego did. Therefore, San Pedro was used by these incoming Australian Saints prior to migrating to San Bernardino.[128] Brigham Young cleverly designated forts and settlements along this specific route. By using these way stations, emigrating Latter-day Saints, passing travelers, and the mail service could find necessary refreshment and security to complete successful journeys. This chain of settlements became known as the Mormon Corridor.[129]

The Mormon Corridor
Map drawn by Kiki Comin

Naturally, Saints who crossed the Atlantic had a longer land route to travel with its own set of inherent dangers. Thanks to international missionary efforts in the early 1850s, Utah-bound foreign converts were pouring into New Orleans and navigating the precarious rivers and overland treks to Salt Lake City. After some time, Brigham determined there were too many spiritual and physical risks inherent to this route. Disembarking at New Orleans presented a serious cholera threat to the European immigrants, and the Missouri River was fraught with apostate and anti-Mormon persons intent on inflicting discouragement and disruption on the pioneers' plans.

Brigham, therefore, announced a new route to help the immigrants avoid "contact with the corrupt apostates and Gentiles that swarm at New Orleans, St. Louis, and Upper Missouri."[130] By 1851, President Young and his counselors issued a general epistle to the Church specifying their intentions for the revised travel:

> It is wisdom for the English Saints to cease emigration by the usual route through the States, and up the Missouri river, and remain where they are till they shall hear from us again, as it is our design to open up a way across the interior of the continent, by Panama,

Tehuantepec, or some of the interior routes, and land them at San Diego, and thus save three thousand miles of inland navigation through a mostly sickly climate and country. The Presidency in Liverpool will open every desirable correspondence in relation to various routes, and rates, and conveniences, from Liverpool to San Diego, and make an early report, so that if possible the necessary preparations may be made for next fall's emigration.[131]

Amasa M. Lyman (left) and Charles C. Rich (right)
Courtesy of CHL

In this same document, Church leaders made members aware of plans for a California settlement that would serve as a receiving station for the Mormon immigrants, be the gateway to the Mormon Corridor, and be "passable during the winter months." Also indicated in the communiqué was the information that Church Apostles Amasa M. Lyman and Charles C. Rich had left Salt Lake City with a company of Saints and 150 wagons "for the purpose of establishing a settlement in the southern part of California, at no great distance from San Diego, and near the Williams' ranche and the Cahone Pass, between which and Iron County we design to establish settlements as speedily as possible . . . to have a continued line of stations and places of refreshment between this point and the Pacific."[132]

After reviewing regional reports drawn up earlier by the

Mormon Battalion and from data collected by Mormon explorer Jefferson Hunt on his southern trips, Lyman and Rich purchased the Rancho del San Bernardino for $77,500. Although short-lived (1851–1857), for the Latter-day Saints this Mormon settlement of thirty-five thousand acres played a key transitional role in Mormon migration by serving "as a port of entry for converts coming from the Pacific missions; as a gathering place for California Mormons generally; and as a rest and supply station for church missionaries going to and from California and Pacific missions."[133]

In the eleventh general epistle from the First Presidency (April 1854), later published for the Australian Saints in *Zion's Watchman*, the following counsel was given: "The Saints in Australia, India, and all countries bordering upon the Pacific, are instructed to gather to California, where they will be directed in their future movements by the Presidency of the Church in that country."[134] If the San Bernardino colony had endured, it probably would have been a long-time gathering spot for these bordering countries, including the Pacific Islander converts.[135]

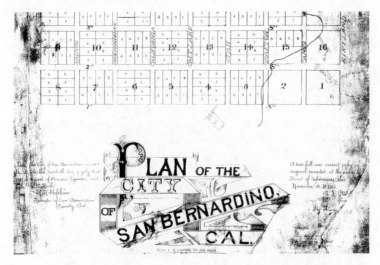

City Plat of San Bernardino (1854)
Courtesy of San Bernardino County Archives

Most of the Pacific converts who made contact with the Mormon settlement at San Bernardino were from Australia. Between 1854 and 1856, several voyages disembarked at San Pedro carrying Australian Saints who temporarily gathered to San Bernardino. Some remained in California while others made their way to the Salt Lake Valley or some other Utah settlement.[136] The San Bernardino colony secured a station for the mail and served as an outpost for goods intended for Salt Lake City coming from Los Angeles, which involved less mileage than routing needed goods via the Missouri River. From San Bernardino in December 1851, Lyman and Rich wrote the following letter to Franklin D. Richards, who oversaw the British Mission, including emigration matters:

> We are situated about one hundred miles from San Diego, seventy miles from the seaport of San Pedro, and fifty miles from Pueblo de los Angelos. Our location here is made in view of forwarding the gathering of the Saints from abroad, and from Europe in particular, by this route, should we be enabled to settle in this country as we wish. You are doubtless . . . apprised of the intentions of the Presidency in relation to this matter, as published in the last General Epistle; and we wish to learn from you, at your earliest convenience, what you may know, or can learn, in relation to the practicability and probable expense of transporting the Saints from Liverpool to San Diego, by any of the present routes across the Isthmus.[137]

MORMON SETTLEMENT IN THE SAN BERNARDINO VALLEY, WITH A VIEW OF THE PEAKS OF SAN BERNARDINO AND SAN GORGONIO.

Drawing titled "Mormon Settlement in the San Bernardino Valley ..." in Lieutenant R. S. Williamson, *Report of Explorations in California and Railroad Routes* Washington D.C.: Corps of Topographical Engineers, 1855, 36

Unfortunately, the change in travel routes would not materialize at this time. The following month, another general epistle explained the obstacles: "By recent communication of President F. D. Richards, of England, we learn that the prospect of immediate emigration of the European brethren to San Diego, as we had anticipated, is in no wise flattering, there being no regular shipping from England to that port; therefore Elder Richards will continue to ship the Saints by way of New Orleans to Kanesville, as hitherto."[138]

James Warby Jr. and Mary Blanch Warby
Courtesy of Bonnie Ames, Dir. of the Beaver DUP Museum,
great-great-granddaughter of James and Mary

There was simply no established shipping route to America's western borders from England. Although probably disappointed, Brigham Young was satisfied that by the mid-nineteenth century, twenty-seven Mormon settlements had been founded along the southern route between Salt Lake and the Pacific, aiding transportation and securing the mail dispatch along the Mormon Corridor.[139] Of all of them, San Bernardino seemed to be of special worth because not only was it at the southern end of the Mormon Corridor, but also its population was second only to Salt Lake City's.[140] In an article published in the *Daily Alta California* titled "The Mormons in San Bernardino," the editor noted that San Bernardino's "population is something more than a thousand, and it promises to increase. In no portion of the State is there a more busy or thriving settlement, or one which, in proportion to number, is working more effectively. . . . Their valley is an exceedingly beautiful place, with great natural advantages."[141] This was a vibrant place where the Australian Saints spent a considerable amount of time: weeks, months, and sometimes even years. For example, the Australian family of James Warby stayed in San Bernardino for two years before migrating to Utah.[142]

Warby felt joyful among the Saints in San Bernardino who laid claim to a portion of Zion's landscape. He wrote home to his family and friends to beckon them to join him:

> Dear Father and Mother,—I feel it a great pleasure to write to you to let you know that we are all well, and in good health at present, for which I feel to thank God.
>
> My Dear Brothers and Sisters I feel somewhat like giving you my testimony to this work, and that is, that Mormonism is true, and that it is the work of the Lord in these last days, and blessed is he that obeyeth it, and lives up to it, and he that doeth it not will be damned, for the Lord has said so, and there is no two ways about it.
>
> I am happy to inform you that I like this country very much; I have been harvesting and have earned as much wheat as will serve us for 12 months, so that we shall not want for bread; I have bought an allotment of one acre in the Township, to build me a house and make a garden.
>
> The produce that is raised here is wheat, barley, maize and loads of garden stuff of all kinds; we are also raising all kinds of fruit, we have a few fruit trees and grape vines of different kinds, this is a very fruitful place.
>
> I never saw one in this place that wished to be back, I would not come back for all New South Wales. My advice to all who wish to serve the Lord in spirit and in truth, is to obey His commandments, and gather with his people before it is too late, for the Lord is about to accomplish His work, that is to gather His people together in one, remember that the Lord has said, that He would gather the wheat into the gardner, and that he would bind the tares in bundles to be burned.
>
> My dear friend cannot you see that the Lord is gathering His people, those who will serve Him from the midst of you, and from all parts of the earth to a place of refuge, whilst the wicked suffer the wrath of an Almighty God.

My dear friends these words are true and faithful, whether you believe them or not, I should like to hear that my father had obeyed the Gospel, if you have not done so, I would beg of you to seek unto the Lord for salvation before it is too late and gather to Zion, wherever it may be, my testimony is that, this is the place that the Lord has appointed for the gathering of his people.

Your affectionate Son, James Warby.[143]

Such letters like Warby's no doubt influenced other Australians to come to Zion.

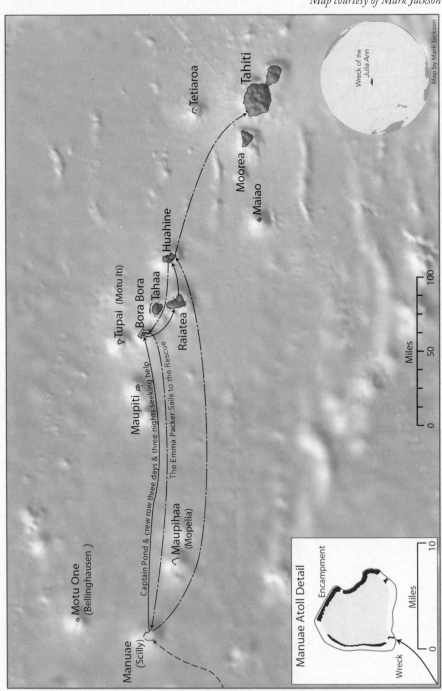

Map by Mark Jackson

Wreck of the
Julia Ann

Tahiti

Tetiaroa

Moorea

Maiao

Huahine

Tahaa

Tupai (Motu Iti)

Bora Bora

Raiatea

Maupiti

Captain Pond & crew row three days & three nights seeking help

The Emma Packer Sails to the Rescue

Maupihaa
(Mopelia)

Motu One
(Bellinghausen)

Manuae
(Scilly)

100

50

Miles

0

Manuae Atoll Detail

Encampment

10

Miles

0

Wreck

CHAPTER FOUR

The Wreck of the Julia Ann and Survival Tactics

"The bell at the wheel, with every surge of the sea, still tolled a knell to the departed, and naught else but the wailings of a bereaved mother broke the stillness of the night."
—Narrative of the Wreck of the Barque "Julia Ann" by Captain Benjamin F. Pond

LESS THAN A MONTH AFTER THE FIRST VOYAGE carrying Australian Latter-day Saints had arrived safely in San Pedro (June 12, 1854), Captain Benjamin F. Pond, the co-owner of the vessel who had traveled with the Saints, wrote a letter to President Augustus Farnham:

> San Francisco, July 7, 1854.
>
> Elder Augustus Farnham,
>
> Dear Sir,
>
> I send by the "Fanny Major" a letter placed in my hands by your friend and brother William Hyde: doubtless he has given you particulars of our voyage, which was a protracted and tedious one. We arrived at Huainea, one of the Society Islands, in 22½ days, the quickest trip on record; but barnacles and grass there gathered on the bottom of the vessel, which affected her speed very materially. We had a succession of head winds for some fifty days. I shall take in a cargo of timber and return at once to Sydney, and should be glad then to make another passenger engagement with you, and do hope that another trip may prove more expiditious and successful than our last. I hope to be with you about 1st of October.
>
> Yours, very respectfully,
>
> B. F. Pond.[144]

47

Captain Benjamin F. Pond holding
a telescope, 1856
Courtesy of Meg Rasmussen

It can thus be ascertained that Captain Pond wanted to begin preparations with President Farnham for another Mormon voyage, over a year before the *Julia Ann* would embark with another cargo of Saints. It is also apparent that Captain Pond was impressed with the Mormon passengers at the time of embarkation on the first passage of the *Julia Ann*. In fact, *Zion's Watchman* reported that Pond, Captain Davis, and the purser had certified "at the time of departure, that they never saw business more correctly and expeditiously transacted, than was the business pertaining to the shipment of that company, and they also stated that they never saw a company who were so easy to be governed, by the voice of one man as that company of Saints were, who, they remarked, were always ready to hear and obey my counsel."[145]

There seems to also be evidence that Pond may have been impressed not only by what he saw on this first LDS voyage aboard the *Julia Ann*, but also by what he heard. William Hyde recorded in his journal just four days after departing Newcastle; "Sunday, 26th [March 1854]. Held meeting on the quarter-deck, Captain and officers present. Spoke on the 1st principles of the gospel, had good liberty. After meeting, the Voice of Warning, Spencers Letters, Book of Mormon, etc., were in good use among the officers and cabin passengers. At night had singing and prayers as usual."[146] The following month, Hyde added, "Sunday, 23rd [April 1854], The passengers and sailors assembled on the quarter deck under an awning erected for the occasion and I addressed them for an hour. Spoke from the 7 and 8 verses of the 26 chapter of Acts. The assembly was very attentive. The Captain and 1st mate are favorably impressed."[147] Though Pond never joined the Church, he seemed to have a good impression of its teachings and members.

Before Pond sailed with the *Julia Ann* again, there was only one other Australian LDS voyage. The *Tarquinia*[148] set sail from Melbourne in the spring of 1855, several months before the *Julia Ann* would leave the Sydney Harbour.

Concerning this voyage, the Victorian newspaper *The* (Melbourne) *Argus* reported in a surprisingly positive tone a letter sent to the editor by an unknown person who used the pseudonym X.Y.Z.:

> The brig *Tarquinia* has been chartered to convey the first lot of them [Mormons] from these shores towards their destination. I believe upwards of seventy souls in all. These (the first fruits of the labors of one of their missionaries . . . a Mr. [Burr] Frost) goes with them. . . . It cannot be said that gain is their object, for most, if not all, of them are making great sacrifices, that they may get to the valleys of the mountains, in Utah, North America.[149]

A week later, in a tone more typical of the Australian press toward the Mormons at the time, *The Argus* reported in an article titled "The Flight of the Mormons":

> For some reason or other . . . they [the Mormons] have suddenly departed to the 'holy city' on the Salt Lake, and the people of Castlemaine remain in the same condition of benighted ignorance from which the disciples of Mormon benevolently endeavored to raise them. We believe the saints of the party found a difficulty in procuring a certain number of the softer sex to constitute a perfect congregation, and to enable the ministers to practise the virtues of polygamy as permitted by the precepts of their prophet.[150]

Such negative views of polygamy and the Saints were not uncommon, as discussed previously.

The leader of this voyage, Elder Burr Frost, explained his *modus operandi* after receiving instructions to conclude his mission and prepare to lead a company of Australian Saints to Zion: "I proceeded immediately to canvas the country to find out how many could emigrate. After visiting South Australia, and the branches in Victoria, I found that I could safely depend on forty-five. I then immediately engaged a vessel to take us to San Pedro, . . . but as the time draws near for sailing it appears probable that we shall have about sixty in passengers, being 75 to 80 souls."[151]

In a letter to European Mission President Franklin D. Richards in Liverpool, Augustus Farnham reported that Absalom P. Dowdle "had gathered up twenty-seven souls out of that [Adelaide] Conference, whom he brought up to Victoria, where they united with the Saints of that Conference, and went on board the brig *Tarquenia*, bound for San Pedro. She sailed on the 27th of April. . . . Elder B. [Burr] Frost had the charge of the company. . . . They numbered seventy-two souls. They were all in good health and spirits."[152] The Australasian Mission Manuscript History further explains that this vessel was forced to stop at Tahiti for a week to repair leaks and had experienced yet additional leakage before arriving in Honolulu. After extra repair work was done in Hawaii, the *Tarquinia* tried yet again to reach California, "but the first night out being a stormy one the old craft, which was virtually unfit for sea, was handled so roughly by the waves and wind that she began to leak worse than ever in consequence of which she was compelled to return to Honolulu, being in danger of sinking" and was condemned as unsafe.[153]

Though it was not recognized at the time, this condemned craft can be considered a foreshadowing of the ominous event which would soon strike the Australian Saints aboard the ill-fated *Julia Ann*. According to his autobiography, Captain Pond, like the crew of the leaking *Tarquinia*, had encountered problems with the *Julia Ann* on a voyage to California, just prior to the second voyage carrying Latter-day Saints across the Pacific. Pond notes that the *Julia Ann* "had been struck by a buster,[154] dragged both anchors across the bay, and thrown broadside on the rocks. . . . We had her heeled down on the beach, surveyed, and her bottom repaired and pronounced all right again. . . . Ship repaired, and . . . with a goodly number of Mormon passengers, we sailed for the Hunter River to load coal for San Francisco."[155] Later he notes trouble with a leak and "the fore rigging and a heating cargo."[156]

Several months before Pond would again launch with another group of Latter-day Saints aboard the *Julia Ann*, the First Presidency of the Church continued to strongly encourage the gathering, which promised sacred blessings reserved for the faithful.[157] Such a fervent push no doubt rallied some of the Australian Saints to make preparations to embark on the upcoming voyage of the *Julia Ann*. Additionally, a letter from Brigham Young to Augustus Farnham, published in this same issue of *Zion's Watchman*, would also have an impact on missionaries destined to board the *Julia Ann*:

> So far as you in Australia are concerned, you are at liberty to return whenever it suits your convenience, and I shall be most happy to again greet you in our mountain home. You may extend the same invitation to all the rest of the Elders who were appointed from here to that mission. You will however organise and regulate matters in the most judicious manner for the continuance of the work; but gather out the Saints and bring them with you as far as you shall be able to do so, leaving a sufficient number to continue the work. We find it best to gather out all the Saints as fast as they can consistantly, leaving only labouring Elders in the field.[158]

John McCarthy and family
Courtesy of Janice Ellis

As a result, President Farnham gave Elders James Graham[159] and John S. Eldredge,[160] who had arrived in the mission field in 1853, permission to return home to Utah with the next company of Australian Saints. Also, Elder John McCarthy, who had immigrated to Australia from Ireland and was then serving as a missionary,[161] "was at liberty to gather with the next company." Elder McCarthy "would therefore visit those with whom he had laboured, to see if he could gather any of them up, and also to collect means to take him to Zion." Thus, these three missionaries would join Australian converts and crew as passengers on the *Julia Ann*, which had been docked at Sydney over a month before departure.[162]

Several days before embarking, local Latter-day Saint John Perkins wrote in his diary as the time of the *Julia Ann*'s voyage drew near:

> Monday 3rd September 1855
> The brethren and Sisters are beginning to come in to go by the *Julia Ann* for the port of San Francisco. . . .

> Tuesday 4th September 1855
> At night attended the Priesthood Meeting. Several things was touched upon by the Presidency and among other things was that in reference to Sister Harris' Passage Money by the *Julia Ann* to San Francisco. Brother Robb seemed quite opposed to it but the President of the Mission succeeded in convincing the brethren that it was a good thing to help her out from this Place if it was for nothing Else but to get her away from her brutal husband.

> Wednesday 5th September 1855
> A fine day throughout. In the Evening attended meeting in Parramatha Street. There was not a very full attendance to night owing to several of the Saints being on board the ship, but we had a very comfortable little meeting and were truly Edified from the remarks that fell from the Presidency. No one else addressed the meeting but the Presidency. The vessel is expected to sail to morrow I believe.

> Thursday 6th September 1855
> A fine day throughout. In the forenoon I got liberty and whent on board the *Julia Ann* to bid farewell to the Saints who are going in this company. . . .

> Friday 7th September 1855
> The *Julia Ann* sailed to day for San Francisco.[163]

At the time of their departure, there were twenty-eight Latter-day Saints on board, three of which were crew members. Eleven other passengers and fourteen more crew members completed a total of fifty-six.[164] Augustus Farnham had appointed Elder John Penfold Sr. to be in charge of the company.[165] The Saints were singing "The Gallant Ship Is under Weigh," a hymn written by the famous LDS poet and hymn writer W. W. Phelps:

> The gallant ship is under weigh To bear me off to sea,
> And yonder floats the streamer gay That says she waits for me.
> The seamen dip the ready oar, As rippled waves oft tell,
> They bear me swiftly from the shore; My native land, farewell!
>
> I go, but not to plough the main, To ease a restless mind,
> Nor yet to toil on battle's plain, The victor's wreath to find.
> 'Tis not for treasures that are hid In mountain or in dell,
> 'Tis not for joys like these I bid My native land, farewell!
>
> I go to break the fowler's snare, To gather Israel home;
> I go the name of Christ to bear In lands and isles unknown.
> And soon my pilgrim feet shall tread On land where errors dwell,
> Whence light and truth have long since fled, My native land, farewell!
>
> I go, an erring child of dust, Ten thousand foes among,
> Yet on His mighty arm I trust, Who makes the feeble strong.
> My sun, my shield, forever nigh, He will my fears dispel,
> This hope supports me when I sigh, My native land, farewell!
>
> I go devoted to His cause, And to His will resigned;
> His presence will supply the loss Of all I leave behind.[166]

Captain Pond recalled, "The first two weeks at sea were altogether exceedingly unpleasant; head winds, accompanied with much rain. We however entered the south-east trades, and every thing again brightened, promising a speedy and pleasant voyage."[167] The following passenger accounts depict life at sea and the unexpected and horrifying outcome of this "pleasant voyage." John McCarthy recalled;

We left the Sydney Heads at 2 o'clock p.m. on the 7th of September, 1855, with the wind blowing from the N.E., and uninterruptedly pursued our course without anything of any consequence occurring until the 4th of October, when Captain Pond, expecting to pass between Mopea and the Scilly Isles, set the watch in the fare-top. The log was hove about 8 o'clock p.m., and the bark was found to be making 11 ½ knots per hour; shortly afterwards the sea became broken, and in about an hour the vessel, with a tremendous crash, dashed head on to a coral reef. She immediately swung round with her broadside to the reef, and the sea made a complete breach over her at every swell.[168]

Charles Joseph Logie
Courtesy of www.findagrave

Crew member Charles Logie remembered, "We were sailing at the rate of about 11 knots per hour. I was at the helm that evening from 6 to 8 o'clock. Captain Pond seemed anxious and told the watch on deck to keep a good lookout, for we were running close to land. I gave the man that relieved me at the wheel the course that I had been steering." Logie then notes, "I was off duty until midnight. I did not go to bed for a short time, and the ship run on the reef before I turned in. The time of the wreck must have been on or about nine o'clock."[169]

Elder James Graham, an American LDS missionary returning home, recorded that the voyage "was successful untill the 3 of october about Nine o Clock pm when the vessel struck on the reefs of the scilly islands."[170]

Andrew Anderson, the second missionary to Australia in the early 1840s and a *Julia Ann* passenger, recounted;

About half-past eight o'clock she struck on a reef of coral rock, . . . this was an awful event in our lives. There was four of our children asleep and in bed; there was very few in the steerage, chiefly on the steerage house, poop, &c. I had been asked two or three times why I was not out,—was I well enough? Yes, well enough thank you, but lazy or something else, (it seems a forboding of what took place,) there was Sister Harris, Sister Logie, my wife and myself in the steerage house at the moment the *Julia Ann* struck, my wife ran to me and said what shall we do, I said I do not think there is much the matter, compose yourself. Mr. Owens, 2nd mate, came in and told us to compose ourselves and remain as we were. . . . Word came out from some one for the passengers to go to the cabin, and by the time I got the four children out of bed, the water was knocking about the boxes, I got my leg very much bruised with a large box, with difficulty we gained the cabin, and about ten minutes after we left, house, gally, and box was all over board, preparations were made to go on the rocks to ascertain whether we could get any footing, as there was no land in sight, the ship was breaking up fast.[171]

In her report to the *San Francisco Daily Herald*, actress Esther Spangenberg,[172] a passenger aboard the *Julia Ann,* said the man who was at the helm at the time of the wreck was Mr. Coffin, who was said to have a rather ominous name. She added, "The night was dark, neither moon or stars visible, when suddenly the chief officer called out to the man at the wheel, 'Hard down your helm,' and in an instant after the ship struck on a reef from which she rebounded, and afterwards we could hear her bottom grate harshly on the rocks. The Captain . . . rushed on deck, but before he could reach it the ship was completely fast on the reef."[173]

Esther Spangenberg, 1856
Courtesy of Meg Rasmussen

Spangenberg further described in detail the great confusion that immediately followed: "The steerage passengers rushed into the cabin—mothers holding their undressed children in their arms, as they snatched them from their slumbers—screaming and lamenting, when their fears were in some measure allayed by a sailor who came to the cabin for a light, and told them that, although the ship would be lost, their lives would be saved, as we were close to the reef." She also noted, "The scene that presented itself to my view, shall never be erased from my memory. Mothers screaming, and children clinging to them in terror and in dread; the furniture was torn from its lashings and all upturned; the ship was laying on her beam ends; the starboard side of her was opening, and the waves was washing in and out of the cabin."[174]

At this time of great urgency, Captain Pond "called for a volunteer to attempt to reach the reef by swimming with a small line. One of the sailors instantly stripped; the log line was attached to his body, and he succeeded in swimming to the reef. . . . By this means a larger line was hauled to the reef, and made fast to the rocks." Pond noted, "I commenced the perilous task of placing the women and children upon the reef. A sailor in a sling upon the rope, took a woman or a child in his arms, and was hauled to the reef by those already there. . . . The process was an exceedingly arduous one, and attended with much peril."[175]

Rosa Clara Friedlander Logie
Courtesy of Dave Moyar

A young seventeen-year-old LDS mother, Rosa Clara Logie,[176] would be the first brave woman to volunteer to be transported to the reef, tying her one-year-old baby daughter, Annie Augusta, on the back of her husband, Charles,[177] before she departed.[178] Spangenberg described how she too struggled onto the deck and managed to haul herself across the line, although she recalled that by the time she reached the reef, "my clothes [were] torn in shreds, and my person bruised and mangled."[179] Another passenger on the *Julia Ann* described the ordeal: "The passengers and crue had to make the best of the way through the foming surf to the coral reef, And when it caim to my lot to test my strenth in brackers, I had to incounter broeken masts and spares in all direc-tions, but through the aid of divine providence I reach'd the reef safe, while its corals shot fourth poison in all directions from their rugit speers."[180]

The following memorable scene occurred, expressed with emotion by Captain Pond as he witnessed a mother desperately crying out for her teenage daughter amidst frantic terror:

> There was a large family on board named "Anderson" a father, mother, three daughters, two sons and an infant. One daughter, a pretty girl, ten years of age, was washed off the deck shortly after the ship struck, and drowned; another daughter "Agnes," sixteen years old, had escaped to the reef, the rest of the family were still on board. The hauling line had parted, the forward part of the ship had broken up, and no hope remained for those who were yet clinging to the quarter deck; but above the roar of the breakers and shrieks of despair, a mother's voice was heard, crying "Agnes, Agnes, come to me." Agnes was seated on the wreck of the main mast, that had floated upon the reef, but no sooner did she hear that mother's piercing wail, than she sprang to her feet, threw her arms up, shrieking "mother! mother! I come, I come," and plunged head-long into the sea. A sailor was fortunately near, seized her by her clothes and drew her back again.[181]

The Penfold family had their own story to tell from the wreck. Peter Penfold told of a harrowing experience that claimed a total of five lives: "Sister [Martha] Humphreys, and sister [Eliza] Harris and infant, were drowned in the cabin. Little Mary Humphreys and Marian Anderson were washed off the poop and drowned. . . . After I had helped to get them all out of the cabin, I came up and found the vessel all broken into fragments, except the cabin, and into that the water was rushing at a furious rate, sweeping out all the partitions."[182]

Concerning another family, Captain Pond recalled,

> There was a mother with six children; the husband and father self-ishly deserted them, and escaped to the reef, before the hauling line parted. I urged the mother to improve the only chance to save her own life. She sobbingly exclaimed, "No, I cannot leave my babes, we will die together". When the husband and father reached the reef,

the sailors inquired where his family were; he replied, "on board the ship". In their indignation at his cowardly desertion of them, they seized and threw him bodily back into the sea. A friendly wave washed him back again, and they allowed him to crawl to a place of safety upon the reef.[183]

McCarthy wrote that he had engraved on his memory "mothers nursing their babes in the midst of falling masts and broken spars, while the breakers were rolling twenty feet high over the wreck." He recalled that some of the men clung to the wreckage. "Soon afterwards the vessel broke to pieces, and the part they were on was providentially carried high upon the rocks, and they were landed in safety."[184]

Later, as he reflected on this trying scene, Pond posed the question of how the accident occurred. From an eyewitness who was also a fellow crew member, he discovered the following:

> On the night of the wreck that fellow was ordered aloft to lookout, taking him along for company. That he saw a long white strip of water ahead and pointed it out, and asked what it could be, but our bright look-out was near sighted, and could not see any thing peculiar, but thought he would go down into the forecastle for his spectacles, and of course before his return the doomed ship had solved the mystery. A startling revelation. Five lives lost, great anxiety and suffering incurred, a large amount of property destroyed, all owing to the near sightedness of a common sailor, and yet did it ever occur to the Captain of a ship to have the sight of his forecastle men examined?[185]

Notwithstanding, the courageous, steady character of Captain Pond, who was both an owner and a master of the vessel, was displayed during this entire ordeal. The *Western Standard* reported;

> Capt. Pond's chief desire throughout the whole sad affair, seemed to be to save the lives of the passengers and crew, as the following noble act illustrates: While the crew were engaged in getting the passengers ashore, Mr. Owens, the second mate, was going to carry a bag containing eight thousand dollars belonging to the Captain, ashore. The Captain ordered him to leave the money and carry a girl ashore; . . . the child was saved, but the money lost.[186]

Captain Pond described in vivid detail their predicament when they finally reached the coral reef:

Our situation on the reef can be better imagined than described. It was about eleven o'clock at night when all were landed; we were up to our waists in water, and the tide rising. Seated upon spars and broken pieces of the wreck, we patiently awaited the momentous future. Wrapped in a wet blanket picked up among the floating spars, I seated myself in the boat, the water reaching to my waist; my legs and arms were badly cut and bruised by the coral. Though death threatened ere morning's dawn, exhausted nature could bear up no longer, and I slept soundly. 'Twas near morning when I awoke. The moon was up and shed her faint light over the dismal scene; the sullen roar of the breakers sent an additional chill through my already benummed frame. The bell at the wheel, with every surge of the sea, still tolled a knell to the departed, and naught else but the wailings of a bereaved mother broke the stillness of the night, or indicated life among that throng of human automata; during the long hours of that weary night the iron had entered their souls, and the awful solemnity of their situation was brooded over in silence.[187]

"Portrait of Captain Peter Martin Coffin 1833–1840," oil on canvas, attributed to Isaac Sheffield (1785–1866)
Courtesy of ANMM, purchased with USA Bicentennial Gift funds

When sunlight broke in the dawn, land was discovered about ten miles away. A row boat was patched up, and spars and driftwood were assembled to make a raft. The women and children were placed in the boat, led by Captain Coffin, while the men were forced to remain on the reef for a second miserable night.[188] The second morning, rafts were prepared for provisions as well as clothing, and the men slowly swam and waded beside them along the reef. The water was up to the men's necks, and the shorter ones had to hold on to the rafts. What appears to be especially terrorizing were the schools of sharks that pursued them in their desperate condition. Pond noted, "At one time I counted over twenty—and not unfrequently we were compelled to seek safety from them upon the rafts." Finally, in a state of complete exhaustion, having had no drink or food for two full days, they reached the island and were soon greeted by the children, who quickly escorted them to drinking water, which had come from holes dug beneath the coral sand.[189]

Three days later, Pond led an exploring party to look for more provisions to sustain the castaways. On another island, some eight miles from their main camp, he found a coconut grove. Turtles were also found to lay eggs on the island at night. Pond noted, "Our hearts dilated with gratitude, for without something of this kind our case would have been indeed desperate. Our living now consisted of shell fish, turtle, sharks and cocoa nuts. We also prepared a garden, and planted some pumpkins, peas and beans."[190] Charles Logie described how pancakes were made by grating the coconuts and mixing them with turtle eggs.[191] John McCarthy added that "too much cannot be said in commendation of the Saints in this trying situation. I have seen an old lady upwards of sixty years of age out at night hunting turtle." He also noted that "while on this uninhabited island we held our regular meetings, dividing the time between worship and labor as we would have done had we been at our ordinary occupations."[192]

With an established routine and provisions now stabilized, the next step for deliverance was to repair the quarter boat.[193] The crew used great ingenuity in pulling strewn materials together in order to construct both a forge and a bellows so that nails could be made and iron work produced. The survivors were also divided into family units, wherein each group built thatched huts using leaves from the pandanus tree.[194] Five weeks later, the boat was ready for launching. The craft was not very sturdy, but there was no alternative; it was either make an effort to escape or remain trapped on the desolate island.

The Society Islands were the nearest inhabited land, a little over two hundred miles windward.[195] Therefore, Pond decided to go leeward (with the wind, instead of against it) in hopes of reaching the Navigator Islands (Samoa), though their distance was about fifteen hundred miles away. Three days were then spent looking for the best place to launch their feeble craft. However, soon thereafter, devastation set in; the weather changed, and a tornado swept the quarter boat away. The hopelessness was so great that "some threw themselves in despair upon the beach; the silent tear trickled down the cheeks of speechless women; others moaned aloud at their sad, sad fate, for our provisions were nearly exhausted, and starvation stared us in the face."[196] Fortunately, the craft was eventually recovered and was not damaged.

Scilly Island
Courtesy of ANMM, 1996

After eight weeks of being stranded on the Scilly Islands, the weather suddenly changed its course and blew windward (towards the northwest), which Pond recognized as "Divine Providence in our favor."[197] Soon every person was recruited to carry the craft about 200 yards across land, where it could be placed on the incoming breakers. It was launched with a crew of ten brave men who would need to row continuously for several days, both day and night.[198] Esther Spangenberg recalled that as the small craft was about to embark on its vital mission, "We invoked God's blessing on the captain and the nine brave men who accompanied him, who boldly risked their lives in an open, crazy boat, to cross an open ocean, to endeavor to bring us succor and relief. As we watched the boat recede from the land . . . there was not one amongst us but was aware that on that boat . . . depended our very existence."[199]

About a week before casting off in the long boat, Pond wrote to his father, Dr. James Otis Pond, a letter dated November 14, 1855, Scilly Island: "All of my property is yours until I am heard of alive & claim it. Witness Peter M. Coffin."[200]

One of the crew was John McCarthy, who described the dire conditions for such an unpredictable voyage: "Our provisions were a little salt pork and jerked turtle, with two casks of water. . . . Our boat was almost level with the water." [201] Pond, recounting the perilous adventure to his niece Orella, explained that those aboard this untrustworthy craft felt that their days were numbered after rowing several days:

> The sea . . . so sluggish, arose in all its might, and power, threatening to engulph us, in its appalling throes. For hours, and hours, the fearful, but unequal contest, was maintained, 'till human endurance could bear up no longer, and we lay exhausted in the bottom of our little boat, now floating at the mercy of the sea. The goal of our hopes, and our very lives, that dim cloud upon the verge of the horizon, gradually faded from our view! Oh! the blank despair of that moment; and as we drew the tarpaulain over the boat, to shelter us from the dashing spray, thoughts of home mingled in our prayers. . . . Thus, for hours we were driven at the mercy of the raging wind and sea, but not forgotten by a kind Providence.
>
> Late in the afternoon, as we lay huddled together, under the protecting cover of the tarpaulin, drenched by the salt spray, faint and exhausted by severe toil, listlessly gazing out upon the combing, raging sea, that threatened instant destruction, the sudden cry of "land! land!" again startled us from the lethergy of despair which seemed, with its cold, icy hand, to gripe our very hearts. . . . Tears of gratitude filled our eyes; our sail was hoisted to the *now favoring* breeze;[202] again the oars were manned, and our little boat fairly trembled at the onward impetus given, by the hope resusitated nerves, of my but recently faint and exhausted crew. . . . As we neared the land, the wind gradually subsided, and the sea no longer broke in heavy combers . . . but rolled, in long, heavy swells, upon a coral reef that encircled the island.
>
> We pulled along outside of the reef about two hours, looking in vain for an entrance, . . . when a native, who was engaged spearing fish inside, guessing our difficulty, motioned to us to proceed

further up the reef, on complying with which we soon found a ship entrance to a fine harbor, and saw the huts of a native village at the head of the bay.[203]

One additional part of the story involving a Mormon elder's prophetic dreams was related by Pond in his autobiography, which was published about four decades later. These dreams were also significant factors in choosing the direction in which the small crew went for safety:

> And now having safely reached one of the Windward [Society] Islands against all human probability when we departed from [the] Scilly reefs, I will give you a peculiar episode in connection with that boat voyage. I can simply vouch for the facts, without any attempt to argue, or explain.
>
> My passengers were mostly Mormons, bound to Salt Lake City, densely ignorant and very superstitious and were bitterly opposed to my first proposition of trying to reach the Navigator Islands. They argued, the distance to be so great, some fifteen hundred miles, that if we succeeded in reaching them they would starve to death before we could hope to send them relief. They could not, or would not understand why we might not steer in face of head wind and sea to the Society Islands which were so much nearer. We, however, as nautical men, determined to act on our own judgment in that matter, and steadily continued our preparations until our plans were blocked in a most unexpected manner. One of their Elders had a dream or vision.[204] He saw the boat successfully launched upon her long voyage, and for a day or two making satisfactory progress. Another leaf in the vision, and the boat is seen floating bottom up, and the drowned bodies of her crew floating around her. This tale, so wrought upon the superstitions that not a man would volunteer to go with me, and I was reluctantly compelled to change my plan.
>
> I then gave strict orders that there should be no more visions told in public unless they were favorable ones, and first submitted to me for my approval. After some days the same Mormon Elder came to me having had another vision. I asked him if it was a good one. Yes, a very good one. He saw the boat depart with a crew of ten men, bound to the eastward; after three days of rowing, they reached a friendly island where a vessel was obtained and all hands safely brought to Tahiti. When I, by compulsion, changed

my plans and decided to double bank the boat and try to pull to windward, only nine men offered, including myself. It was useless to start short handed, and I had been waiting unsuccessfully to get one more man to complete my crew. On hearing this very good vision, I looked my man over. He was a fine, athletic fellow, and asked him if he believed his vision. "Yes, indeed, was it not a revelation from God?" I then suggested that it would be a good way to prove his faith by volunteering for the boat. "Of course he would," and he did with alacrity, and thus was my crew completed. You have heard the account of how literally his dream was fulfilled against every probability.[205]

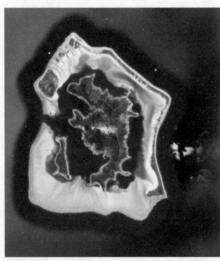

Bora Bora
Courtesy of Aerial Google Map

After finally reaching Bora Bora in late November, Pond records that he and his nine-man crew "could not walk for some time after being removed from our boat by the natives."[206] Pond went for help and eventually found it with the aid of the British Consulate, who recommended Captain Latham, docked with the schooner *Emma Packer*,[207] waiting for oranges at the nearby isle Huahine.[208] On December 3, the castaways on Scilly Island were rescued.[209] Recalling this joyful, redemptive event, John S. Eldredge expressed his profound gratitude:

We were delivered from our exiled and desolate situation by the untiring perserverance of Captain B. F. Pond, master of the barque *Julia Ann*, connected with the charitable good feeling of Captain Latham, master of the schooner Emma Packer, that came to our relief. We were taken off the Scilly Isles, where we were wrecked, on the 3d of December, making it two months that we were left in this lonely situation on an uninhabited island. I need not attempt to describe our feelings of gratitude and praise which we felt to give the God of Israel for His goodness and mercy in thus working a deliverance for us; for I have not language to express my own feelings, much less the feelings of those around me, suffice it to say, I am thankful to know that His mercy endureth for ever.[210]

There were additional offers of help to rescue the *Julia Ann* castaways as well. Captain H. Eldredge, master of the ship *Oregon*, in a letter from Huahine dated November 29, 1855, wrote to Captain Pond offering the assistance of his ship in the rescue of the passengers. In a note that Pond wrote referencing the letter from Eldredge, he stated that the *Oregon* arrived at the Scilly Islands shortly after the *Emma Packer* and rescued three people: "The Oregon reached Scilly reefs, after the pas-

John Sunderlin Eldredge
Courtesy of William Knudsen

sengers had been taken off by schooner 'Emma Packer' but was fortunate in rescuing the 2 Mates and one passenger of the Bark '*Julia Ann*' who were found on an outlying reef abandoned by their boat, and would undoubtedly have perished had not the ship 'Oregon' providentially put in an appearance. B.F.P."[211]

Although they were rescued from the Scilly Islands, the former *Julia Ann* passengers' voyage home was not yet over, nor were their problems. Peter Penfold explained; "We embarked on the 3rd [of December], and arrived at the island of Una [Huahine] on the 11th, where we saw the grave of sister Allan [Esther Allen, an LDS passenger on the first LDS voyage of the *Julia Ann*], who was buried on that island. We stayed there three days; we then went on to Tahiti; we landed on the 19th."[212]

After the stops in Huahine and Tahiti, Penfold further explained in a letter to his brother that upon their arrival at Tahiti, the consuls would do nothing for these castaways: "The American Consul said he had nothing to do with us, because we were English; and the English Consul said he had nothing to do with us, because we were in an American ship;[213] so we were in a very peculiar situation,—without friends, without money, without home, without clothes, without food, and in a strange land, under the French Government."[214] Yet delivery came in the form of the Freemasons of Tahiti. Penfold notes, "By the charity of the Free-masons' Lodge we were found in food until the 19th of January, after which they could feed us no longer."[215]

When news reached Augustus Farnham and other Saints in Australia via Peter Penfold's letter, it was read at the April 6, 1856 conference and later published in the *Watchman*:[216]

> President Farnham presented the case of the sufferers surviving the wreck of the *Julia Ann*, who were still at Tahiti, without any prospects of getting away from there, and called for an expression of the feelings of the Brethren, in reference to their case. The unanimous feeling of the Brethren was, that every possible exertion should be made for the relief of the suffers. Several of the Brethren who had prepared to gather with the next Company, expressed their willingness to donate the whole of their means and stop behind to work for more, so that their suffering Brethren at Tahiti might be relieved. It was proposed, seconded, and carried, that a subscription be opened for the relief of our Brethren and Sisters, who survive the wreck of the barque *Julia Ann*, and that President Josiah W. Fleming be appointed to receive the same. [217]

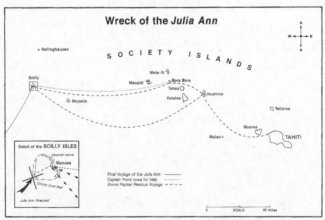

Map showing route and wreck site of the *Julia Ann*
Courtesy of Mark Jackson, BYU

A letter that Peter's father, John, wrote from Tahiti to President Farnham, dated March 21, 1856, was also published in the

Watchman. It explained the dire situation of some of the Saints, with Penfold's query, "How Brother Anderson or myself will get away I know not, for we are surrounded here with enemies on every hand, and have not the slightest chance of getting away, except you can prevail upon the Captain of the vessel that brings out the next company, to call at Tahiti and take away us poor castaways."[218]

At a special conference of the Australasian Mission held in Sydney on May 4, 1856, President Farnham again "laid before the Brethren the condition of the distressed Brethren at Tahiti, and called upon them to assist them; he also called for means to take the poor Saints and also to assist the Elders."[219] In this same issue of the *Watchman*, it is evident that immediate action was taken:

> We regret to have to record the wreck of the barque *Julia Ann*. She struck on a hidden coral reef near to Sicilly Island, on the evening of 3rd of August [October] last. She left this port on the 7th of September, with a company of Saints consisting of 27 souls, five of whom perished in the wreck, two adults and three children, one of those who perished was Sister Eliza Harris, formerly of the London Conference. Let the Editor of the *Star* be pleased to notice this.
>
> Our readers will perceive that the survivors are still at Tahiti without any prospect of being relieved, until we go along with the next company and call for them.
>
> Arrangements have been made with S. F. Sergent, Captain of the Clipper Schooner, "Jenny Ford," for the departure of the next Company. This vessel will sail about the 25th instant, and will call at Tahiti to take on board our brethren there.[220]

On May 28, 1856, a group of 120 Australian Saints led by Augustus Farnham did indeed leave Sydney on the *Jenny Ford* bound for Zion. Their minds were also fixed on rescuing their stranded fellow-Saints in Tahiti on the way.[221] Soon after departure, however, the *Jenny Ford* nearly followed the path of the *Julia Ann*. Josiah W. Fleming,[222] one of the LDS passengers, noted the following when the vessel came near wrecking:

> While we were yet in full view of Sydney, the wind ceased to blow so we had no control of the vessel, which was thrown before the waves toward the shore, which was a fearful looking sight as the waves were beating against the breakers, flying and foaming high

in the air, every sail was set and every possible means was used to save the vessel from the approaching danger, but to no purpose. In a short time we discovered a huge rock toward which our vessel was drifting, we saw our fearful danger, without any earthly way to prevent it, Every soul on board was waiting to see the vessel dashed to pieces. At this critical moment I called some of the Elders to come and stand on the side of the vessel nearest the breakers, and by the power of the Priesthood and mighty faith, we might have power with our heavenly Father to turn the vessel in another direction, as it did not seem possible we should come to such a fearful death, yet the vessel continued to drift broadside toward the rock, as one more wave passed, and the vessel lowered within a short distance from the rock, only waiting the next wave to be dashed to pieces, I lifted my eyes to my Father in Heaven for, perhaps, the last time in this life, I felt the power of God immediately rest upon me and I said—O God, the eternal Father in the name of Jesus Christ Thy Son, I command this vessel to stand still and go no farther toward this rock. The next wave came rolling along and raised the vessel to the full height, which soon passed and the vessel lowered in the same place. When I saw this, I again lifted my voice to my Father in Heaven and in the name of Jesus commanded the wind to blow and fill the sails, which it did instantly and we were soon out of danger. This power had been placed on my head by Joseph Smith Sen., and John Smith Patriarch, who said, I should have power over the winds and waves of the sea and they should obey my voice.[223]

This near disaster may have served as an omen of good things to come; the Saints did not encounter any other major problems on their voyage. They safely reached Tahiti less than one month later. One of the passengers aboard was John Perkins, who recorded their arrival at Papeete:

Monday 23rd June 1856. . . . At 4:30 P.M., we came to an Anchor in the Harbour of Papete, the capital of Tahiti. The captain went on shore but there was no one else allowed to go on Shore owing to liberty from the authorities not being given. After tea, Elder Addison Pratt came on board. President Farnham called a council meeting of the Elders above which was held in the cabin. Brother Pratt afterwards attended prayer between decks. All the brethren and Sisters was in attendance. We sang two or three Hymns and were then addressed by Elders Pratt, Farnham, and Fleming. There was also another of the Brethren with Brother Pratt who came from San Bernardino with him. They Seemed to quite enjoy themselves at Meeting with us. . . .

Thursday 24th June 1856. A fine night throughout. Still laying in the Harbour of Papete alongside the wharf. All our brethren and sisters that was [illegible] in [missing] [Julia] Ann had left Tahiti before we got [missing] is one family left behind who was passengers in the *Julia Ann* by the name of McGee, formerly of the Uncle Tom's Cabin in Woolloomooloo Street, Sydney. They are to come on board the *Jenny Ford* to go to San Francisco in her.[224]

Papeete, Tahiti in 1859
*Collection Museum of Tahiti and the Islands - Te Fare Manaha" or
"Collection Musée de Tahiti et des Îles - Te Fare Manaha"
Papeete, Tahiti in 1859. Photography G. VIAUD*

About two weeks earlier, President Farnham had Elder John Jones, the clerk for the voyage, prepare a letter of thanks to the Freemasons at Tahiti prior to their arrival at Papeete:

[June] 9, [1856] Monday. . . . President Farnham having requested me to draw up an address to the free mason's at Tahiti. The following was known drawn up by me: To the most worshipful grand master and other officers and members of the most honorable fraternity of free and accepted Masons. Beloved Brethren: It is with the greatest feelings of pleasure that I embrace the opportunity offered by our calling at Tahiti to tender to you. The most worshipful grand master and all other officers and brethren of our honorable Fraternity residing at this port. On the part of myself and brethren of the Church of Jesus Christ of Latter-day Saints the sincere and deep felt gratitude of our hearts for the assistance rendered by you to our distressed brethren and sisters who survived the wreck of the Barque *Julia Ann* that was lost near to Scilly Island on the 4 of October last. And I do assure you, that your charity is so deeply enstamped upon our hearts that it will ever live in our memories and we shall ever pray that God may bless you. So might it be, your affectionate brother, Augustus Farnham M.M. [meaning Master Mason] President of the Australian Mission of the Church of Jesus Christ of Latter Day Saints. Clipper schooner, *Jenny Ford*, 1856.[225]

Like Perkins, Jones also described their arrival:

[June] 23, [1856] Monday. At 4 a.m. the captain, chief mate and second mate all on deck. The ship. . . . entered the harbor about 4 p.m. alongside Harts wharf. Many thronged to look at us. A message having been sent by President Farnham, Mrs. McGee who was a passenger [on] *Julia Ann* came alongside from her. We learned that all the Saints had left the Island for San Francisco also her husband and eldest son. President Farnham was in conversation with a person named Morse from whom we learned that Elder A. [Addison] Pratt was on the Island. President F. [Farnham] requested to communicate to Elder Pratt our presence in the Port permission having been obtained from the customs. President Farnham and Fleming went ashore to Mrs. McGee. They returned about 7 ½ p.m. called a meeting of the priesthood in the cabin. At this time Elder A Pratt came on board and participated in the councils of the priesthood. This meeting having been called for considering the case of Mrs. McGee and family who though not members of the Church were the only survivors of the wreck that were left on this Island. It was determined that as our brethren and sisters had been assisted to leave through the charity of the Free Masons since Mr. McGee being a mason that therefore they be taken to San Francisco by us. They numbered three and a half passengers besides an infant three weeks old. Elder Pratt cordially agreed with us on this matter.[226]

The Mr. McGee spoken of here was Thomas Magee, whom the Tahiti British Consulate passenger list notes as being "born in Dublin; age 35, shoemaker by trade, 18 years settler in Australia." The list also notes that his wife, Eliza, was thirty-two years of age and that their children were Thomas, age fourteen; Ann, age twelve; John, age ten; James, age eight; Constantine, age five; and Margaret, age two.[227] Passenger Alonzo Colton on the *Jenny Ford* mentioned taking the children back to San Francisco:

> We found all our shipwrecked bretheren had got off one after another in fruit vessels to San Francisco aided by the benevolence of the free Masons. A letter of thanks was tendered them by the Presidency of the Mission which was handsomely responded to just as we were going out of the harbour and we brought away the Wife and five Children of a Free Mason who were the last of the sufferers wrecked from the *Julia Ann* whose Husband had previously left for San Francisco with the hope of earning money to send for them.[228]

Anchor excavated at *Julia Ann* wreck site
Courtesy of Paul Hundley

Magee, as noted above, belonged to the masonic fraternity, and it appears quite likely he was the person who probably initiated the request for aid from the masons in Papeete due to the mutual brotherhood he shared with them.[229] In keeping with a promise he made to Captain Latham, Magee spearheaded an article to the *San Francisco Herald* from Tahiti, Jan. 6, 1856:

> "The Wrecked Passengers of the *Julia Ann*."
> To Jno. Latham, Esq. Captain of the American schooner Emma Packer—Sir: We, the undersigned, being a portion of the passengers who were unfortunately wrecked upon the Island of Scilly, on board the American bark *Julia Ann*, whilst on her voyage from Sydney to San Francisco, in the month of October last, and who,

after a residence of two months upon that miserable Island, were rescued by you from it, and brought up to this port on board your vessel, cannot allow you to depart from amongst us without at least thus publicly tendering to you our most sincere gratitude for the promptness and disinterestedness you have evinced by immediately getting your vessel under way after you heard of our situation; sincerely regretting that we have it not in our power to tender to you a more substantial acknowledgment of our thankfulness, (having lost all we possessed at the time the wreck took place.) Hoping that "He who commands the storm and the calm" will grant to you a happy and prosperous voyage through life, and that when you may be called to "another and a better world" you may receive the reward due to those who act the good Samaritan, we are, Sir, your most obedient and ever thankful servants;

[Signed]

Thomas Magee, for self and family; Jno. Anderson, for self and family; Jno. Penfold, wife and two sons; Peter Penfold, Stephen Penfold, Jno. Symmonds, Jno. Eldridge, Jno. Graham, Chas. Gumric, wife, and two child'n; Sarah Wilson and son; Eliza Humfries and brother; Thomas Clagger Tahiti, Jan. 4, 1856. [230]

Dr. James Otis Pond received a letter from his son Capt. B. F. Pond about a week before the ten-man crew went for help at Bora Bora, which stated, "All of my property is yours until I am heard of alive & claim it." Dr. Pond wrote back to his son: "I shall preserve this letter as a memento of filial affection."
Courtesy of Meg Rasmussen

The profuse thanks to Captain Latham was accompanied by one thousand dollars, paid by the American Consulate, although Esther Spangenberg explained that "Capt. Latham, who on hearing of our condition, immediately started to our assistance, . . . not knowing if he would receive any reward for so doing."[231] Thus, through incredible bravery on the part of Captain Pond and his crew of nine, coupled with the timely and charitable efforts of Captain Latham and others, those who survived the wreck were rescued.

CHAPTER FIVE

Aftermath

"Though we have lost all our worldly goods, and all that we had; yet we have faith in God, and trust He will deliver us. . . . Do not forget to come along the first opportunity; though we were shipwrecked, that is no reason you should be. I hope to see you all before long in the land of the free, surrounded by the saints of the Most High God."
—Letter of Peter Penfold [232]

CONCERNING THOSE WHO SURVIVED THE WRECK of the *Julia Ann*, Sarah Wilson is thought to have gone to San Francisco and married Captain Russell Latham, who brought the *Emma Packer* to the rescue of the *Julia Ann* survivors.[233] Thomas Magee reunited with his family, but apparently abandoned his family and died as a result of excessive drinking four years later in San Andreas, about one hundred miles from his wife and children in San Francisco.[234] Further, it is apparent that Magee also temporarily abandoned his family at the time of the wreck when he swam for a coral reef and left his wife and children on the *Julia Ann*, the event that was noted in the *Autobiography of Captain B. F. Pond*. Immediately after arriving in Tahiti, the actress Esther Spangenberg, a cabin passenger; Captain Coffin, first officer; and the rest of the crew departed on board the *Lucas*, another vessel owned by Pond. Spangenberg bought and ran a boarding house in San Francisco and later became a school teacher. As a token of bravery, Pond assigned Mr. Owens as first mate onboard the *Fremont*, which was also owned by Captain Pond. Unfortunately, the *Fremont* crew had a much worse fate than those aboard the *Julia Ann*: "After leaving San Francisco this ship was never heard from again and is presumed to have been wrecked. The rest of the crew all signed on a vessel travelling up the west coast of America. This ship was wrecked, with all the crew drowned. Captain Coffin returned to New England and never went to sea again. Captain Pond . . . returned to his family home in New York." Pond did not return immediately to his home in New York, but rather sailed for Callao, Peru, Panama, San Francisco, and then back to Australia before returning home to New York.[235] The paths of the other passengers not of the Mormon faith are not known.

Peter Penfold
Courtesy of Audrey Chappell
in "I Sailed to Zion," 124

The other Mormon passengers slowly made their way across the Pacific to San Francisco on any vessel they could find. The Anderson and Penfold families chose to settle in California and are later listed as members of the Reorganized Church of Jesus Christ of Latter-day Saints (known today as the Community of Christ).[236] Some of the other passengers took a direct passage to San Francisco on the brig *G. W. Kendall* and arrived on June 27, 1856.[237] Elders Graham and Eldredge chose not to travel directly back home to Utah but rather took a detour when they came into port in Honolulu on March 12 and traveled over to Lahaina to meet with Utah missionaries stationed there as part of the Hawaiian Mission.[238]

While it is known that Graham and Eldredge and others eventually reached their homes in Zion, it is not known what happened to John Pegg. John McCarthy immigrated to Utah, married his neighbor Eliza Telford, and moved to Bountiful, Utah. The Logie family eventually made their way to American Fork, Utah, and now have a large Mormon posterity.

Over the years, descendants of the survivors have recounted the story of the *Julia Ann* in bits and pieces to family members and friends; scholars and storytellers have also related this captivating narrative with awe. Historian Paul Hundley, wanting to know more, excavated the wreckage, and later, to his credit, displayed the story and his findings in a traveling museum exhibit. But what about those who were aboard the vessel? How did they view their experience before and after the accident took place?

Captain Benjamin F. Pond, 1886, age 67
Courtesy of Meg Rasmussen

Reflecting on the wreck and rescue of the *Julia Ann*, Captain Pond no doubt felt it important to view this event in the proper prospective. As noted earlier, Pond in his accounts often referred to the manifestation of "Providence" and no doubt felt that the hand of God should be acknowledged. Clearly, Pond's experience confirmed to him the reality of God.

Did the Mormon converts aboard the ill-fated *Julia Ann* voyage regret the trip when tragedy arose and five lives were lost? Perhaps this question can be answered best by the additional witness of two of the passengers, one who barely survived and the other who lost her life. Their letters exemplify the faith and fortitude so common among Saints who attempted the sail and trail journey to follow what they perceived as inspired counsel to gather to Zion. Writing to his son from Tahiti, Peter Penfold noted; "Father and mother and we all are in good health and spirits, though we have lost all our worldly goods, and all that we had; yet we have faith in God, and trust He will deliver us soon from this place. Do not forget to come along the first opportunity; though we were shipwrecked, that is no reason you should be. I hope to see you all before long in the land of the free, surrounded by the saints of the Most High God."[239]

The other letter was penned by Martha Humphreys before she departed Australia aboard the *Julia Ann* and her subsequent drowning:

> And now my dear Mother, I will answer that question you put me, of when, are we are going. . . . We leave Australia, with all its woes, and bitterness, for the Land of Zion next April. . . . Perhaps you will say, I am building on worldly hopes, that never will be realized, not so, Mother, . . . knowing what I know, I tell you, if I knew for a positive certainty, that when we get there, persecutions, such as have been the portion of the Saints before, awaited us, I would Still insist upon going, what are a few short years in this present state, compared with Life Eternal.[240]

APPENDIX A

Autobiography of Capt. Benjamin F. Pond

*Extract from "Autobiography of Captain B. F. Pond
Written at the Request of His Wife and Children," printed in Tenafly,
NJ, June 15, 1895. Courtesy of National Archives.*

Chapter XVII.

WRECK OF THE JULIA ANN AND TWO MONTHS RESIDENCE OF THE SURVIVORS ON A CORAL REEF IN THE SOUTH PACIFIC OCEAN.

THE ACCOUNT OF THE WRECK OF THE JULIA ANN given in the following chapter is a rescript of an address given before the "Tenafly Literary Society," November 10, 1893, on an assigned subject, viz: "Perils of the Sea," illustrated by an account of the wreck of the Barque *Julia Ann*, and two months residence of the survivors on a coral reef in the South Pacific, eliminating only the introductory remarks giving a description of the vessel and incidents already recorded in the preceding pages:

We sailed from Sydney on Friday, September 7th, 1855, with fifty-six souls on board, men, women and children. The day seemed very unpropitious and gloomy, and before our anchor was weighed, it commenced blowing and raining, and in getting out of the harbor, we met with very many annoying accidents.

The first two weeks at sea were altogether exceedingly unpleasant; head winds, accompanied with much rain. We, however, entered the South East trades, and everything brightened, promising a speedy and pleasant voyage.

Twenty-seven days out, October 3rd, I was on [p200] the lookout for land all day, and carried a press of sail, in order to pass

77

certain dangerous islands before night. At that day those seas were very incorrectly surveyed. At one time, bound from San Francisco to Australia, about sundown, we raised a reef crossing our course directly ahead of us, about ten miles long, not noticed or marked on any chart extant. Had we been an hour later, the ship would have been a helpless wreck. About two P. M., we sailed directly over the position given on my charts of the Scilly reefs on which the vessel was wrecked, and on my arrival at Tahiti, on looking the matter carefully up, I found that my calculations were correct, and that the position given on the charts was from sixty to ninety miles too much to windward.

At sundown no land could be seen from the royal yards, and I judged myself at least thirty miles past them, and after my arrival at "Bora Bora," I found that I was correct.

However, in compliance with my usual custom of precaution, when in the vicinity of reefs or islands, at eight o'clock I charged Mr. Coffin, my first officer, to have a good lookout kept, and went below to get some rest.

I had been in the cabin not over half an hour, when the alarming cry of "hard down your helm" was heard; I sprang to my feet, but my heart failed me, as I was nearly thrown upon the floor of the cabin by the violent striking of the ship, and before I could reach the deck, she was thumping hard. On deck the scene was terrific.

It was blowing a trade gale, a high sea was running, the vessel was in the breakers of the coral reef, and no land in sight. I instantly saw there was no hope for the ship, and very little for the lives of those on board. You can form some idea with what force the ship struck. At eight bells, the wind about two points free, port studding sails set alow [p201] and aloft, we logged the ship, and she marked over eleven knots.

I, however, kept sail on the vessel to force her as high as possible on the reef, and then cut away the masts, to relieve her from the immense strain. And now the lives of those on board were my first care, and the prospect was gloomy enough. The sea was making a complete breach over the ship, she had fallen on her beam ends, seaward, and threatened to be rapidly torn to pieces by the enormous seas that were rolling in upon her. There was no land in sight, and not a dry rock visible upon the reef. One of our quarter boats was stove when we first struck. I endeavored to secure our only remaining boat, but it soon broke adrift from the davits and plunged bows on, into the sea.

The second mate and three or four sailors nobly plunged after. The boat was stove and turned bottom up, and they were all thrown upon the reef together; Mr. Owens, the second officer, very badly injured and disabled from further exertions.

I now called for a volunteer to attempt to reach the reef by swimming with a small line. One of the sailors instantly stripped, the log line was attached to his body, and he succeeded in swimming to the reef, under the lee of the vessel. By this means a larger line was hauled to the reef and made fast to the jagged coral. A small one for a hauling line was also rove, and I commenced the perilous task of placing the women and children upon the reef.

A sailor in a sling upon the rope took a woman, or a child, in his arms, and was hauled to the reef by those already there, and then hauled back again by myself and others. The process was an exceedingly arduous one, and attended with much peril; but our boats had they not been destroyed would have been useless in such a surf, and it was [p202] the only means left us.

In the meantime, the vessel was laboring and thumping in a most fearful manner, and it was almost impossible to cling to the iron railing of the quarter deck. One or two persons had already been hurled far seaward by the awful throes of the ship. The passengers were collected in the aftercabin, where they were compelled to remain, though the sea breached in and half filled it; and presented themselves as their names were called, to be passed to the reef upon the rope. There was no confusion, up to the last all were subservient to my orders. But the scene rapidly drew to a crisis.

The vessel had fallen off the reef to more than double her former distance; the rope attached to the reef was stretched to its utmost tension, the hauling line had parted for the third time; the crew were all on the reef and after repeated efforts to join us, the attempt was abandoned. At every surge of the sea I expected the vessel would turn bottom up; two large families still remained on board of her with Mr. Coffin (my first officer) and myself; five had been drowned, two washed off the deck, and three out of the cabin; the sea had broken in the forward part, and it was with the utmost difficulty that any one could keep from being washed away.

I urged those remaining to try to reach the reef on the rope before it parted, it was a desperate but only chance for life. The women and children could not, and the men shrunk from the yawning gulf as from certain death. Captain Coffin and I however watching our opportunity as that last destructive roller struck the ship, breaking her in two just abaft the main mast, we slid down on the slack of the rope, and there rolled in a kind of trip sea, tearing off the quarter deck on which the few persons still on board were clinging, washed it completely over us, and anchored it upon the reef, [p203] and the lives of those on board were most providentially saved. The sailors who were in charge of the reef end of the rope finding that it had parted from the ship and was adrift, mechanically hauled it in, and to their surprise and delight found Coffin and myself clinging to the end of it.

And here I will pause a moment in the direct narrative to relate a few of the most graphic incidents occurring upon the ship before we had all effected our escape to the reef.

When the ship first struck, Mr. Owens, my second officer, came to me and inquired whether I had not considerable gold on board. I told him I had. He then offered, with my consent, to make an effort to save a portion of it. I went into my stateroom and opened the iron safe in which I had $15,000 in English sovereigns, and much other treasures and valuables. I took two bags of gold containing about $8,000 or $9,000, and gave them to him. I was in great haste, for the sea was breaking over the ship, and my presence was very necessary on deck. I thought it very doubtful whether we could save our lives, and therefore considered the gold of little importance; but as I was closing the safe, I happened to notice a roll of sterling exchange for $10,000 lying before me utterly forgotten. I picked it up and stuffed it into my pocket; it was well that I put it into my pantaloons pocket, for when I left the ship I threw off all my clothes except my pants.

This was the last time I was in my stateroom, or saw the iron safe, which was lost with all its valuable contents. I will here state the somewhat romantic circumstances attending the recovery and preservation of those bills of exchange. The responsibility thrown upon me of preserving and saving human lives during the wreck and up to our final deliverance was so overpowering that I gave no [p204] thought whatever to the pecuniary loss, and this roll of exchange stuffed in my pantaloons pocket was entirely forgotten. About two weeks after the wreck, a sudden thought struck me to investigate the contents of my pockets, if perchance something useful might be discovered. I found it no easy matter to effect an entrance, the pocket being hermetically sealed by its long immersion in salt water. I was engaged in picking out and throwing on the ground the obstruction, when Captain Coffin, standing behind me, suddenly called out, "Look out Captain, what are you tearing up?" And when I saw the yellow scraps of paper, for the first time the thought of that exchange flashed across my mind. The pocket was carefully cut out, the money was in one solid wad, much mutilated (all three sets, pounds, shillings, and pence were there). We picked up the torn pieces, wrapped all together in canvas, and sewed it up securely. When I left the island on that boat voyage, I deemed my chance of life and success so very slim that I wrote a farewell note to my parents in New York, giving a brief statement of my pecuniary affairs in shape of a will, wrapped it up with the package of sterling exchange, and gave it to my first officer, Captain Coffin, to be delivered to my father in New York, in the event of his escape from the island. After my arrival in San Francisco, it became necessary for me to return to Australia to settle up my business affairs. I therefore chartered and loaded the ship "Horihant," and prosecuted my last voyage to Sydney, sailed thence for New York in the ship "Sea King," via Callao and Panama. On my arrival in New York, I found the package of sterling exchange, preserved more as a keepsake than for any special value. I however sent it intact to the Bank of Liverpool, and by return mail received a check for about $11,000, no unwelcome windfall just then in the face of so great pecuniary loss.

When I stationed Mr. Owens and some men to endeavor to

save our only remaining boat, he put the two bags of sovereigns in his stateroom, and when the boat was washed away with Mr. Owens and his crew there was no time to think of gold. After a while, the sailor who was on the rope taking passengers to the reef, told me that he must have a pair of boots before he could go again, as his boots were cut to pieces by the sharp coral. I went down to my stateroom to get him a pair, but something had fallen against the door inside, and I could not open it. I returned to the deck for the purpose of getting an axe to break it open, when "hold on all," rang in my ears, and I had barely time to seize hold of the mizzen rigging when an awful sea struck the ship, tearing up the bulwarks, threatening death and destruction to every thing within its reach. A fearful shriek arose from the cabin, and when I returned not a vestige of my stateroom, or its contents, remained. That resistless sea had stove in the forward part of the cabin, washed away the starboard staterooms, with two women and a little child. The poor mother had lashed her infant to her bosom, and thus they found a watery grave together.

There was a mother with six children; the husband and father selfishly deserted them, and escaped to the reef, before the hauling line parted. I urged the mother to improve the only chance to save her own life. She sobbingly exclaimed, "No, I cannot leave my babes, we will die together." When the husband and father reached the reef, the sailors inquired where his family were; he replied, "on board the ship". In their indignation at his cowardly desertion of them, they seized and threw him bodily back into the sea. A friendly wave washed him back again, and they allowed him to crawl to a place of safety upon the reef. [p206]

There was a large family on board named Anderson, a father, mother and three daughters, two sons and an infant. One daughter, a pretty girl, ten years of age, was washed off the deck shortly after the ship struck and drowned. Another daughter, Agnes, sixteen years old, had escaped to the reef, the rest of the family were still on board, the hauling line had parted, the forward part of the ship had broken up, and no hope remained for those who were yet clinging to the quarter deck; but above the roar of the breakers and shrieks of despair, a mother's voice was heard crying "Agnes,

Agnes, come to me." Agnes was seated on the wreck of the main-mast that had floated upon the reef, but no sooner did she hear that mother's piercing wail, than she sprang to her feet, threw her arms up, shrieking, "Mother! Mother! I come, I come," and plunged headlong into the sea. A sailor fortunately near, seized her by her clothes, and drew her back again. The family were eventu-ally saved, when the quarter deck was washed upon the reef. The mother said she felt as though she wanted Agnes with her, and then all would die together.

Again, when the ship first struck the reef, I took my nautical instruments and gave them to one of my most reliable men, and sent him the first one to the reef upon the rope with the charge that, "all of our lives might depend upon their safety, and if I found him alive, I should also expect to find those precious instruments in his possession." I also had barrels of bread and other provisions thrown overboard, but all that we eventually gathered was ruined for use by the salt water.

Our situation on the reef can be better imagined than described. It was about eleven o'clock at night, when all were landed; we were up to our waists in water, and the tide rising. Seated upon spars and broken pieces of wreck, we patiently [p207] awaited the momen-tous future. Wrapped in a wet blanket picked up among the float-ing spars I seated myself in the boat, the water reaching to my waist, my limbs and arms were badly cut, and bruised by the coral.

Though death threatened ere morning dawn, exhausted nature could bear up no longer, and I slept soundly. It was near morning when I awoke. The moon was up and shed her faint light over the dismal scene, the sullen roar of the breakers sent an additional chill through my already benumbed frame. The bell at the wheel, with every surge of the sea, still tolled a knell to the departed, and naught else, but the wailings of a bereaved mother, broke the still-ness of the night, or indicated life among that throng of human automata; during the long hours of that weary night, the iron had entered their soul, and the awful solemnity of their situation was brooded over in silence.

At morning's dawn low islands were discovered, distant about ten miles. Again all was activity. I immediately set about patching the boat, whilst others collected spars and drift stuff to form a raft, on which to place the women and children. A little after sunrise, I started for the land, though our boats would scarcely float.

The first island on which we landed presented a very barren appearance; it was covered with the banana tree; birds were plentiful and very tame, but after a diligent search no water, fruit or vegetables could be found. We proceeded to another, and nothing but disappointment awaited us. Water was madly sought for in vain; and late in the afternoon we returned disappointed and unsuccessful to our companions of the reef.

I then placed the women and children in the boat, and sent them in charge of Mr. Coffin to the land, while the rest of us remained on the reef for [p208] a second night. A small raft had been found, but not large enough for all to sit upon.

Early on the morning of the second day, Mr. Coffin returned to us with the boat, and I immediately dispatched him again in search of water, for the want of which we were nearly famishing; while the rest of us commenced in earnest preparing a couple of rafts, on which we placed what provisions and clothing could be collected. And about ten o'clock made an attempt to reach the island, by wading along the reef, our boats in tow, the old and helpless men, of whom there were several, being placed upon them. Energy, perseverance and above all, necessity, can accomplish almost impossibilities, and we were successful.

Most of the water for a distance was deep. In one place, for over a mile, it took us to our necks, the shorter men being compelled to cling to the rafts. Several deep inlets had to be crossed when our best swimmers were called into requisition. In one of these attempts I nearly lost two of my best men. Large numbers of sharks followed in our wake, at one time I counted over twenty, and not infrequently we were compelled to seek safety from them upon the rafts. Late in the afternoon we reached the island, completely exhausted, but our hearts swelled with gratitude as we were conducted by the children to some holes dug in the coral sand on the beach, where they had obtained drinkable water. We had been forty-eight hours in the salt water, two days exposed to the rays of a tropical sun, without food or drink. We never found any fresh water supply on any of the small islands other than by digging; the water we obtained in this way was brakish, but fairly good.

The island that we reached with our rafts, and where we made our permanent camp was a low, oblong coral reef, rising just above the surface of the sea, perhaps fifty rods long by twenty rods at its widest [p209] point, covered quite thickly with a low tree of the banyan species. Our first great anxiety was a search for something to eat. Remember, we had been literally fasting for forty-eight hours, without a morsel of food. Under such circumstances you may well believe that we were neither very particular nor squeamish. We found the island fairly swarming with a small red land crab, about half the size of one's first, not a crab, but we knew no other name, and so dubbed them crab. They were a crawly affair, naturally disgusting to the touch or taste, but they were food to the famishing, and we seized upon them with avidity. In about a week we cleared the entire island, not one more of the creeping things could be found.

I well remember the excitement and glorification among our little party of castaways on the discovery of our first turtle. About five days after our landing, I was seated with my officers at our camp fire discussing the situation, the rapidly diminishing supply of our only food, the delectable crab, was causing the keenest anxiety, when a loud shout from a party of sailors some distance from us up the beach attracted our attention. They were shouting and dancing in a circle around something to us invisible. Every one rushed to the spot, and there found a large turtle in the hands of the Philistines. And this find meant to us a new lease of life. Knowing the habits of the sea turtle during the incubating season of seeking the land at night and depositing their eggs in the dry sand on the beach, we organized parties, watch and watch, to patrol the beach during the entire night on the lookout for turtle, and when one was found, they would turn him over on his back, and the following day the night's catch would be brought to camp. Our largest find in any one night was five turtles. Every turtle killed was carefully divided among the [p210] several messes, first saving a portion to be jerked and dried in the sun, for the purpose of accumulating provisions for our proposed boat voyage. We soon began to gather more turtle than we needed for our daily consumption. We therefore built a stockade turtle pen to keep them, to be used as needed, believing that they would live on land as well as on the deck of a ship at sea, where they can be kept for months alive by simply throwing sea water over them occasionally during the day. But in this we were disappointed, for every morning we found a dead turtle or two in our pen, and as we could not afford to lose any, we lived on turtle, butchered, a la mode, after death.

And right here I will correct a misstatement made by Miss Spangenberg, in a letter published in the *San Francisco Daily Herald*, in which she says that we obtained fire by rubbing barro together. Not so. On the night of the wreck, when I found the ship was hopelessly doomed, I tried to provide as fast as possible for just such circumstances as we were finally placed in, among other things, the need of matches. I therefore put a large quantity in my overcoat pocket, but on leaving the wreck I threw off my overcoat and all surplus clothing. Afterwards this coat was found floating on the reef, but the matches were water soaked and spoiled. Fortunately a sailor had three or four matches in the lining of his hat, where he had been in the habit of keeping them to use in an emergency for lighting his pipe. With these we started a fire, and took good care to never allow it to go out while we remained on the reef.

Three days after our landing I took an exploring party in the boat, and upon an island some eight miles from the one on which we had located, discovered a grove of cocoanuts. Our hearts dilated with gratitude, for without something of this kind, our [p211] case would have been indeed desperate. Our living now consisted of shell fish, turtle, sharks and cocoanuts. We also prepared a garden and planted some pumpkins, peas and beans. They came up finely and flourished for a few weeks, then withered and died, for lack of deepness of soil. I have been asked where we got seeds to plant. The damaged provisions, such as bags of peas and beans found upon the reef furnished seeds that when planted grew; a pumpkin was also picked up on the reef, from which we obtained seeds.

Having found means of present subsistence, my next object was to repair the boat. It was one of our quarter boats, small and badly stove, but no other hope seemed to offer for a final deliverance from capitivity. We constructed a forge and smith's bellows to make nails and the iron work necessary. Several trips were made to the wrecks, from which we obtained canvas, boards and many necessary articles. A lookout was also established at the cocoa island, as perchance a passing vessel might be signaled, and at night parties were sent out to hunt turtle. We built a small punt, or batteau, for use on the lagoon, while our larger boat was being repaired, and fitted for sea service. We also gathered broken barrel staves on the beach and made kegs and vessels to hold water.

We divided ourselves into families, built huts and thatched with the leaves of the pandanus tree. All the provisions found were thrown into one common stock, and equally divided among each mess every morning, and we gradually became reconciled to our sad fate.

And here I will anticipate a question that has probably already suggested itself, and that had occasionally troubled me, but which in the crowding anxieties and perplexities that pressed upon me, I had found no opportunity to investigate. And that [p212] was, how it happened that with a good lookout on the foreyard, the ship should have dashed so recklessly and without warning to her destruction. However, the answer came to me unasked in this manner: Our night patrol had captured five large turtle on one of the outlying island, and I sent two men in the punt across the lagoon to bring them to camp. The sailor in charge, against the protest of his companion, undertook to bring them all in one trip, the consequence was the boat was swamped in the middle of the lagoon. With my glass I saw the men struggling in the water, but was quite powerless to help them. When night set in, I had a large beacon fire kindled, in the hope that it might possibly be of use to them, and about nine o'clock one of them came puffing in half drowned. He had supported himself with an oar, and thus succeeded in reaching land. He came to me with a grievance. Said that he would never trust himself afloat again with that man, (his sailor companion) that he had nearly drowned him twice, and he would take good care not to give him another chance. Said that on the night of the wreck that fellow was ordered aloft to lookout, taking him along for company. That he saw a long white strip of water ahead and pointed it out, and asked what it could be, but our bright look-out was near sighted, and could not see any thing peculiar, but thought he would go down into the forecastle for his spectacles, and of course before his return the doomed ship had solved the mystery. A startling revelation. Five lives lost, great anxiety and suffering incurred, a large amount of property destroyed, all owing to the near sightedness of a common sailor, and yet did it ever occur to the Captain of a ship to have the sight of his forecastle men examined?

Five weeks after our unfortunate wreck our boat was ready. The attempt to launch forth upon the [p213] treacherous sea, in so frail a thing was desperate, but we knew no choice between death encountered in a manly effort at escape, or a life-long captivity upon that desolate reef. To satisfy the passengers, I offered to remain with them and send one of the officers with a portion of the crew for assistance. Mr. Coffin objected to going in the boat, said he was an old man, and preferred to die where he was, and the crew likewise to go without me, but volunteered to follow my lead.

The nearest inhabited islands were the Society Group, supposed to be three hundred to five hundred miles dead to windward of us; for more than five weeks it had been blowing a steady trade gale from the east, and I reluctantly abandoned the hope of ever reaching them, and turned my eyes to leeward. The Navigator Islands seemed our only chance, and though the distance, some fifteen hundred miles, was appalling, I determined to steer for them, trusting to a kind Providence for our success. I selected four of my men for a boat's crew, and fixed the day for our departure.

Nothing now remained for us but to survey the opening from the lagoon to the ocean, which had been neglected owing to the want of a suitable boat, but the existence of which had never given me any uneasiness. And you may judge of our dismay when, after two days diligent search, no passage could be found, and the fact that we were imprisoned in a circle of angry breakers became apparent. Gloomy despair seemed to fill every breast; those most active and energetic heretofore seemed prostrated; but bewailing our unhappy lot and future prospects would never effect a deliverance, and I summoned all of my flagging energies to the task. I scattered the ship's crew and officers in every direction over the reef, and commenced a systematic search for any break in the rocks that might [p214] offer a chance for the launching of a boat. Three days were spent in this manner upon the reef, and a spot finally selected, where by carrying the boat some two hundred yards and in favorable weather offered a hope of success.

On the following day I determined to make the trial. But my own spirits now seemed crushed. I felt like one going to the stake, a foreboding of evil came over me. The weather was unsettled and threatening, and I retired to my tent as I thought for the last time, unhappy and without hope. The clouds gathered in gloomy grandeur, and finally broke in a tornado over the island. In vain I sought repose and sleep. About three o'clock in the morning I arose and walked down upon the beach, and there indeed was experienced the climax of my distress, for the boat upon which all our hopes centered had disappeared.

I called the second mate, and as the report spread from tent to tent, men, women and children, yet in the gray dawn of morning, gathered upon the beach, and gazed upon the spot where the night previous, they had seen the priceless boat so snugly moored. Their great misfortune could hardly be realized. Our compass, nautical instruments and everything of value had been exhausted in its construction. The loss of all these banished hope from every breast, and seemed to seal the doom of the entire party. Some threw themselves in despair upon the beach; the silent tear trickled down the cheeks of speechless women; others moaned aloud at their sad, sad fate, for our provisions were nearly exhausted, and starvation stared us in the face.

I endeavored to cheer them with the hope that the boat had dragged her anchor into deep water, and after drifting across the lagoon would anchor herself again off one of the leeward islands. This eventually proved to be the case, and the boat was re- [p215] covered, nearly full of water, but not injured. The weather now seemed to be breaking up; the trade winds blew less steadily, and all appearances indicated change. Secretly influenced by a gloomy, undefined premonition of evil and disaster, as the result of my proposed attempt to reach the Navigator Islands, I was now determined on the apparently more desperate course of double banking the boat with a crew of ten men, and watching a favorable opportunity, endeavor to pull to the nearest windward islands.

Against this course Captain Coffin, an old whaler, opposed [with] all his influence and experience. Said, he would rather venture alone than with ten mouths to feed, that it would be impossible to pull our boat, so deeply loaded, against a head wind and sea, and there was no place under our lee where we could make a harbor in the event of our encountering what we might expect—easterly weather; that in fact, it was a life or death undertaking, success or certain destruction awaited us. But desperate diseases require desperate remedies. I proposed it to my crew, and with but a single exception, they all volunteered. We now impatiently waited for a suitable opportunity to launch our boat.

At daybreak on the morning of the third of December, just eight weeks from the day of our wreck, I was aroused by Mr. Owens. The wind was blowing in gusts from the northwest; the night had been stormy; heavy clouds hung in the western horizon; the whole firmament was overcast, and a drizzling rain rendered the entire aspect of nature chilling and unpromising. I hesitated long, but it was the first westerly wind we had had since our residence on that island, and I gave the orders for our departure.

And here I will pause for a moment to state [p216] another of what we recognized as direct special Providence in our behalf. Considering our resources, we had succeeded admirably well in fitting up our boat; had gathered jerked turtle meat and cocoanuts for provisions; had succeeded in making tight kegs from old barrel staves and hoops found upon the reef to carry the water needed. But how to secure light for our binnacle at night was an unsolved problem. We had damaged matches that could be only used as applied to a spark. We had also the steel and tinder, but the needed flint to get the spark could not be found. We had searched every crook and crevice as we thought on the reefs and islands unsuccessfully, and no light for our binnacle meant probable aimless steering at night and loss and destruction of the boat's crew.

On the day before our departure, with a small party of sailors, still in the prosecution of what seemed a hopeless search for a stone that could be used with steel and tinder, I had reached a small island, the most distant one from our camp and somewhat difficult of access, and in consequence had been seldom visited by us. Working our way through a thick tangle of underbrush, we came to an open space, and I believe that my eyes fairly bulged with astonishment as I descried a small pool of fresh water, beside which lay a bucket and large flint stone. I seized the stone, and with a shout, exclaimed, "A gift from God, boys we are saved, we are saved."

On our subsequent arrival in Tahiti, I met the man to whom the stone and bucket belonged. Some years previously he had visited those reefs in search of pearl oysters, and made his camp by that pool of fresh water, and left his flint and bucket on his departure.

You understand our situation; we were on a chain of small low islands, connected from island [p217] to island by a coral reef and angry breakers, inclosing a beautiful lagoon, perhaps ten miles across; at low water we could pass from one island to another by wading.

Every man, woman and child, capable of service, started on foot, while the crew pulled the boat with water and provisions across the lagoon to the place selected to try the reef, distant about eight miles. The boat was carried over the reef some two hundred yards, and placed in the breakers, where she was held securely by the united strength of fifteen to twenty men, while her water and provisions were stored, her crew at their stations, and at the word, we were safely launched once more upon the open sea.

And just here again, please emphasize another of those wonderful interpositions of Divine Providence in our favor. For the eight weeks that we had been on those reefs the wind had blown incessantly from the east, accompanied with a heavy choppy sea. But on the night previous to our departure, it hauled to the south west, very squally, with occasional heavy dashes of rain. The sea was dark, boisterous and altogether presented a very dangerous outlook, and this was the condition of the weather when we finally put to sea, its only redeeming feature to us was the fact that the wind, such as it was, and if we could stand it, was favorable to the course we desired to steer.

Having cleared the boat from the reef and obtained the open sea, we were almost immediately compelled to throw overboard a large portion of our water, provisions and every article that could possibly be spared to lighten the boat. And thus our boasted liberal supply that we had collected and saved with so much perseverance and economy suddenly vanished in the sea, leaving us a scant pittance for perhaps five or six days. [p218]

Having made everything snug as possible, we shaped our course, proposing to scud before the wind, but suddenly the wind lulled, a dense black cloud rolled up, covering the entire firmament, shutting out the day, and enveloping us in almost Egyptian darkness, and such a downpour of water burst from the cloud—in the language of scripture, it seemed as though "All the fountains of the great deep were broken up, and the windows of Heaven were opened." The rain seemed to fall in solid sheets; though intensely sharp, far beyond any previous experience of ours, the downpour was very brief in its duration. The clouds cleared as suddenly as they arose; the sun burst out upon the face of the great deep; the rain had beaten down the boisterous sea, which now rolled in long smooth swells. It was a dead calm, and for three days and nights there was not breeze enough to blow out a candle. I will also mention another curious fact. We were all of us, for a day or two, very seasick. The men labored at their oars, and vomited over the thwarts. Mr. Owens, my second officer, was so intensely sick that he lay stretched in the bottom of the boat, and for the first twenty-four hours I had to cun the boat without relief, before he could take his trick at the helm.

After three days of incessant toil, hope, fear and despair alternately predominating, "Land ahead." Oh, how the cry, the thought, the reality thrilled our every nerve, and our anxious longing eyes gazing at the dim, cloudlike outline of a far distant island, gradually lit with renewed fire, and hope again shone out, bright and clear, and yet the most fearful portion of our voyage had still to be experienced, for now old Boreas blew out fresh and strong, contrary to our course, and the sea yesterday so sluggish arose in all its might and power, threatening to engulf us in its appalling throes.

For hours and hours, the fearful but unequal [p219] contest was maintained, till human endurance could bear up no longer, and we lay exhausted in the bottom of our little boat, now floating at the mercy of the sea, the goal of our hopes, and our very lives, that dim cloud upon the verge of the horizon, gradually faded from our view.

Oh, the blank despair of that moment! And as we drew the tarpaulin over the boat to shelter us from the dashing spray, thought of home mingled in our prayers. Late in the afternoon, as we lay huddled together under the protecting cover of the tarpaulin, drenched by the salt spray, faint and exhausted by severe toil, listlessly gazing out upon the combing, raging sea, that threatened instant destruction, the sudden cry of "Land, land," again startled us from the lethargy of despair, which seemed with its cold icy hand to [grip] our very hearts.

And true enough, as the sun emerged from the dark storm cloud to sink into the sea bright and beautiful in the far west, lighting up the circling horizon, the clear outline of an island mountain peak could be distinctly seen in the southeast. Tears of gratitude filled our eyes. Our sail was hoisted to the now favoring breeze. Again our oars were manned, and our little boat fairly trembled at the onward impetus given by the hope resuscitated nerves of my but recently faint and exhausted crew. The darkening shades of night soon shut from our view that lone mountain top, rising as a beacon hope from the sea, and in its stead, the mariner's compass served as our sure guide till morning again dawned, and discovered to our enraptured gaze the fertile slopes of a mountain island, distant about fifteen miles. As we neared the land, the wind gradually subsided, and the sea no longer broke in heavy combers as on the day previous, but rolled in long, heavy swells upon a reef that en- [p220]circled the island. We pulled along outside of the reef about two hours, looking in vain for an entrance, and in our impatience, once more to tread a hospitable shore, and partake of the luxurious fruit that hung so temptingly beyond our reach; we had about made up our minds to attempt to land upon the reef through the breakers, when a native who was engaged spearing fish inside, guessing our difficulty, motioned to us to proceed further up the reef. On complying with which we soon found a ship entrance to a fine harbor, and saw the huts of a native village at the head of the bay. And now having safely reached one of the Windward Islands against all human probability when we departed from Scilly reefs, I will give you a peculiar episode in connection with that boat voyage. I can simply vouch for the facts, without any attempt to argue, or explain.

My passengers were mostly Mormons, bound to Salt Lake City, densely ignorant and very superstitious and were bitterly opposed to my first proposition of trying to reach the Navigator Islands. They argued, the distance to be so great, some fifteen hundred miles, that if we succeeded in reaching them they would starve to death before we could hope to send them relief. They could not, or would not understand why we might not steer in face of head wind and sea to the Society Islands which were so much nearer. We, however, as nautical men, determined to act on our own judgment in that matter, and steadily continued our preparations until our plans were blocked in a most unexpected manner. One of their Elders had a dream or vision. He saw the boat successfully launched upon her long voyage, and for a day or two making satisfactory progress. Another leaf in the vision, and the boat is seen floating bottom up, and the drowned bodies of her crew floating around her. This tale, so wrought upon the superstitions that not a man would volunteer to go with [p221] me, and I was reluctantly compelled to change my plan.

I then gave strict orders that there should be no more visions told in public unless they were favorable ones, and first submitted to me for my approval. After some days the same Mormon Elder came to me having had another vision. I asked him if it was a good one. Yes, a very good one. He saw the boat depart with a crew of ten men, bound to the eastward; after three days of rowing, they reached a friendly island where a vessel was obtained and all hands safely brought to Tahiti. When I, by compulsion, changed my plans and decided to double bank the boat and try to pull to windward, only nine men offered, including myself. It was useless to start short handed, and I had been waiting unsuccessfully to get one more man to complete my crew. On hearing this very good vision, I looked my man over. He was a fine, athletic fellow, and asked him if he believed his vision. "Yes, indeed, was it not a revelation from God?" I then suggested that it would be a good way to prove his faith by volunteering for the boat. "Of course he would," and he did with alacrity, and thus was my crew completed. You have heard the account of how literally his dream was fulfilled against every probability.

We were met on our landing by a crowd of copper colored natives, and escorted to a large bamboo house in the centre of their village. We could communicate only by signs, and I endeavored to make them understand who and what we were, but evidently our reception was not very cordial. They seated us on the ground in a distant corner of the long room, stationing half a dozen stalwart men, suspiciously like a guard, in front of us, and we began to experience not a little anxiety as to what kind of company we had fallen among. By and by those who [p222] seemed to us chiefs, or men in authority, gathered around a table on which was placed bread, fruit for their noon meal, and much to our relief one of them bowed his head and asked a blessing. Our anxieties at any rate were allayed, for we found that we were among Christians, and we quietly awaited events. Later in the afternoon a new comer appeared upon the scene, one who could speak broken English. It seems that he was absent in a distant portion of the island when we arrived, and they immediately dispatched a messenger to summon him. He informed us that we were on the island of Bora Bora, the most westerly of the Society Group. That the king was on a visit to a neighboring island. The reason that we had been treated with so much incivility and suspicion was the fact that only a short time previously a boat's crew landed on their island, claiming to be shipwrecked mariners. They were received with the greatest cordiality and kindness, but had proved themselves treacherous: kidnapped some of their women and endeavored to escape in their boat. Had been pursued, and a bloody conflict occurred. They were said to have been escaped convicts from a British penal settlement, and our boat's crew appeared to them like a second edition of the same sort.

The missionary belonging to this station was the only white resident on the island, and he was absent on a visit to his home in England.

A small yacht was lying at anchor in the bay, belonging to the king, and through the interpreter, who professed a great desire to aid us to the best of his ability, I endeavored to persuade the Captain to carry us to Tahiti distant some sixty to seventy miles further to windward, where an American Consul resided, but he refused to have anything to do with us; seemed to fear that we would take possession of his vessel. However, after a good deal of dickering, he finally offered to take me alone, [p223] starting the next day, if I would immediately, that same afternoon, send off my crew to Riatia, lying some fifteen miles to the southward of Bora Bora, where they informed me a British Consul lived. I felt this to be pretty hard lines for me personally, but it was the best, and in fact, only thing to be done under the circumstances, and I reluctantly consented. And now I encountered almost as much difficulty in persuading my own men to leave me alone on that island. They had no confidence whatever in the "surley" natives. However, to use their own words, "The Captain knew best, and they would obey orders." But I will confess to an awful feeling of loneliness and desertion creeping over me as I stood upon the beach and watched them pull away to sea again, leaving me behind and alone. At daybreak on the following morning I was astir, hoping to get a bright and early start for Tahiti, only to find that during the night the yacht and my friendly interpreter had disappeared, gone to parts unknown. I sat down quietly in my tracks, making no effort whatever to communicate with the natives, sick, heart-sick, discouraged, utterly helpless. A little after mid-day, I observed a six oared whale boat pulling rapidly across the bay, apparently a new arrival from the sea. As I lay there listlessly watching their movements as they stepped ashore, the natives gathered around them pointing towards me, as I supposed, telling the story of my advent among them. Presently one of the new comers started towards me, and as he approached, the scales seemed to fall from my eyes, the blood shot through my veins, as I recognized the face of an old familiar friend, a Mr. Barfe, whose home was in Huania. He

96

had come across to collect cocoanut oil. He was profuse in offers of assistance; gathered his men, and we immediately started in his boat, in an effort to overtake my men at Riatia. About half way [p224] across we met my boat's crew returning to me, bearing a letter from the British Consul full of sympathetic expressions for my disaster, and requesting me to remain in Bora Bora, as he had dispatched an express to Huania, where several American vessels were lying, containing the assurance that I might expect one at the earliest possible moment to call for me and proceed to the rescue of the castaways remaining on Scilly Reefs. In response I returned with my boat's crew to the island of Bora Bora, and there awaited the promised assistance.

The day following a large number of boats arrived at Bora Bora from Riatia, the news of the wreck having spread like wild-fire in all directions, to visit the scene of the disaster, but they were all too small to be of any service. However, on the morning of the second day, the fine large schooner, Emma Packer, appeared off the harbor, Captain Latham having received the British Consul's dispatch while lying at Heuania made no delay in getting his vessel to sea, and coming to my relief. He also brought a letter to me from the Captain of the ship *Oregon*, saying that I might expect his vessel to be under way for Scilly Reefs within a few hours after the departure of the Emma Packer to render any needed assistance.

I boarded the Emma Packer, and sailed for the rescue of my poor, distressed fellow-voyagers of the *Julia Ann*. We sighted Scilly Reefs about ten days after our departure therefrom, and much to our surprise, with our glasses we could discover no signs of life on the islands, though we sailed entirely around them, and Captain Latham was quite disposed to return, arguing that the people must have been taken off by some other vessel. He, however, in compliance with my earnest request, remained off the reef over night, for I was determined not to return without first effecting a landing, and personally [p225] inspecting my old camping grounds, and we were rewarded early the following morning by discovering a group of people gathered on the point of reef nearest to our vessel, frantically waving a signal. Words simply fail me in any attempt to describe the scene that met me, as I sprang from the relief boat into the outstretched welcoming arms of those more than half-starved castaways.

They were speedily embarked, and taken to Tahiti, where the American and British Consuls took charge of their different nationalities, and provided for their necessities.

And now answering one or two questions that are almost invariably asked, when the incidents of wreck have been the subject of conversation, and I will close.

In the face of such experiences were you not cured from all desire of ever again venturing upon the ocean? This question is asked without much reflection, or consideration of human nature. And I will answer it, in the good old Hibernian style, by asking another. A young man drives out upon the highway with a pair of young mettlesome horses, affrightened by a passing train; they dash furiously along the road beyond control, until horses, vehicle and driver are piled in one heterogeneous mass by the wayside, the driver glad to escape with his life and broken limbs, does he for all future time ignore the use of fine blooded stock, and choose the drone cart horse, or the staid plow team, that require a constant "gee up, go long" and application of the whip to secure the most moderate trot, because perchance in the use of one there is assured perfect safety and of the other, possible danger? Your answer is mine, most emphatically, "No."

On the contrary, while toil, exposure and hardship, peculiarly incident to the life of the sailor, [p226] may possibly drive some to the abandonment of their profession, it is this very sense of peril and danger to be encountered and overcome that proves almost its sole attraction; courage and true manhood are as inseparable as light, and the sun's rays pass an object between the sun and our earth and daylight is obliterated, 'tis all obscurity and darkness, and so likewise, take from man the principle of courage, and you have a human monstrosity.

While no man may assume to himself credit for the possession of physical courage, the want of it is a most unpardonable disgrace. The exposed coward is invariably hooted from the society of decent men; courage in man is the element that commands the love of woman, and its opposite, in the gentler and more delicately toned nature of woman, is that which wooes and wins to her embrace and protection man, all rugged and hardened in life's battles though he be, as the balmy summer's wind bends to her will the mighty oak.

The keenest and most tangible sense of enjoyment of my entire life has been experienced standing upon the quarter deck of my ship in the morning watch after a night spent in battling successfully with the driving temptest, my ship under storm sails riding safely to the gale, and as my eye stretched out over the vast tempest-tossed ocean, and then peering into the heavens, thickly studded with stars, and there, selecting one, countless millions of miles distant, and with it marking out a sure highway over that trackless waste of waters to our destined port, it is then, and amid such scenes, that man realizes in himself his mortality and his immortality, his wonderful capacity, and his utter dependence.

Infidelity and skepticism are dethroned, and he knows the truth, the reality beyond all cavil, that God created man in his own image, but a little [p227] lower than the angels, breathing into his nostrils the breath of Eternal Life, and that man, redeemed from the taint of sin, might indeed be a fit associate of those celestial beings, who sing God's praises around the throne of Heaven. [p228]

Chapter XVIII

FIFTH VOYAGE TO AUSTRALIA. SHIP HORIZONT, RETURN VIA SOUTH AMERICA TO SAN FRANCISCO, THENCE TO NEW YORK.

The protest recorded on the closing page of this book, filed with the American Consul, against my unwarranted detention in Tahiti had its desired effect in obtaining from the Government a permit for my departure in the French ship "Africaine," bound for Callao, though not for some hours after she had left the harbor.

Fortunately however for me the wind was light, and my hardy crew were ready with the *Julia Ann*'s boat that had brought us from the reef, and they pulled out in pursuit of the Africaine, overtook her and placed me on board. I gave them the boat and its contents as a small expression of my regard for their fidelity. Poor fellows, it was a final parting, for they all, to a man, lost their lives in pursuit of their calling but a few months subsequently.

Three days after my departure from Tahiti, our own ship *Lucas* appeared off the island, en voyage, to San Francisco. My fellows recognized the ship, and, faithful to my interests, they rowed out to her, and warned the Captain against bringing his ship into the harbor, for the authorities, on discovering that she belonged to the same owners as the *Julia Ann*, would be likely to compel her to take all of the wrecked passengers who were then [p229] being comfortably provided for and in charge of the British Consul, on a free ticket to California. Hence, the Captain of the *Lucas* took Miss Spangenburg, the only cabin passenger of the *Julia Ann*, her officers and crew, and proceeded on her voyage to San Francisco, where he arrived only three days before me, bringing the first intelligence of our disaster.

The brig *John C. Fremont* was then lying in the stream, ready for sea. A vessel that my partner, Mr. Wetherbee, had bought and fitted up during my mysterious absence, and Mr. Owens, who had made for himself such a splendid record for bravery and efficiency as second officer of the *Julia Ann*, was placed on board of the *Fremont* as first officer, having hardly an hour's shore leave between arrival of the *Lucas* and sailing of the *Fremont*.

This vessel was never heard from subsequent to her departure, though a rumor reached us that a vessel answering her description had been wrecked on "Christmas Island," and all on board perished.

The foremast hands of the *Julia Ann* shipped in a body on a vessel bound up the coast. It was wrecked, and crew drowned. Captain Coffin, my first officer, returned to his eastern home, and retired from the sea.

To return to my own personal experience on leaving Tahiti. The Captain of the Africaine, a Frenchman, received and treated me like a brother, gave me a free passage and of the best his ship afforded. On arriving at Callao, the American Consul received me with many expressions of sympathy at my misfortune, provided me with free quarters at the hotel Americana in Lima, and also with a free passage on the British steamer to Panama, and here again the American Consul interested himself in my behalf, and a free passage was given me on the American steamer "Golden Age," Commodore Watkins, to San Francisco. [p230]

My long and mysterious disappearance had caused intense anxiety among my relatives and friends. The papers of the world were daily scanned for any intelligence of the missing ship, and when my letters, written at Bora Bora, and mailed from Panama, reached my parents in New York, all hope had been abandoned, and brother Metcalf was busy packing his trunk preparatory to sailing for California to hunt up and settle my scattered business affairs. Dear mother, however, said that she never gave up hope that her son Franklin was somewhere alive, and would eventually be heard from. Who can fathom a mother's love and faith in an only son.

My prolonged absence had considerably embarrassed my partner, Mr. Wetherbee, who really knew very little of the details of the foreign end of our business, and in fact Mr. Randall, of Sydney, knew nothing about Wetherbee as a partner of mine, and though I had advised Wetherbee by the schooner *Carbon* of the contract I had entered into, yet all of the papers were with me in the *Julia Ann*. I also had $15,000 in gold and $10,000 in bills of exchange, the insurance policies and memoranda of extreme importance to him as surviving partner in my safe in the *Julia Ann*.

He had, however, at a venture dispatched the *Carbon* with a cargo of timber to Sydney, and also the *J. C. Fremont*, but it was an unspeakable relief to him when I made my appearance three days after the arrival of the ship *Lucas* in San Francisco.

It was no small undertaking to pick up the threads of our interrupted business affairs and start things running again smoothly.

After conferring with my partner for a few days, and in a measure shifting the burden of a mass of business from my own to his broad shoulders, it seemed as though my nerves collapsed utterly. I was not conscious to what a terrible strain and tension [p231] they had been subjected to until the reaction came, leaving me physically and mentally for a week or two, well, if I may so express it, a vacuum. I would retire at night and lie with my eyes open, and arise in the morning, not having had a wink of sleep. Mr. Wetherbee became quite alarmed at my condition, and in conjunction with the landlord of the hotel took me in hand, and applied a remedy perhaps somewhat primitive and characteristic of the country and age, and which I would hesitate to recommend to others. They put me to bed, then administered glass after glass of hot whisky. It put me to sleep most effectually, and certainly I awoke after a season, but "Richard was himself again."

I very much desired to take a vacation, and make a visit to the Eastern states, but Mr. Wetherbee insisted on the necessity of my returning to Sydney to look after our insurance and other business, which had become quite disjointed. However distasteful this was to me personally, I could but concede its importance, and therefore set about making preparations for another voyage to the antipodes. The large French ship "St. Anns," having a carrying capacity of 300,000 to 400,000 feet of timber, was chartered and dispatched to Puget Sound, to load for Sydney. We also, a little more leisurely, chartered the Dutch ship "Horizont," and laid her on for passengers, for which she had fine accommodations, and general cargo from San Francisco direct to Sydney. In this vessel I sailed as supercargo. We had for fellow-passengers some quite prominent theatrical and musical stars, Mrs. Sinclair, the separated wife of Edwin Forrest, the world-renowned tragedian; a Mr. Sedley, also a Mr. Loder, prominent in the musical circles of the day.

This voyage was without special incident, pleas- [p232] ant and rather monotonous, except one startling affair. Fire at sea is always a present danger, but its actual occurrence will undoubtedly stir the blood of the most sluggish, and we had this experience which really aroused our sleepy Dutchmen for a day at least, to something like old fashioned Yankee go. It was caused by one of our Dutch passengers falling asleep while smoking his pipe, and the fire ate its way into the baggageroom before it was finally extinguished, with no serious damage other than the salt water soaking of a considerable quantity of theatrical furbelows. This reminds me of an incident that happened to me on a voyage while in command of the *Julia Ann* that I failed to note.

It was a wet, drizzly day. The ship was lazily moving ahead

before a light breeze, dead aft, head sails set, main course and top sail hanging loose in their clews, spanker and gaff topsail furled when suddenly, like a flash, fire burst out forward, the flame in a broad sheet of fire, leaping clean up to the foretop. I was standing aft by the wheel. Of course at such an apparition every one naturally rushed forward. Before reaching the break of the quarter deck, my hat blew off, and instinctively I turned to chase that hat. Well, the fire was occasioned by the boiling over of the cook's pot of fat in the galley. The rigging was fortunately soaking wet, nothing ignited, and the fire disappeared almost as suddenly as it appeared, but it was a standing joke poked at me the remainder of that voyage, the Captain chasing his hat with the forward part of his ship in a blaze of fire.

The Captain of the Horizont had with him his young wife, a bride, not yet passed their honeymoon, and his handling of the ship was so different from what I had been accustomed to in the *Julia Ann*, as to keep me fretted and nervous most of the time. Instead of being on deck and taking advantage of wind [p233] and weather in the prosecution of his voyage, he was too frequently in his cabin billing and cooing with his young wife. If the wind freshened to a stiff sailing breeze, he would shorten sail in response to her nervous fears, when I, on the contrary, would wish to pack on all the more. His wife was of the nervous kind, and it became proverbial among the passengers that she was the real captain.

While the ship was under charter to me, yet I was powerless. Personal etiquette kept me silent, for no greater offense could be given than open criticism of the captain in actual charge by one, a mere passenger, in the same vessel. I therefore possessed my soul in patience to the best of my ability.

We approached Sydney heads before a fine leading breeze, and I was busy in my stateroom, making preparations, and fully expecting to land the same afternoon, when several passengers, having donned their shore toggery, rapped at my stateroom door, and in great excitement informed me that the captain had tacked ship, and was standing out to sea again, and begged me to interfere; said they had stood such nonsense long enough. I hastened on deck, and to my astonishment, true enough, the ship was heading off shore.

The wind was fitful, blowing to the land, a peculiar unearthly sigh-
ing seaward, the darkening firmament and the rising sea plainly
indicated the near approach of a storm of threatening proportions.
Indeed, I felt it quite time for me to interfere vigorously, for it
seemed to me that the Captain's course was almost an act of lunacy,
and I promptly demanded an explanation. In response, he claimed
that he had stood into the land quite as far as was prudent, that
no pilot had appeared, and he was afraid of being caught on a lee
shore at night in a rising gale, and determined, [p234] as the more
prudent course, to claw off the land, and get his ship well out to
sea before the gale broke. I protested in no measured words against
such a lunatic course, told him that I knew that coast well, that
if he did not put his ship inside of Sydney Heads with all speed,
his opportunity would be lost, that in the face of a rising tempest
we might be detained weeks at sea, and that as charterer of that
vessel, I would hold him responsible for unwarrantably prolong-
ing his voyage; that Sydney pilots only boarded vessels well inside
the Heads from whale boats, they never cruised outside looking
for ships. The passengers had gathered around during this heated
controversy, and vigorously applauded my onslaught. They had frequently expressed to me their gratification that I was on board, on
whom they might rely, as they expressed it, in case of any great
emergency, for they had but little confidence in their Dutchman,
under petticoat government.

The Captain grumbled at such unwarranted and "insolent"
interference, threatened to hold me responsible in case of disaster, but nevertheless, gave orders to tack ship, and headed up for
Sydney light. It was nearly night when we were fairly inside the
Heads; no pilot appeared, and, confused by the roaring of the surf
on the rocks to le'ward, the boiling and seething of the sea on the
ragged reef that apparently obstructed all entrance to the bay dead
ahead, the threatening rising gale seaward, our Captain utterly
lost his head, and in a vain attempt to tack, the ship was caught
aback, and threatened to drift broad side upon the rocks, where
the cliff towered perpendicularly hundreds of feet above the water.
The passengers frantically shouted to me to take charge. I sprang
to the helm, and with the greatest difficulty succeeded in getting

the ship righted, and sails drawing a rap full none too soon, as she gathered headway, and pulled out from [p235] the extremely dangerous vicinity to the breakers close aboard under our lee. The captain meekly went forward, pulled and hauled with his men, in obedience to orders given by me from the quarter deck. The ship was pointed directly to the reef known as the "sow and pigs," by which we swung less than a half cable's length, and safely dropped anchor in smooth water under its lee. It was an exceedingly narrow escape from wreck and certain death.

A large ship, the season before, had been wrecked under very similar circumstances. She drifted upon the rocks, and entirely disappeared during the night. The disaster was first discovered on hearing a human voice, by persons on the cliff above the day after the wreck, and, on investigation, a man, the only survivor, was discovered clinging to a crevice in the rocks, and he was finally rescued only by a rope let down from the top of the cliff, which he succeeded in seizing, and was hauled up safely over the brow of the cliff.

I did not blame the Captain so much as many. He evidently relied on getting a pilot, and had failed to study the chart for himself, and I well remember the thrill that shot through my nerves the first time I entered Sydney Heads with a pilot in charge. I felt certain that the ship was rushing to destruction on that seemingly impassable barrier, the sow and pigs, until she swiftly passed them close aboard to starboard. With a fair wind there is no danger. It only requires a clear head and firm hand, but it is the very worst place in the world for a man to become addled, to lose his head and the control of his vessel.

My stay in Sydney this time was quite prolonged. My old friends welcomed me as one almost returned form the dead. Such insurance as we had on the *Julia Ann* and cargo was promptly paid. [p236]

APPENDIX B

Crew and Passenger Lists

Adapted from Paul Hundley Research and List

CREW TOTAL=17

Captain Benjamin Franklin Pond (36) Captain
Captain Peter Martin Coffin (59) First Officer
William Owens (25) Second Officer
C. J. Clark (40) Cook
Henry Perkins (35) Steward
James Anderson (37) Ship's Carpenter
John Elder (40) American Seaman
Charles H. Duncan (35) American Seaman
William W. Eggert (29) American Seaman
John Evans (30) American Seaman
Fernando Victs (26) American Seaman
N. Cliff (45) American Seaman
William Sutton (32) American Seaman
Bully Williams American sailor
Charles Logie (26) Aus. LDS member
John McCarthy (25) Aus. LDS missionary (elder)
John Pegg (32) Aus. LDS member

AMERICAN PASSENGERS TOTAL=8

Miss Ester M. Spangenberg
John Sunderlin Eldridge (24) American LDS missionary (elder)
James Graham American LDS missionary (elder)
J. Cohen
W. Limmores
John Bull
Miss Logan
Mr. McCahme

AUSTRALIAN/BRITISH PASSENGERS TOTAL=33

23 LDS Passengers

Cabin   John Penfold (58)
       Elizabeth (61) (wife)
Steerage   Peter (24)
       Stephen (19)
       Andrew Anderson (44)
       Elizabeth (44) (wife)
       Jane (19)
       Agnes (17)
       Alexander (14)
       Marian (10)
       John (10)
       Andrew (8)
       Joseph (5)
       James (3)
       Rosa Clara Logie (19)
       Annie Augusta (14 mo)
       Eliza Harris (30)
       Maria (2)
       Lister (6 mo)
       Martha Humphreys (44)
       Mary (9)
       Eliza (12)
       Francis (7)

10 non-LDS Passengers

       Thomas Abel Lawrence (21)
       Thomas Magee (35)
       Eliza Magee (32) (wife)
       Thomas Jr. (14)
       Ann (12)
       John (10)
       James (8)
       Constantine (5)
       Margaret (2)
       Sarah Wilson

Passengers lost:

> Washed off deck:
> Miss Marian Anderson
> Mrs. Eliza Harris
> Lister Harris
> Mary Humphreys
> Mrs. Martha Humphrey (washed out of cabin)

Total=56
Crew=17
Passenger=41
LDS=28
Non-LDS=28

Note: There is a discrepancy between the passenger list and the signatures on the thank-you letter from Thomas Magee and other passengers. The thank-you note included the following names that are not indicated as being on the *Julia Ann* in any other document: Jno. Symmonds, Chas. Gumric, and Thomas Clagger.[241]

APPENDIX C

Biographical Register

Anderson, Andrew and Elisabeth. Andrew was born on July 26, 1810, in Edinburgh, Scotland; he married Elisabeth Crabbe on November 21, 1834, at St. Cuthbert's in Edinburgh. Elisabeth was born on August 10, 1810, in Dalkeith, Scotland. [242] A Presbyterian dissenter,[243] Andrew was one of the first baptized into the LDS Church in Edinburgh by Orson Pratt.[244] Elisabeth joined the LDS Church with her husband. Andrew was trained as a paper maker,[245] mason laborer, and was able to read and write. He had "a view to better the condition of his family, and took advantage of a free passage for a year's servitude at moderate wages."[246] Andrew was recruited to be a bounty immigrant and moved to Monteflores, New South Wales (NSW).[247] He, Elisabeth, and their three children sailed on the *James Moran*, arriving in NSW on October 6, 1841. Elisabeth was listed as a house servant on the passenger list of the *James Moran*. [248] Andrew, the second missionary in Australia,[249] faced much opposition from the government.[250] Following the call to gather to Zion, the Andersons again set sail in 1855 aboard the *Julia Ann*. Six of the children—Jane, 20; Alexander, 14; John, 10; Andrew, 8; Joseph, 5; and James, 3[251]—arrived safely; however, ten-year-old Marian died during the *Julia Ann* wreck.[252] The family finally made it to California, and in 1868 Anderson joined the RLDS Church (now known as the Community of Christ). He was baptized by W. W. Blair on August 2, 1868, and was ordained a priest by the same on September 26, 1869. Andrew attended the Irvington California Branch, most likely with his wife, though there is no record of Elisabeth also

111

joining the RLDS church.²⁵³ Andrew died on January 1, 1891, in Petaluma, California; Elisabeth died on January 21, 1894, also in Petaluma, California. ²⁵⁴

Anderson, James. James was the carpenter aboard the *Julia Ann* and was from Scotland.²⁵⁵ He was thirty-seven at the time of the wreck, thus born in 1818.²⁵⁶

Barratt, William James. William was born on January 25, 1823, in Burslem, North Staffordshire, England. Religion was part of his upbringing due to his father's religious curiosities. William was taught by Alfred Cordon and baptized in late 1839 or early 1840. When his mother and stepfather moved to Australia due to difficult economic conditions in England, Barratt went along,²⁵⁷ but not before being ordained an Elder by George A. Smith and Alfred Cordon at the age of 17.²⁵⁸ He was encouraged to share the gospel in Australia, though not specifically called to do so. He and his family left London for Australia on July 17, 1840, aboard the *Diadem.* In Australia, he helped his stepfather set up shop, sharing the gospel where he could and corresponding with Church leaders for the first few years. He befriended and baptized Robert Beauchamp, who later became a president of the Australasian Mission. Because of little Church contact and no support system in Australia, William eventually followed more conventional religious paths, holding religious services in his house throughout his life. He married Ann Gibson, and they had seven children. He died on September 10, 1889, at Bald Hills, Australia, and is buried in a nearby churchyard cemetery at Victor Harbor.²⁵⁹

Bull, John. John was an American passenger aboard the *Julia Ann*'s second voyage.²⁶⁰

Clark, C. J. Clark was the cook aboard the *Julia Ann.* He was 40 at the time of the wreck, which means he was born in 1815. He was from New York City.²⁶¹

Cliff, N. Possibly William Radcliffe from Massachusetts. Cliff was an American seaman, one of the older crew members on the *Julia Ann* at 45 years of age.²⁶²

Coffin, Peter Martin. Coffin was born March 31, 1796, in Edgartown, Dukes County, Massachusetts, the second oldest of thirteen children.[263] Coffin, a descendant of one of the first Nantucket settlers, was a log keeper and master on various whaling vessels. In 1826 he married Margaret Mayhew in Edgartown, Dukes County, Massachusetts.[264] He was referred to as a "master mariner" in a listing in 1839 that declared he was the owner of an estate in Edgartown.[265] In 1846, as master of the *Ann Eliza*, Coffin had to abandon his ship due to severe damage caused by heavy gales.[266] In October 1849 he voyaged to California aboard the ship *Martha* during the gold rush. On this same voyage was Henry Wetherbee, who later became a business partner with Captain Benjamin F. Pond. On both voyages of the *Julia Ann* (1854 and 1855), Coffin served as the first officer.[267] At the time of the *Julia Ann* wreck, he was 59 years old and an experienced sailor; he felt it was foolhardy to sail into the wind for help, and he knew he was too old to be one of the ten men who left Scilly Island. He therefore stayed behind with the other survivors.[268] After the wreck and rescue of the *Julia Ann*, he took advantage of an offer for a free passage on the ship *Lucas* to San Francisco, on which Esther Spangenberg, the only cabin passenger on the *Julia Ann*, was also a passenger.[269] According to Captain Pond, after the *Julia Ann* incident, Coffin "returned to his eastern home, and retired from the sea."[270] By mid-August 1856 Captain Coffin is listed as one who has mail unclaimed at the New York City post office.[271]

Cohen, J. Cohen was an American passenger aboard the *Julia Ann*'s second voyage.[272]

Duncan, Charles H. An American seaman aboard the *Julia Ann* from Rochester, New York, Charles was 35 at the time of the wreck, putting his birth year at 1820. He was paid US$20 per month as a seaman.[273]

Eggert, William W. An American seaman aboard the *Julia Ann* from Providence, Rhode Island, William was 28 or 29 at the time of the wreck, putting his birth year around 1826. He stood five feet nine and a half inches tall and was paid US$20 per month as a seaman.[274]

Elder, John. A British seaman aboard the *Julia Ann* from St. Andrews, John was 40 at the time of the wreck, putting his birth year at 1815. He was paid USD20 per month as a seaman.[275]

Eldredge/Eldridge, John Sunderlin. John was born on April 30, 1821, in Sennett, Cayuga County, New York.[276] He was baptized in Far West, Caldwell County, Missouri, in 1838 with his father, Alanson, and brother, Horace. Due to troubles with Missourians in Far West, he and his family fled Missouri and migrated to Indianapolis, Indiana. They later emigrated to Nauvoo, but left there soon after due to additional persecution and migrated to Winter Quarters, Nebraska. On March 24, 1849, John was married to Sinah Ceneth by Brigham Young. They had a baby girl later that year and migrated to American Fork, Utah, in 1851, where he rendered Church service as a clerk and choir director.[277] It is claimed he was one of the first to use a plow to prepare the desert land for food.[278] Two years later, he joined James Graham as a missionary in Australia, arriving with him and eight other elders in Sydney on April 9, 1853, and surviving smallpox on the voyage over.[279] After surviving the wreck of the *Julia Ann*, John and James Graham are listed as steerage passengers aboard the bark *Francis Palmer*, which left Honolulu on April 1, 1856.[280] He returned to his family and eventually moved to Charleston, Utah, which was plagued by contentions with Indians. While plowing one day, he died suddenly of a heart attack on May 5, 1871, in Charleston, Wasatch County, Utah.[281] He was survived by his wife Sinah and four children, who ranged in age from 13 to 24, as well as his second wife, Rhoda Silvia (Collett), who had three children who ranged in age from 9 to 14.[282]

Evans, John. An American seaman from New York aboard the *Julia Ann*, John was 30 at the time of the wreck, putting his birth year at 1825. He was paid USD20 per month as a seaman.[283]

Farnham, Augustus Alwyn. Farnham was born on May 20, 1805, in Andover, Essex County, Massachusetts. He was baptized on April 21, 1843, and ordained a Seventy on August 17, 1845. Called to serve an Australasian mission, he arrived in Sydney on April 1, 1853, aboard the *Pacific* and became president of the mission by vote nine days later. Farnham left for home aboard the *Jenny Ford* on May 28, 1856.[284] He married Caroline Pill on February 7, 1858. He was an exceptionally talented carpenter by trade; he built a secure roof for the East Bountiful Church after it had been blown off twice by the east wind.[285] His handiwork is best seen in the Bountiful Tabernacle, which he designed in 1857. Farnham also introduced alfalfa from Australia to Bountiful.[286] He died at Farmington, Utah, on May 2, 1865.[287]

Fleming, Josiah W. Josiah was one of the ten American LDS missionaries who arrived in Australia in the spring of 1853.[288] He is also listed as a counselor to Augustus Farnham in the Australasian Mission presidency by 1854.[289] Fleming was falsely charged with the abduction of a young woman by her father but was found innocent the following year.[290] In 1856, he was sustained as the president of the Sydney Branch.[291] He left that same year on the *Jenny Ford* to return to Utah.[292] In the history of the Las Vegas Mission, it is recorded that Fleming, Farnham, and others from the Australasian mission arrived in Las Vegas in late October 1856, where they conducted some meetings and related experiences about their missions in Australia.[293] Fleming died in Provo, Utah, on January 6, 1873.[294]

Frost, Burr. Frost was born on March 4, 1816, at Waterbury (New Haven), Connecticut. On August 16, 1843, he married Mary E. Potter for time, and they were sealed for eternity in the Nauvoo Temple on February 6, 1846.[295] He was one of the original pioneers, having traveled west with a company in 1847. A blacksmith by trade, he was an important part of the pioneer trek, often erecting a bellows to make necessary repairs along the way.[296] After arriving in the Salt Lake Valley, he had two responsibilities: the first was to protect the settlements from marauding Indians; the second was to exterminate dangerous animals. Frost made his home in Salt Lake City.[297] He served a mission to Australia from 1853 to 1854, and in April 1854 he is listed as a counselor to Augustus Farnham in the Australasian Mission presidency.[298] He was also a president of the 70th Quorum of the Seventy. He died on March 16, 1878, survived by a large family.[299]

Graham, James. James was born on October 11, 1804, in Enniskillen, Ireland and grew up in Delaware. He married Mary Ann Butler around 1824. They had twelve children.[300] He joined the LDS Church in Illinois in about 1840. They left Nauvoo, Illinois, in 1846 and traveled to Winter Quarters, where Mary Ann passed away. He crossed the plains in 1849 carrying a printing press for the Church. He married Hannah Tucker Reed on September 13, 1849, in Salt Lake City, Utah; they had two children together.[301] He was called to serve a mission to Australia in 1853 and served there for two years (1853–1855) as a traveling elder,[302] returning to America aboard the second voyage of the *Julia Ann* in 1855. After the wreck, he found passage home with John Eldredge; both were listed as steerage passengers aboard the *Francis Palmer*, which left Honolulu on April 1, 1856.[303] He reached San Francisco on June 27, 1856.[304] Jensen's "History of the Las Vegas Mission" also notes that he passed through the Las Vegas mission on October 26, 1856, where he spoke and "sang a piece he had composed on his mission to Australia."[305] About a year after returning to Ogden, Utah, he died on December 9, 1857.[306]

Harris, Maria. She accompanied her mother, Eliza, and younger brother, Lister, aboard the *Julia Ann* in 1855 due to her mother's strong desire to emigrate to Zion; her mother and brother died in the wreck, and she was taken in by the Penfold family, who traveled to San Francisco with her and Francis and Eliza Humphreys, who also orphaned during the wreck.[307] Her father, Edmond, traveled to Utah aboard the *Lucas* in 1857, but it's unclear whether they reconnected.[308]

Harris, Eliza Barrett. Eliza was born on October 9, 1824, in London, Middlesex, England.[309] She married Edmond John Harris on May 9, 1847, in London. Edmond worked as a carman (a laborer who moved merchandise with a horse-drawn cart) and Eliza as a housemaid. They joined the Church in 1847 and immigrated to Australia in 1849.[310] Eliza traveled alone aboard the second voyage of the *Julia Ann*, perhaps due to the discontinuance of the Perpetual Emigration Fund—assistance for members trying to immigrate to Zion via the Church. This meant the family did not have enough funds to allow her husband Edmond to travel as well.[311] She took with her their two young children. After the wreck, she tied her six-month-old baby, Lister, to her back to descend the rope to the safety of the coral. As she struggled down the line, a huge wave swept her and the baby to sea. They were two of the five casualties of the *Julia Ann* wreck.[312] Her husband sailed later on the *Lucas*, arriving at San Pedro on October 12, 1857.[313]

Humphreys, Eliza and Francis. These children survived their mother, Martha, and sister, Mary, who were swept overboard during the crash of the *Julia Ann*. Eliza was 12 at the time of the crash, which puts her birth at about 1843; Francis was 7, born around 1848. Their father, William Humphreys, a British subject, remained in Australia while the children and their mother traveled to Zion. They were cared for by the Penfold family directly after the wreck, as was Maria Harris, although no information about them is known after they left Tahiti for San Francisco. [314]

Humphreys, Martha Maria Bucknell. Martha was born on August 22, 1812, in London, England. In 1826, her family moved to Sydney, Australia, where her father, a jeweler, was allotted two land grants in Hunter Valley. Martha married William Humphreys on February 14, 1837. [315] They settled in Williams River, New South Wales, Australia.[316] Martha came into contact with the LDS Church in mid-1852, when John McCarthy spent a year preaching in the Hunter Valley area. She was baptized on December 17, 1852, followed soon after by her son John and her sister-in-law Susannah Barker Bucknell. Her husband did not join and often worked away, but Martha had a desire to go to Zion, as expressed in letters to her parents and husband. While she did not go on the first voyage of the *Julia Ann*, she did travel on the second, accompanied by her three youngest children. Martha and her ten-year-old daughter, Mary, were swept out of the cabin of the *Julia Ann*, becoming two of the five lives lost at sea when the *Julia Ann* wrecked.[317]

Hyde, William W. Hyde was born September 11, 1818, in York, Livingston County, New York. His parents' farm was adjacent to Warren Cowdery's land. Warren introduced the Hydes to the

Book of Mormon, and on April 7, 1834, William and his father, Heman, were baptized, and were soon followed into the waters by the rest of the family. The family followed the directions of the LDS Church leaders by moving to Kirtland, Ohio; Far West, Missouri; and Nauvoo, Illinois. In Nauvoo, Hyde was ordained a Seventy and called to serve a mission to Maine, accompanied by Elder Herrett. These were followed by missions to Vermont and New York. He married Elizabeth H. Bullard on February 23, 1842. He also volunteered to serve with the Mormon Battalion, with which he marched from the Missouri River to Los Angeles. After he was relieved, he returned to his family in Council Point, Missouri, and made the trek with them back to the Salt Lake Valley, arriving on September 22, 1849. In 1852, he was called to serve a mission to Australia.[318] Hyde is listed as a counselor to Augustus Farnham in the Australasian Mission presidency.[319] He was appointed to oversee the 1854 voyage of Latter-day Saints aboard the *Julia Ann*.[320] He helped found the settlement Hyde Park in Cache County, Utah, in 1860, and became bishop of the LDS church there.[321] He worked as a farmer, had a co-partnership with Thomas Ricks and William Hendricks in building and operating a gristle mill, and aided in laying 100 miles of railway track for the Central Pacific Railroad.[322] His poetic ability is evidenced in a poem he wrote when he set sail for Australia, as well as a song he composed regarding the death of Joseph and Hyrum Smith.[323] Near the end of his life, Hyde was ordained a Patriarch. He died on March 2, 1874.[324]

Jones, John. Born in 1813, John married Jane Howard on May 19, 1834,[325] and they emigrated from Liverpool on the ship *Agnes Ewing,* arriving in Sydney, Australia, on January 18, 1842.[326] He was a former Welsh Calvinistic Methodist. In the fall of 1851, his conversion commenced through the first sermon John Murdock ever preached in Australia at the Race Course in Sydney. Following Murdock's address, Jones asked, "Does your Church profess to receive revelation, suited to the present condition and character of man?" Jones received a spiritual manifestation of the divinity of the Latter-day Saint work as Murdock was speaking.[327] He served with Elder John McCarthy as a missionary to the Maitland region and became a counselor to Charles Wandell in the mission presidency.[328] Jones later served as the sub-editor of the LDS periodical *Zion's Watchman*.[329] His literary talent and scriptural depth are evident in arguments he made in defense of Mormonism to the editors of the *Sydney Morning Herald* and the *Empire*, as well as his instruction to the Saints.[330] Jones later published an article in these Australian newspapers titled "Where Shall I Bury My Dead?" when a minister refused to allow him to bury his daughter in a Presbyterian cemetery because of his Mormon faith, even though two of his sons were already buried there.[331] Though later "brutally assaulted by four ruthless ruffians, who . . . rushed upon him with all the ferocity of fiends just let loose,"[332] he continued to be firm and steadfast in the faith and afterwards wrote a historical sketch of the development of the Church in the Australian colonies during the 1850s.[333] In addition, Jones is listed as the president of the Sydney Branch in 1854–1855, as well as the clerk of the Australasian Mission, 1854–1856.[334] Jones showed his poetic ability by composing a poem for Augustus Farnham at the time Farnham left to open missionary work in New Zealand.[335] At the age of 43, he emigrated from Sydney to San Pedro with his wife, Jane Howard Jones, and their four children—Janet McKinnon, John Robert, Martha Jane, and Thomas—in the *Jenny Ford* company of 1856.[336]

Latham, Russell. John S. Eldredge recalled, "We were delivered from our exiled and desolate situation . . . with the charitable good feeling of Captain Latham, master of the schooner *Emma Packer*, that came to our relief."[337] The British Consulate had recommended Captain Latham, who had been docked with the schooner *Emma Packer* waiting for oranges at the isle of Huahine.[338] He was paid $1,000 for his detour to rescue the *Julia Ann* survivors on the Scilly Islands.[339] Afterwards, a letter written and signed by some of the rescued passengers referred to Latham as a "good Samaritan." One of those who were rescued by Latham was Sarah Wilson.[340] It is thought that she married Captain Latham and later changed her name to Elizabeth Sellars or Fields.

Lawrence, Thomas Abel. Lawrence was born in 1834 in Plymouth, England. He traveled to Australia and was a gold digger. He traveled aboard the *Julia Ann* as a passenger, bound for San Francisco; after the wreck, he was "forwarded homeward via Valparaiso," Chile, aboard the *Dido*.[341]

Limmores, W. An American passenger aboard the *Julia Ann*'s second voyage.[342]

Logan, Miss. An American passenger aboard the *Julia Ann*'s second voyage.[343]

Logie, Charles Joseph Gordon. Charles was born at Chelsea, Middlesex, England, on October 15, 1829. His father, following government assignments, moved the family first to Sydney in 1839 and the following year to New Zealand. Charles became a sailor at age 18 and never returned to New Zealand.[344] While on shore leave in Sydney, he saw Rosa Friedlander and declared he would marry her. He was taught the gospel by James Graham and John S. Eldredge and was baptized in April 1853, a month before marrying Rosa. He worked as a carpenter after they were married.[345] He was ordained an elder on October 3, 1853.[346] Responding to the call to gather to Zion, Charles worked as a crew member aboard the *Julia Ann* to pay his way. Charles worked in Tahiti to pay the family's fares to San Francisco; he then worked on a ranch near Reno, Nevada, until the family finally made it to American Fork, Utah.[347] There Charles worked on the farm of John Eldredge. A skilled carpenter, Charles eventually built a home for his family, became a coffin maker, and served as the town undertaker. Charles died in 1903 in American Fork, Utah.[348]

Logie, Rosa Clara Friedlander. Rosa was born on the English island of Guernsey, off the coast of Normandy, on June 16, 1837. Rosa's father died when she was a child. Her mother remarried, and the family lived in London and later moved to Sydney. She lived in Sydney, and according to a newspaper that reported her death, she was "in charge of Mission President Brother Farnham, her parents living in Melbourne,"[349] due probably to the fact that she did not get along with her stepfather. In early 1852 she joined The Church of Jesus Christ of Latter-day Saints with her stepfather, mother, and younger brother. They were baptized by Charles Wandell. She married Charles Logie in May 1853 at the age of 16. They were aboard the *Julia Ann* with their one-year-old daughter, Annie Augusta, when the ship wrecked. She was the first woman to traverse the rope that attached the sinking ship to the treacherous reef. The family eventually settled in American Fork, Utah, where they had an additional eight children, two of who died as children.[350] Rosa died after a six-month illness at age 76 in American Fork on June 15, 1913.[351]

Logie, Annie Augusta. Annie was born on June 27, 1854, in Sydney, Australia, to Rosa Friedlander and Charles Logie. Traveling to America to follow the call to gather to Zion given by the LDS Church leadership, Annie's parents took her aboard the *Julia Ann* when she was one year old. After the wreck, she grew up in American Fork, Utah, and was a second mother to her younger brother and sisters. Annie married Lee Clark outside the LDS faith in 1878, and they moved to Fort Canyon to help settle it. They had five children. She died on August 25, 1938.[352]

Magee, Thomas and Eliza. Thomas was born in Dublin, Ireland, around 1820—he was 35 at the crash of the *Julia Ann*—and had lived in Australia for many years when he boarded the *Julia Ann* to travel to San Francisco with his family. However, this was not his first voyage from Australia to San Francisco. Magee had previously gone there alone, several years before, to see how he would fare as a shoemaker, which proved to be profitable and a trade he enjoyed for the rest of his life until his untimely death in 1860. Eliza was also born in Ireland in 1823, being 32 at the time of the wreck. They had six children with them aboard the *Julia Ann*: Thomas Jr., 14; Ann, 12; John, 10; James, 8; Constantine, 5; Margaret, 2. After the crash when the rescued passengers were brought to Tahiti, Thomas and his son James left for San Francisco before Eliza left Tahiti with the rest of the children on the vessel, *Jenny Ford* in 1856, among a group of 120 Mormons who were under the direction of Augutus Farnham.[353] After they arrived back in San Francisco, a letter from

Thomas Magee and his family, as well as some of the other passengers from the *Julia Ann*, appeared in the *San Francisco Daily Herald* addressed to Jno. Latham (Russel Latham), captain of the *Emma Packer*, thanking him profusely for their rescue.[354]

McCahme, Mr. An American passenger aboard the *Julia Ann*'s second voyage.[355]

McCarthy, John. McCarthy was born on April 6, 1830, in Ulster County, Northern Ireland, to a staunch Catholic family. He was "well educated for a man of his day; he spent hours at his desk writing, often leaving his bed at night to record thoughts. He loved to write poetry. . . . He was able to converse in seven languages." As he was studying to be a priest, he was introduced to Mormonism and rebelled against the religion of his family. His family disapproved greatly; family lore says that his parents forced him to wear a coat of horsehair dipped in lime, which resulted in scars he wore for the remainder of his life. He left Ireland as a stowaway. He eventually settled in Australia, where he was baptized into the LDS Church by Charles W. Wandell on May 2, 1852. He and John Jones served as traveling missionaries in Maitland, New South Wales, about 80 miles northeast of Sydney, where they established a small branch. A letter from Brigham Young in 1855 informed him that he could end his missionary work and travel to Zion, which he did via the *Julia Ann* and subsequently wrecked. McCarthy was one of the nine that went with Captain Pond to get help for the castaways, and it is thought that he was the Mormon who had the dreams referred to by Captain Pond, as there were only two Mormons in the rescue crew and the other (Charles Logie) was already a crew members when the voyage of the *Julia Ann* commenced. He was 26 when he finally arrived in Utah, and he settled in Bountiful, Utah, where Augustus Farnham had also settled. There he met Eliza Victoria Telford, who was picking berries near the home of Anson Call, where he first found lodging. Soon thereafter, on March 13, 1857, they were married. They had nine children. He was called to take part in the Utah War (1857–1858). John became a US citizen in 1868. He was called to serve another mission to the British Isles in 1877. While his message was rejected by his own people in Ireland, he taught extensively on Jersey Island at the suggestion of Joseph F. Smith, president of the Liverpool Mission. He returned home in 1878. He lost sight in one eye later in his life, though he continued to read and write poetry. John died from a stroke at his home in Smithfield when he was sixty-eight years old on August 24, 1898.[356]

Murdock, John. Murdock was born July 15, 1792, at Kortright, Delaware County, New York. He was a first-generation American, his father having emigrated from Scotland in the mid-eighteenth century. Murdock moved west when he was 27 and settled in Ohio. He marryed Julia Clapp four years later. He was baptized by Parley P. Pratt on November 5, 1830, and was confirmed and ordained an elder by Oliver Cowdery on November 6. His wife was baptized a few weeks later on November 14, but died the following year, shortly after giving birth to twins, leaving him with five small children. The twins were adopted by Joseph and Emma Smith. Murdock spent much of his life as a missionary, serving missions in Missouri, Vermont, and New York and establishing branches in Geauga County, Ohio, and Delaware County, New York. He was a member of Zion's Camp. He married Amoranda Turner on February 4, 1836, but she died of fever on August 16, 1837. Arriving in Nauvoo in 1839, he was ordained and set apart as a bishop in 1842. He remarried again to Electa Allen on May 3, 1838, but she passed away in October 1845. He traveled west with his fourth wife, Sarah Zufelt, and they arrived in the Salt Lake Valley in September 1847. There he acted as a high councilor and was again set apart as a bishop of the 14th ward. He was also involved in the legislature of Deseret until he resigned to serve a mission to the Pacific in 1851. Leaving the valley on March 12, 1851, he traveled with Charles Wandell to Sydney, where they landed as the first American LDS missionaries in the country. He labored there until June 2, 1852, when his poor health required that he travel home early. He returned to Sarah in Lehi, Utah, and settled there from 1853 to 1867, where he was ordained a patriarch. Murdock lived in Beaver, Utah, with his children for the last few years of his life and passed away there on December 23, 1871.[357]

Owens, William. Owens was from New York and twenty-five years old in 1855 at the time he was employed as second officer of the *Julia Ann*.[358] Captain Pond mentioned that at the time of the wreck "Mr. Owens, the second officer, [was] very badly injured and disabled from further exertions."[359] Owens was one of the ten men who rowed in a small craft for help, and Pond noted that at the time of this arduous task, Owens "was so intensely sick that he lay stretched in the bottom of the boat . . . for the first twenty-four hours . . . before he could take his trick at the helm."[360] Pond further recalled, as a token "for bravery and efficiency as second officer of the *Julia Ann*, [he] was placed on board the *Fremont* [brig *John C. Fremont*] as first officer. . . . This vessel was never heard from subsequent to her departure, though a rumor reached us that a vessel answering her description had been wrecked on 'Christmas Island,' and all on board perished."[361] According to one source, at Christmas Island, "November, 1856, the lumber vessel, *J.C. Fremont*, was cast ashore in the Bay of Wrecks," and this is probably when Owens lost his life.[362]

Pegg, John. Pegg was born on April 20, 1826, most likely in England, the first child of James and Frances Pegg.[363] The family traveled to Parramatta, New South Wales, on the *Orpheus* with the Royal Veteran Company on May 6, 1826, arriving in Sydney on September 13, 1826.[364] James was a soldier that was discharged in Sydney in 1829 and had been entitled to a land grant at Banksmeadow. Upon arrival, it was found to be a swamp, and John's father spent the rest of his life trying to get compensation.[365] John was 32 when he worked as a sailor on the *Julia Ann*, likely working to pay for his passage to California.[366] While John's family eventually immigrated to America in 1877, John may have returned to New South Wales, where there is record of his death on June 16, 1866, in a government asylum at Parramatta, New South Wales.[367]

Penfold, John Sr. and Elizabeth. John was born on January 9, 1797, in Goudhurst, Kent County, England.[368] He was a farmer by trade.[369] Elizabeth Thompson was born in 1794 in Burwash, Sussex County, England. They were married on March 9, 1817, in Lamberhurst.[370] They traveled with their eight children aboard the *Palmyra* to Sydney, arriving on September 26, 1838.[371] They settled in Clarence Town, New South Wales.[372] He joined The Church of Jesus Christ of Latter-day Saints while in Australia and became president of the Hunters River Branch there.[373] He was chosen to be the company leader of the Saints who were traveling to Zion aboard the *Julia Ann*.[374] Elizabeth and John took their sons Peter and Stephen with them aboard the bark; the ship subsequently wrecked, and the family made their way to San Francisco, accompanied by the children made orphans by the wreck: Eliza and Francis Humphrey and Maria Harris.[375] The family settled in Oakland, Alameda, California.[376] While in California, John was converted to the Reorganized Church of Jesus Christ of Latter Day Saints (RLDS, now known as the Community of Christ) by Morgan and Faulk. Elizabeth died before the 1870 census was taken. John died on December 23, 1884, in Santa Ana, Los Angeles County, California.[377]

Penfold, Peter. Peter was born on January 22, 1830, in Lamberhurst, Kent, England. Peter was a miller by trade. He traveled with his parents, John and Elizabeth Penfold, on the *Julia Ann* in 1855 to come to America;[378] after the wreck, the family settled in Oakland and then El Monte, California.[379] He was baptized into the RLDS church on June 6, 1864.[380] It appears that Peter lived with his father until the 1880s and never married.

Penfold, Stephen. Stephen was born on May 25, 1835, in Lamberhurst, Kent, England. He was only three when his family made the voyage to Australia in 1838, and twenty in 1855 when he, his brother Peter, and his parents, John and Elizabeth, fatefully boarded the *Julia Ann* to travel to America. He was a miller by trade.[381] On June 22, 1864, he was baptized and confirmed a member of the Reorganized Church of Jesus Christ of Latter Day Saints by H. H. Morgan; he attended the Newport California Branch.[382] He married Rebecca Varley between 1870 and 1880; there is no evidence of any children. By 1880, his brothers Peter and John were living with him and Rebecca in El Monte, California.[383] The 1910 census shows him and Rebecca, now both in their mid-70s, living in Santa Ana, California.[384] He died on July 10, 1916, in La Puente, Los Angeles, California.[385]

Perkins, Henry. The steward aboard the *Julia Ann*, Henry was born in Massachusetts around 1820. He was 35 at the time of the wreck.[386]

Perkins, John. Perkins was born on June 28, 1821, at Bath Somerset, England. He was "a college bred man, and was educated for the Christian Ministry [and] he studied Pitman Shorthand." At twenty-one, John left home for the gold rush and married Mary Conway in Sydney. At the request of his mother, he returned home to England to visit, but without Mary. He never saw her again. He returned to Sydney in December 1853, where he settled down to employment as a "store keeper for a Wine and Spirit merchant" in the city.[387] He was ordained to the office of a priest in 1855[388] and as treasurer of the Sydney Branch the same year.[389] He came to San Pedro aboard the 1856 voyage of the *Jenny Ford* and travelled on to Salt Lake. He remarried to Jane Benson in March 1860. He passed away March 31, 1870, at the age of 49, leaving Jane with two little daughters.[390]

Pond, Benjamin Franklin. Pond was born on November 30, 1819. As a boy, Pond did not enjoy school, particularly when it was suggested he (the only son) follow in his father's footsteps to become a physician.[391] He suffered from arthritis in his youth[392] yet left home at age 19 to make his fortune. The adventurous Pond recalled, "I was young, very hopeful, ambitious, and certainly esteemed my personality and abilities up to their full measure, probably much beyond."[393] Pond meandered west, first coming into contact with the LDS Church in Nauvoo in the early spring of 1842. Throughout his autobiography, written at the request of his wife and children, he often acknowledges the hand of God as "divine providence." He was a successful entrepreneur who worked as a clerk, bookkeeper, and brick manufacturer; in banking, ranching, and bakery businesses; as a silk merchant, master ship owner, cotton factory proprietor, and in the shipping trade and other endeavors.[394] He was one of the forty-niners for the California gold rush[395] and was captain of the *Julia Ann* with routes between San Francisco and Australia.[396] He never sailed as a captain after the *Julia Ann* wreck. Pond finally married in 1866 to Caroline Frost and lived in Bloomvale, New Jersey.[397] They had five children, two of whom died in childhood from scarlet fever.[398] While in Bloomvale, they attended the Millbrook Reform Church and also arranged for a Sabbath school and religious service in one of the tenant houses connected with their cotton factory. Pond wrote, "About forty from among the factory people were received into the Millbrook church on confession of their faith in Jesus Christ as their personal Saviour."[399] The couple moved to Tenafly, New Jersey, in 1874, where they lived the rest of their days.[400] They were members of the Tenafly Presbyterian church. Pond started a rubber factory called the Pond Manufacturing Company, which experienced an explosion that demolished the building and all goods inside.[401] Pond was active in the Tenafly community, elected for Commissioners of Appeal in early 1895.[402] The Pond Manufacturing Company was later run by Charles J. Everett in 1901.[403]

Pratt, Parley Parker. Pratt was born on April 12, 1807, at Burlington, Otsego County, New York. He grew up as an avid lover of books, which manifested itself later in his life as he became the editor for the *Millennial Star* and wrote several books and pamphlets, including *Voice of Warning* and *Key to Theology*.[404] He grew up working as a farmer and went west towards Ohio to acquire land with his brother in 1823. He joined the Baptist Church in 1825 and married Thankful Halsey in 1827. After reading the Book of Mormon, he was baptized by Hyrum Smith in September 1830. Parley served many missions throughout his life, from most of the New England states to the countries of Chile, England, and Canada, where he was able to establish thriving branches.[405] In 1831 he was ordained a high priest by Joseph Smith. He was ordained an apostle in 1835. He experienced severe persecution with the body of Saints in Missouri and Illinois, including eight months spent in jail in Missouri.[406] As a member of Brigham Young's Vanguard Company, he entered the Salt Lake Valley in 1847.[407] He was instrumental in drafting the constitution of the state of Deseret (now Utah) and served on the state legislature. Parley was the president of the Pacific Mission and sent the first full-time American missionaries to Australia in 1851. He was serving a mission in the eastern states when he was murdered near the boundary of Arkansas and Indian Territory on May 13, 1857.[408]

Sutton, William. An American seaman aboard the *Julia Ann* from New Jersey, William was 32 at the time of the wreck, putting his birth year at 1823. He was paid USD20 per month as a seaman.[409]

Spangenberg, Esther M. Spangenberg was born in Wilkes-Barre, Luzerne County, Pennsylvania, around 1830. She moved to California in the 1850s, where she joined Lola Montez' Dance Troupe. The group traveled to Australia aboard the *Fanny Major*.[410] Once in Australia, Lola Montez was told that her planned tour throughout Australia, India, and China would not be profitable, and she promptly disbanded the troupe, to the dismay and misfortune of all members, including Esther.[411] Esther sought passage on the *Julia Ann*, becoming the only cabin passenger on the vessel.[412] She was about 25 at the time it ran amuck on a coral reef.[413] Esther returned to San Francisco onboard the *Lucas* with Captain Coffin and produced a play satirizing Lola Montez.[414] She spent the rest of her life in San Francisco, where she owned a boarding house and became a teacher.[415]

Victs, Fernando. An American seaman aboard the *Julia Ann* from New York, Fernando was 26 at the time of the wreck, putting his birth year at 1829. He was paid USD20 per month as a seaman.[416]

Wandell, Charles Wesley. Wandell was born on April 12, 1819, at Courtland, Westchester County, New York. He was baptized into the LDS Church by Hugh Herringshaw on January 5, 1837, and was ordained an elder on April 6, 1837, by L. R. Foster.[417] He served as a missionary through several states, particularly in New York, where forty-eight elders were under his direction, including Augustus A. Farnham. After the martyrdom of Joseph Smith, he worked as an officer with a steamboat company out of St. Louis.[418] As the historian for the Church in Nauvoo, he felt disillusioned with some of the Church leaders' decisions. He eventually traveled to California by boat, and in 1851 became the first missionary called to Australia, along with John Murdock. He was president of the Australian Mission from 1851 to 1853. He made his way back to California with the first group of Saints traveling to America from Australia aboard the *Envelope* in 1853. After living in San Francisco for a time, he traveled to Salt Lake City in 1857. He was baptized into the RLDS Church (now known as the Community of Christ) by Glaud Rodger on July 6, 1873, and was called to serve a mission in Australia again.[419] He died while on that mission in Sydney, Australia, on March 14, 1875, most likely of heart disease.[420]

Warby, James and Mary Blanch. James was born in Kent, England, on November 15, 1822.[421] He married Mary Blanch on March 10, 1846,[422] and they had eighteen children. They likely traveled to Australia because of the Poor Law, which helped agriculture workers move to Australia, where they were promised land.[423] James was baptized on June 22, 1853, by William Hyde and emigrated from Sydney, Australia, on March 15, 1854, to San Bernardino, California.[424] He settled in Beaver County, Utah, for a time.[425] He was ordained a high priest on April 11, 1886, by Daniel Tyler in Beaver. He died in Manila, Utah, on December 14, 1906, after being sick for two years.[426]

Williams, Bully. Not much is known about this American sailor except that it was said he saved the life of Charles Logie and his baby daughter, Annie. One account notes, "When they abandoned ship, Charles had handed Rosa over the gunwale of the ship into the hands of one of the sailors while he tied his baby daughter, Ann to his back with a brown shawl. In the crush of the moment, Charles and Ann were pushed overboard and would have drowned except for one of the sailors. Bully Williams dove overboard and grabbed Charles by his long black hair and pulled he and Ann to the reef. Even though Charles was a sailor, he had never learned to swim and thus Bully truly saved their lives."[427] Despite this heroic account, a later newspaper account refers to Williams as a "ruffian" who should be "expelled from the important position he has disgraced." Williams was in command of the Twenty-ninth Precinct, and the public felt he should no longer be in control there. He was also eventually made a captain.[428]

Wilson, Sarah. Sarah was born in Sommerset, England. She had been in Australia for several years before she went aboard the *Julia Ann* in 1855. During the time the survivors of the wreck were in Tahiti, the British Consulate at Tahiti distressed-person log records, "A young female, a native of Sommerset under the charge of Mr. & Mrs. Penfold, had been for some years residing in the Australian colonies."[429] Sarah departed for San Francisco on January 7, 1856. It is thought that she may have married Russell Latham, captain of the *Emma Packer*, who rescued Sarah and the other survivors from Scilly Island.[430] Her name is listed "Sarah Wilson and son" in a thank-you letter written to Captain Latham, who is called "the good Samaritan" by the grateful *Julia Ann* survivors.[431] It is thought she might have changed her name to Elizabeth Sellars or Fields and settled in New Zealand.[432]

APPENDIX D

Petition and Protest of Capt. Benjamin
F. Pond to Tahitian Consul.

———

Letter

Addressed by Capt. Pond to the United States Consul at Tahiti

WHEN CAPT. POND ARRIVED AT TAHITI, THE United States Consul assured him that his obligations towards his passengers were dissolved by the entire loss of his vessel. However, on the representation of the British Consul, Mr. Kelly soon changed his mind, and insisted that the captain should although in want of money, clothes, credit and friends— take his passengers to California. On this view of the case, he was actually detained a prisoner on the island, for some time, and it was only at the latest moment that he was permitted to go on board the French ship, "Africaine," bound to callao, although he had fully discharged his duty, by offering to charter the "Emma Packer," for the purpose of taking the people to California. His bond for the charter charge was, however, refused and it was absolutely impossible he could do that on which the British Consul so pertinaciously insisted.

The Captain address Mr. Kelly thus:—

Papeeta, Tahiti, December 25th 1855.
   To H. Kelly, Esq., Consul of United States of America:—

The American barque "*Julia Ann*," from Sidney, bound to San Francisco, was totally lost on the 3d of October last, on a reef off Scilly Island, and five persons drowned. The remainder of the passengers and crew escaped to the [p.33] adjoining island in a most destitute condition. After remaining on the island seven weeks, I repaired the ship's boat, and started for this group with nine of my crew, and succeeded in reaching Bora Bora four days after my departure from Scilly Islands.

The British Consul at Riatea, hearing of the disaster, and the deplorable condition of the passengers and crew, immediately despatched an express to Capt. Latham, of the schooner "Emma Packer," lying in Huaines, who started without delay to their relief. He called at Bora Bora and took me on board, thence proceeded to Scilly Island, rescued the passengers and crew, and brought them in safety to this port.

On my arrival here you assured me that my connection with the passengers ceased: that they were off my hands.

On the 21st inst., the captain of the French ship "Africaine," kindly tendered to me a free passage in his vessel.

I immediately applied to you for information, whether it was necessary to notify the French Government of my intended departure. You assured me, that in my case, they would waive such formality.

I being a stranger to the customs of the port, having full confidence in your knowledge, and the position occupied by you, as representative of my country, I anticipated no interference from the authorities, but busied myself with necessary preparations for my departure; and you may judge of my astonishment on being informed by government officials, to-day, that I could not be permitted to leave this island. [p.34]

Sir, I was brought here a passenger on board the "Emma Packer" shipwrecked and in distress. The clothes on my back, were a loan from Capt. Latham. My ship, cargo and gold, amounting to some fifteen thousand dollars, were totally lost on scilly reef. I have no funds and no credit to raise any whatever. I have incurred no indebtedness in the dominions of this government. I have at all times conducted myself decently and in order; I have infringed no law or regulation, and it is of the utmost pecuniary importance for me to reach San Francisco, where my business interests centre, at the earliest possible moment. Further delay may be attended with utter ruin and bankruptcy, and there is not another opportunity for that place expected for the next two months. I therefore respectfully request your interference and assistance officially, as representative of my country, to demand of the Governor a permit for me to leave in the "Africaine," which vessel is expected to sail at 10 o'clock tomorrow. I make this application in full confidence, not deeming it possible that this government has the power to detain shipwrecked, unfortunate American citizens, who have landed on their shores in distress, from their native country, for no crime or breach of law.

I remain, sir, very respectfully, yours, &c,

B. F. Pond,
American Barque, "*Julia Ann.*"[431]

Protest of Captain Pond

Capt. Pond filed the following Protest with the American Consul, at Papeeta, Tahiti

Tahiti, Dec. 26th, 1855

Wm. H. Kelly, Esp., Consul U.S.A.

Being informed by you, that the British Consul, in this place, has protested to the French Government, against my departure from this island, and that in consequence, the Governor has refused me permission to leave, and knowing no law or authority by which the British or French Governments can forcibly detain an American Citizen from his own native country—no charge of any kind, either criminal or civil, being made against him—I hereby enter my protest against the British Consul, officially and personally, also against the French Governor, officially and personally, for my forcible detention, and shall hold them responsible for all damage or loss that may accrue to me from such detention, reserving to myself the right of extending this protest, at some future time. Very respectfully, B. F. Pond

Captain Pond returns his warmest thanks to the commander of the "Africaine," for his kind attention and gentlemanly treatment of him when on board his ship, as well as for a free passage to Callao. Also, to Captain McLain and Commodore Watkins, of the Pacific Mail Steam Ship Company's service, for gentlemanly attention, and a free passage on board the Steamer "Golden Age," from Panama to San Francisco.

APPENDIX E

Extracts of Interviews regarding the Julia Ann

John Bailey

Great-great-grandson of James and Mary Warby
Sydney Region, New South Wales, Australia, January 23, 2013

M Y FAMILY HAS A HISTORY OF BEING INVOLVED with the Mormon Church. And it goes back to 1853 when my great-great-grandfather [James Warby] was walking home from work and he met the two missionaries from America. They said they were having a meeting that evening and would he be interested in returning with his family. He agreed and went home. Met his wife [Mary Blanche]; she agreed to come as well. She . . . handled two of the children. He had two on his back and they went into town. . . . James and Mary were so touched with the information that was passed by the missionaries, and they felt that in their heart that it was from God. . . . Later, through greater investigation . . . my great-great-grandmother [Mary] was baptized in April of 1853. And shortly after, on the 28th of June, my great-great-grandfather, James Warby, was baptized. . . .

All of their friends cast aspersions against them for joining this "awful cult." And then three days after he [James] was baptized, their first child died. Then within the next three weeks three of their children died. How do you cope with that? What infrastructure of a support do you have? . . . Many of their neighbors had criticized them for having anything to do with this religion that was . . . regarded as . . . an American religion. . . . We've admired them through all of those difficult times of staying close to the feelings that they had felt, to the point where they went with twenty-eight other likeminded members of the Church with leader William Hyde, who had been, in fact, the one who baptized James Warby. He led the party on the ship the *Julia Ann* on its March 22nd, 1854, voyage . . . to San Pedro, California.

They worked hard in San Bernardino, California, and eventually James wanted to encourage those who . . . remained behind in Australia in Raymond Terrace, North of Newcastle . . . to come likewise. . . . He wrote a wonderful letter . . . that encouraged many of them to take the second . . . voyage on the *Julia Ann*. . . .

James and Mary held fast to . . . their belief that families can be together forever, even beyond death, but that that could only occur when certain earthly ordinances [were] completed within a temple of the Church. The temples at that time were in Utah. They went to Utah to join other members and to go through the ordinances where they could see their lost children even after death as an eternal family. . . .

Membership from around the world was encouraged by those that converted them to join with likeminded members . . . in Salt Lake City, Utah, [which] was regarded as coming to Zion and building the strength there. In fact, that same [gathering] of converts happened around the world until 1955. My father and mother had their names in to become immigrants to the United States and were on the list for twelve years. In February of 1955 we had the new-called . . . president of the Church, David O. McKay, visit us in Sydney. He met with about one thousand members from . . . Australia. And he commissioned all the members that now Zion is to be established in your own countries, where you now live. I was only eleven, and I can remember that family home evening whereby we knelt in prayer, and we agreed that we would follow the direction of the living prophet and remove our names from our immigration list. That is why I'm still here today, in that same city, along with my wife. . . .

My direct grandfather was a descendant of Mary Blanch. He met the missionaries in 1917 and he and my grandmother were baptized in Raymond Terrace. Because they had joined this "awful cult" as the neighbors had told them, they were threatened with tarring and feathering. They fled to the great city of Sydney, and established their home in the security of being right next door to the only church in Sydney at the time in Enmore, with the missionaries across the road with the mission president. My grandfather and my uncles and aunts, my father, all grew up with missionaries. We have had a great, enormous respect for these young people that would leave their homes at the age of nineteen, travel 12,000 miles, taking two to three months by boat, to come out here and travel around Australia by train, the enormous sacrifice of being on their own, so far from their own families for those two years, two and a half years. When I was called as a young missionary, at the age of nineteen, I was sent and assigned from Sydney to go to New York City, and I worked with the same fervor that I had witnessed from having the missionaries in our home, three and four times a week. We fed them, we took them to activities, and we felt the Spirit of these young men that gave up so much for those people that they loved. . . .

I think of the sacrifices of my grandfather when he as a new convert. The first World War was on and all the American missionaries were taken back to America in 1917. They were left on their own without leadership, but they kept the Church together during that time until the Americans could return. Likewise I think of my grandfather when he was . . . in the branch presidency in the Enmore Branch, and the missionaries were taken away again in

1941, taken back into the war. They [the branch presidency] had to manage the Church those four or five years until the American missionaries could return. I think of the sacrifices and the faith and the commitment to seek God's direction and guidance, without the assistance of those that had the knowledge. I think of my own father and what he went through in the 1950s in the major roles of the Church here. I think of myself, just wanting to serve wherever called. . . .

We used to have Family Home Evening every Monday night, and for one of the exercises we were to cut up a piece of paper, and we were to join it with a piece of sticky-tape, and my father would do one little circle, then my mother would put her piece of cut paper through, then my eldest sister, then myself, and we had six children. And the message was, we are an eternal family; no one has the right to break this chain. I've never forgotten that small lesson at the age of thirteen, that through our ancestry there is a link, and that no one is to break that chain.

Brittany Chapman

Coeditor of Women of Faith in the Latter Days,
Salt Lake City, Utah, December 27, 2012

ROSA CLARA FRIEDLANDER WAS BORN ON THE Guernsey Islands off the coast of England. Her father passed away when she was a young girl. Her widowed mother tried to make a good living but it was difficult in England at that time, especially as a widowed woman. So Rosa [and] her younger brother and widowed mother made their way to Sydney, Australia, to try to make a better life for themselves. They lived there for several years before Rosa's mother remarried and they found the gospel. They converted to the LDS faith when Rosa was fifteen years old. . . .

They actively embraced the faith. . . . Rosa walked twelve miles to her meetinghouse weekly, and sometimes more than once a week . . . to participate in different events [and] to sing in the choir; they met weekly to practice. . . . They hosted cottage meetings where people who were interested in learning about the faith met [and] were taught by the missionaries. [They] were actively involved in help[ing] others learn about Mormonism.

At age sixteen, Rosa was standing on a raised platform outside of the church meetinghouse. Two sailors were walking along— they were friends—and commented to one another about how beautiful Rosa was. They were both anxious to meet her. One of

the sailors ran around the front door of the meetinghouse to meet
her, and her future husband Charles Logie climbed up the trellis
and met her on the platform, introduced himself, learned about
the gospel, and he, too, was converted. They were married shortly
thereafter. Rosa was sixteen years old and Charles was twenty-
three. . . .

Like so many Latter-day Saints, they wanted to gather in
Zion with likeminded believers. . . . The doctrine of the gathering
encouraged people to come to Zion and build up the kingdom in
Utah. Charles and Rosa felt this same desire to gather with the
Saints in Zion. So they made preparations, were able to secure
passage on the ship *Julia Ann*, and in 1855 began their voyage. . . .
There were about fifty-six people on board, twenty-eight of whom
were Latter-day Saints.

They had been on the voyage about four weeks, and it had
been a relatively peaceful passage. Then about 8:30 PM—Rosa
may have just finished putting her young daughter to bed—there
was a great crash and water started rushing into the ship. Rosa and
her husband gathered together, grabbed their daughter, and began
thinking of how to escape from the sinking ship. . . . The ship had
run into a coral reef, which ended up being something of a blessing . . . because the passengers had place where they could go. . . .
The environment was chaotic. Women and children were screaming. Men were trying to gather everyone together. A rope was
secured from the ship to [the] coral reef where passengers could
reach safety. They were having trouble convincing the women and
children to get on the rope and go the coral reef. . . Rosa was
brave enough to go first and show the other passengers that it was
doable. She reached the coral reef in safety. . . .

Once on the island, the shipwrecked passengers had to create
a life for themselves. There was very little food. Often we think of
tropical islands as having [an] abundance, but here there was not.
Charles did his best to provide for his family. Shortly after they
arrived on the island, Rosa became sick, and he did his best to help
her and the baby. From an old trunk, he was able to get a large silk
skirt and create bands, created a shelter for Rosa and her daughter
to stay in. That helped to provide a little bit of shelter from the

elements before they could build a more substantial structure. . . .

Charles was one of the crewmembers. During the two months that the passengers were stranded on this island, crewmembers had been repairing a rowboat, and Charles was one of the ten members chosen to row on this small boat to an island about 200 miles away where they eventually found help. . . . During their time on the island, the wind was blowing in the opposite direction than they needed to reach other islands for help. They had been waiting and waiting for wind blowing in the direction they needed to embark on their journey. At last Captain Pond decided, "We're going to go the opposite direction, following the wind." There was opposition among the Mormons and crewmembers. A Mormon elder had a dream that if they went the way that the wind was blowing that they wouldn't make it to their island destination for help. . . They postponed leaving the Scilly Island. That very night there was a storm and the rowboat that they were going to take was driven to another part of the island. . . . They were very grateful that they had not left the day before. They may very well not have made it. With the storm, the wind moved into the correct direction that they needed and, under miraculous circumstances, they were able to get in the rowboat and make their way to the island of Bora Bora where they received help. . . .

Rosa was one of the many women who sacrificed to come and gather in Zion. Her story is filled with extra adventure; her story is one of faith and endurance. And that faith set her up for the rest of her life in remaining a faithful Latter-day Saint. Her legacy would be with many women—women who kept the faith amidst very dire, uncomfortable circumstances that required a lot of sacrifice. . . . She established a legacy for her eleven children, and . . . joined the ranks of faithful Mormon women upon which the LDS [Church] is built . . . today.

John Devitry-Smith

Author of Australian Mormon History
Smithfield, Utah, December 27, 2012

S O PROVIDENCE SEEMED TO HAVE INTERFERED directly in our behalf," states Captain Benjamin Pond. This was a sentiment verified in other firsthand accounts about the wreck of the *Julia Ann*. . . . We hear "kind providence," "divine providence," and it is highly unlikely we'd be here at all discussing this story of the wreck of the *Julia Ann* and John McCarthy if not for this "providence" they so often talk about. . . . In all likelihood we'd probably be reading a brief footnote in history . . . stating how the bark, the American bark the *Julia Ann* left Sydney on September 7, 1855, and was never heard of again. . . .

Pond knew he was in a dangerous area. The charts weren't real reliable and he knew there were low coral reefs and lower areas. . . . He'd thought he had passed them, and he was out of the way. . . . Then about eight thirty at night—it's just gone dark—they slam into the reef. What's so amazing is that the guy that's on lookout supposedly didn't have his glasses. . . . By the time they go and check, they clam head on [with] this coral reef. The boat lifts up out of the water with . . . 350 tons of coal. It hit the reef and it swung around on its broadside, and then the waves start pounding it. . . . McCarthy and Spangenberg talk about these twenty-foot waves hitting the vessel. A lot of people were out at deck about that time—at night . . . people are bored and they're just sitting around and they're singing songs. . . . Two young girls [are] up on the deck and a huge wave sweeps over and washes them off and both of them are drowned . . . .

Also about this time, the mothers are putting their other children to bed, the younger kids and the babies. A couple of the women are inside when the boat hits the reef, which swings the boat around, and it starts getting pounded until a huge hole opens up. Initially it was the size of a barrel and . . . water is pouring in. Pond didn't cut the sails initially—a really wise thing to do. He tried to let the wind push the ship up a little higher on the reef so it wouldn't fall off and sink.

The boat's still getting slammed against the rocks. Water's pouring in. Everything is coming undone. . . . This is a chaotic scene. . . . Martha Humphreys is down below, and she knew she couldn't get out of there. She had two young children and she says, "I'm not going to get out of here, so I can at least get my kids out." She gets her children and someone takes [them], and the boat keeps slamming against the reef; she and Eliza Harris . . . get washed out, and they drown. . . .

The boat is getting smashed to pieces and they've got to get off. A sailor jumps over and gets a rope to the reef. They start to move people along this rope—a daunting task. The younger, the healthier, the stronger—they could get off there. But the older people, the younger children, the mothers—they couldn't get off here, leaving quite a large group on the boat. . . .

Sister Anderson is stuck on the boat, and she can't find all of her children. She will not leave the boat until she finds them. . . . She's trying to get her children together, [not knowing] that her ten-year-old daughter is already washed off the boat. . . . The captain's saying, "If you don't get off the boat now, this is your last chance to get off here. You've got to try to get off." Sister Anderson wouldn't leave. She says, "I'm not leaving without all my children." . . . As the boat's falling apart, there's a part on the ship that sits up higher on the boat. The remaining passengers were stuck there. Sister Anderson's calling out to her children, and Agnes, her sixteen-year-old daughter, had already made it to the reef when she heard her mother crying out, "Agnes! Agnes! Come to me, come to me!" How many sixteen-year-olds would just jump and go, "Mother! Mother! I'm coming! I'm coming! I'm coming!" And she jumps headlong into the sea to try to get back to her mother. Her mother made the comment that she wanted the family to die together—a simple request. That is a beautiful touching story in Mormon history . . . . Often you hear these miraculous stories and these amazing events and it's witnessed by Latter-day Saints. But here you have one of the more touching scenes in Mormon History illustrating the bond of love between a mother and a daughter. This bond, enough to get a girl to give up her place of safety and dive into this crazy, raging sea to try to get back to her mother— that's a beautiful thing. . . . Captain Pond writes this story, not another member of the Church.

The captain was very artistic, well-mannered, chivalrous. . . . McCarthy spoke so highly of Captain Benjamin Pond, the way he reacted to this situation, and the way he handled the whole situation throughout. . . .

In essence what we have is a ship miles off course, in dangerous, poorly charted waters, slamming into a coral reef, resulting in the total loss of the vessel. The survivors are stranded on this barren, uninhabited island, nothing more than a series of sandbars, with . . . just a few things they saved from the wreck. They were miles off course in an area seldom visited by anyone, except by the occasional whaler. . . . They've got a quarter boat—that's all that's left. It needs to be patched together. The quarter boat's about twenty-two foot long.

They get to an island. It's deserted. There's no food; there's no water. Initially there's a few crabs. But . . . there is no hope of getting off this island except for the quarter boat. . . . The captain has some of his nautical equipment, and they figure out the Solomon Islands are about 1,000 miles away with the wind. Tahiti is only 200 miles away . . . but the trade winds are blowing straight at them from Tahiti. . . . It was not even an option to try to row into a strong headwind. It's like if your car breaks down on the hill. It's a lot easier to just let your car roll ten miles down the hill then try to push it one mile up the hill. And so, although appalling, they all agreed: "We need to try to make it to the Solomon Islands." . . .

McCarthy has a dream. . . . It's shared with the rest of the survivors and the captain's rather annoyed about this. . . . McCarthy says, "Oh no, I see the boat heading towards the Solomon Islands, and you get off to a good start but a day or two later the boat's capsized and all dead bodies around it." This has got to nothing short of terrify . . . the crew that's going in the boat. . . . Pond maybe said, "I'm still going to go that way," and he gets ready to go. He's getting ready to head out, the boat's all packed, the provisions are ready to go, and the night before there's a big storm, and the boat gets washed to who knows where. [Everyone] panics: "The boat's gone, we can't find the boat." It's a bad omen. They finally find the boat half full of water. . . . A few days later, McCarthy comes back to report to the captain: "Captain, I've had another dream." "Is it a good one?" McCarthy goes on to share this dream: "Captain, I see the boat rowing straight towards Tahiti. You get in the boat, ten crewmen in the boat, and you row directly towards Tahiti." . . . Chief Officer Coffin, when he heard that, said, "I'd rather die where I am. That's ridiculous. You can't row directly into the trade winds, into this rough sea." . . . This . . . highlights the spirituality of Captain Pond and the interaction between McCarthy and Pond. McCarthy had great respect for Pond; obviously, Pond had some sort of respect for McCarthy to give credence to what he was saying. . . .

Pond decides on this desperate course to double bank the boat and sail directly into the wind if it dies down. Providentially, the wind dies down. They get ready to go when Pond notices they only have nine members. He approaches McCarthy and says, "I'm short one guy. Do you believe this dream that you had?" "Absolutely. Was it not a revelation from God?" Pond says, "So, if you believe that then you'll be more than happy to get in the boat with us." This is where the rubber really hits the road. . . . McCarthy's response is beautiful: "Absolutely, yes." . . . That's remarkable! That McCarthy stands by this dream and he boldly exclaims that and tells the captain and everyone else that could hear. . . . He was more than happy to say, "Yes, I believe we're going to get rescued. I believe the vision that I saw is real and I'm more than happy to get in that boat with you." . . .

McCarthy proved prophetic. They get in this boat, and they start to row; it's pretty deep in the water. It wouldn't have taken very much to tip [it] over. They're rowing straight into the wind. Their hands were bleeding after a few days—they're exhausted. They sort of have an idea where they are, but after three days this huge storm comes in. They're getting blown around, so they pull a tarp over [the boat], and they think they're done. Amazingly, they look up and they see an island about fifteen miles in the distance. . . .

Personally, I think it's quite amazing and rather unusual in Latter-day Saint history to find someone that's not a member of the Church, who has referred to the Mormons as ignorant and superstitious, and who then turns around and vouches for this revelation from God. . . . Pond says, "You have heard the account of how literally his dream was fulfilled against every probability." And Pond also states, "I can simply vouch for the facts without any attempt to argue or explain." What an amazing statement! . . . .

Looking at this account from today's perspective, it's a strange interaction between a sea captain and a Mormon missionary. This is an odd meeting of men from different backgrounds but who also share something in common. McCarthy and Pond share this belief, a belief in the divinity of man and God. We hear over and over again the word "providence," not only from the members of the Church, but from the non-members, and especially from Captain Pond. Now I feel this quote by Captain Pond about life on the sea really sums it up. He talks about his days on the sea, "peering into the heavens thickly studded with stars and there selecting one, countless millions of miles distant, and with it marking out a sure highway over that trackless waste of water to our destined port. It is then and amid such scenes that man realizes in himself his mortality and his immortality, his wonderful capacity and his utter dependence." . . .

I think people assume that when the Mormon missionaries first went to Australia in late 1851, they did all the heavy lifting. But you can't discount what the local members did. . . . Nobody stands out in Australian Church History like John McCarthy. The missionaries got there, late 1851 . . . . and McCarthy within seven months is baptized, ordained an elder, and set apart as a traveling missionary. He's the one that goes to Maitland. He went to the areas in Australia where most of the people on the first, successful trip of the *Julia Ann* came from. He was an excellent missionary. He worked with the American missionary William Hyde, and he was there working for at least three years as a missionary. And that's as long, or longer, than any of the Americans or locals. McCarthy did a number of other amazing things when he was a missionary in Australia. Some amazing events that are documented in Australian Church History were from John McCarthy. They were documented by Charles Wandell, an American missionary there at the time, and so sometimes people could cast doubt. But here . . . the captain of the ship is standing by what McCarthy says. . . . What an amazing story and event in Mormon Church History. . . .

How many people going through such an ordeal could forget themselves as John McCarthy did? As soon as he knew everyone was rescued, John McCarthy looks at opportunities to preach the Gospel. . . . As this story unfolds, we find out that McCarthy baptized on that island—[he visited and] he baptized a number of people. This made the members of the Church much stronger, and it didn't shipwreck their faith. That's the beautiful thing. It made them better people. It made McCarthy a better person. . . . There are stories of people coming from miles around to talk to John McCarthy, to get a blessing, to talk to him. . . . What an inspiration McCarthy and many other members of that wreck went on to become.

Kieran Hosty

Curator at the Australian National Maritime Museum,
Sydney, Australia, January 24, 2013

IN THE . . . LATE EIGHTEENTH CENTURY, AUSTRALIA was occupied by the Europeans. The first twenty or so years of Australian occupation was taken up with a penal colony, a convict colony. However, about 1810, free migrants started to come to Australia, drawn by land [and] incredibly high wages. For instance, a carpenter in Sydney in 1810 could earn between fifteen and twenty shillings a day, whilst the . . . wage in England was about three or four shillings a week. So [immigrants] could earn ten, twelve, fifteen times their salary by just coming to Australia. Land was also very cheap; food was readily available. There's many great things drawing people here. The only downside was the convicts. There's a growing awareness in Australia about the problems of having a convict colony here, and from about 1820 onwards there's a growing movement to stop convicts [from] coming to Australia. By 1840 . . . convicts being forced to the east coast of Australia had just about stopped and there were certainly no convicts coming into Sydney in the 1840s. . . . [After] about 1840 there was a problem with a shortage of labor. Convicts had been providing a fantastic source of labor. The governments in New South Wales, in Victoria, and in Western Australia, tried to encourage free migrants to come to Australia by offering them land grants. If you came out here with your family, . . . you were given so many acres per child and so many acres per wife. That became very attractive to someone growing up in London, starving—they can get a good job in Australia and they can get access to land. . . .

Australia, a colony of New South Wales . . . was just coming out after a really big depression. [During the] 1840s, the price of wool had collapsed. People were leaving the land. There's a jail depression in Australia. In 1851, however, gold was discovered, originally in Bathurst, East South Wales. . . . The population in Australia at the time, probably around two hundred thousand Europeans, almost quadrupled in a decade—population went from two hundred thousand up to a million. Sydney went from a sleepy little ex-convict town of around thirty thousand to a world metropolis of almost two hundred and fifty thousand in a very short length of time.

The port of Sydney grew alarmingly. They had so many people coming in here. And the gold rush created a lot of problems here as well because . . . crews were coming here with supplies for the gold fields and [were] abandoning their ships and going off to seek gold, because of course gold was more attractive than working for months at a time for very poor wages on board a ship. The port of Sydney was getting clogged with shipping; crews [were] very hard to obtain, and it was an incredibly vibrant place in 1851, 1852, all the way through to the end of the 1850s. Sydney was also known as a very safe port. It's a massive harbor. There's always protection no matter which way the wind is blowing in Sydney Harbour. There's only one real hazard, which is what they call "Sow and Pigs Reef." Everywhere else you can basically pull up close to shore, quite deep water and anchor your vessel. It had a good reputation as a safe port as well as a very vibrant place in the 1850s.

We tend to think nowadays of ships as being either passenger ships or cargo ships. . . . But in the nineteenth century ships were very much general purpose carriers. They could carry cargo, they could carry passengers, they could carry livestock. And because the majority of ships were made of timber, they're very easy to adapt. A ship that could carry coal one minute with a bit of . . . planking and a [with] a bit of carpentry work could all of a sudden be turned into a passenger vessel. . . . It wasn't uncommon for ships to carry both passengers and cargoes, such as coal and wheat—more like a combination of a semi-trailer and a bus on the road today.

The coal trade out of Sydney was quite a complex thing. It started in the early 1800s. [By] 1803, Australia was exporting coal to places like India, quite surprisingly, and also back to England and to the United States. The coal supplies here were quite abundant and they were easily obtained from a place called Newcastle, only seventy or so miles north of Sydney. In the 1850s, ships needed a paying cargo to go back with. . . . Once they dumped their supplies in Sydney, they needed passengers and they needed . . . a cargo to make the voyage profitable to return to their home port. In the case of the *Julia Ann*, they took a mixture of passengers and over 350 tons of coal from Newcastle.

There [are] lots of perceptions about how people traveled around the world in the nineteenth century. We have this belief that sailing in the nineteenth century was quite hazardous. But in fact, it was relatively safe. About 1 in a 1,000 vessels . . . never succeeded in their voyage, was shipwrecked by storm, or captured by pirates, or disbanded, or lost at sea. . . . However, the Pacific was a different kettle of fish. The Pacific, specifically where the *Julia Ann* was going, was incredibly isolated. It'd only been opened up to European exploration [in] the last hundred years. Charts were quite poor considering . . . because of the problems of actually calculating where you were in such a vast ocean—problems with calculating longitude and latitude, very few large landmarks once you got past the New Zealand coast. . . . It was quite easy to sail all the way across the Pacific without seeing another land mass. So there's nothing to check your calculations as you were sailing. . . Unfortunately for Captain Pond, his charts were inaccurate. He believed that he was fifteen or so miles away from the Scilly Isles, and unfortunately he was a lot closer. Because he had problems [with] calculating latitude and longitude, the chronometer might have been only a second or so out and that was enough to put him on the rocks at the Scilly Isles.

One of the major hazards in the Pacific Ocean [is] the reefs.

We have to remember that a lot of these reefs are not marked by islands. They're just coral reefs, low lying. You have no idea, especially if the sea's calm, that they're there. Even if you had a seaman . . . actually taking soundings in the water, the reefs can rise . . . 500 fathoms to 0 in less than a nautical mile. They can really jump out at you. At night, there'll be no warning at all. The lookout wouldn't see it breaking up the surf. The . . . person taking sounding would have no idea they are getting close to land; if their navigation is only slightly out they could end up on one of these very isolated coral atolls.

When the *Julia Ann* went up on the Scilly Isles, the captain, Captain Pond, and First Officer Coffin would have realized that they were in desperate circumstances. . . . The ocean was so vast it was very unlikely that another ship would actually sail very close to the Scilly Isles. . . . The very first thing that Pond and the other officers on board would have done was organize food and water into the boats and also to bring their navigation equipment along. They realized that because they were so isolated, they were going to have to sail themselves out of this problem. They were going to have to keep one of the boats, modify the small ship's boat, get their navigation equipment, and then make an incredible ocean voyage in order to organize rescue for the remaining people left behind. . . .

We have people who barely knew each other thrust up onto a coral atoll and then . . . these people on an isolated atoll had to survive for sixty days. How I would do it if I was shipwrecked, and how I would survive for sixty days in a coral atoll? I don't think I could. And it makes me think how wonderful these people were and how strong they were. Both the people of the faith and the people who were not Mormons, just how incredibly strong and resilient they were. . . . It's an amazing experience. As an archaeologist I would really like to explore the survivors' camps to see how they survived on the island . . . and also look at the shipwreck itself to see how it's changed over time, over 150 years. . . .

I know there has been a number of accounts, survivors' accounts, written about what happened to *Julia Ann* and what happened on the island, and how [they] eventually got off the island, and [were] saved. In some of those accounts they talk about a divine providence, some outside influence, which allowed them to survive. In the nineteenth century, people were very superstitious, and sailors amongst them incredibly superstitious. Looking back at what happened . . . they were certainly incredibly lucky in what happened to them (if you can call being shipwrecked on an island lucky). The ship did actually, instead of breaking up in deep water, manage to bounce on top of the reef, and the survivors managed to get off. Instead of being a totally isolated coral atoll, there was actually a place where they could land and eventually take sustenance from the sea around them. The weather conditions could've been a lot worse. There could have been hurricanes; there could have been cyclonic activity happening. They were actually very fortunate with the weather. . . . They shouldn't have been able to sail for four days against the current, against the wind, but they managed to do that. So I don't know if it's lucky, or I don't know if it isn't actually someone else looking after them, some sort of divine providence if you like, that actually helped them on their way.

There's a cluster of small islands on the Scilly Isles. . . . Many coral atolls have no islands at all. But when they got ashore on these atolls there was some small trees. There was bird life on the island and there's also turtles coming ashore. To the passengers on board, they may have looked on the turtles as being quite a strange fare. To seafaring people, turtles were actually quite fair game. It was quite common practice to carry turtles as food on board ship. They could actually take turtles, and they knew that if they turn them on their backs, . . . they would keep for three or four days. There's no need to cure them until they needed the food. This is the way they carried them on board ship at the time. No doubt when the sailors saw the turtles coming ashore they realized that, in fact, they were saved. There was a good sustainable source of food, because with turtles not only do you get turtle meat, you also get turtle eggs. . . .

The passenger rate from Sydney to San Francisco was quite an arduous trip because of the navigational hazards facing those passengers and facing the crew on board. . . . Shipping at the time had to take an S-shape, from Sydney, thread their way through the

Coral Islands of the Pacific and eventually up on to the northeast coast of America. Now that voyage, depending on the weather, could take anything from seventy to one hundred and ten days. Often the ships had to call in on port to pick up additional food and supplies, usually water, but also hardtack and preserved meats as well. There's a couple of places they could do that. They could do it in Tahiti, but the more popular place was what used to be the Sandwich Isles, which is now Hawaii.

People have different impressions of what a shipwreck should look like underwater. If you're a non-diver you would assume that when a ship sinks it sinks into the sand. . . . Unfortunately, the marine environment is very harsh on shipwrecks. Particularly timber shipwrecks. If they go off on a hard surface like a coral reef, if they go off in an area which is very rough with huge seas, like you get on the Scilly Isles, those timber ships begin to break up quite quickly.

In the case of the *Julia Ann,* we know from the survivors' accounts that . . . the wrecks stayed on the reef for a couple months. . . . Within about a year or eighteen months the ship would've been dispersed across the seabed, most of it into the lagoon. But hopefully [for] an archeologist some of it would have gone down into the deeper water at the front of the reef. . . .

When the archeologists went there in 1997, they found the remains—the fragmented remains—of what they believed to be the bow of the *Julia Ann.* They found the anchor, they found the windless, which was at the bow of the ship—the front end of the ship—they found copper sheeting; they didn't find timber and that's not surprising because there's a number of underwater organisms that actually chew their way through timber. Things like *teredo navalis*, which is a ship worm, will quite happily eat timber until there's nothing left. As an archeologist, the interesting thing about the *Julia Ann* is that we believe that part of the vessel, the stern of the ship, actually slipped off of the reef into the deeper water at the back of the reef. And if that's the case you've got a fantastic time capsule of 1855 sitting on the sea bed.

Paul Hundley

*Former Senior Curator for the USA Gallery of the Australian National
Maritime Museum in Sydney, Australia.
Doha, Qatar, June 7, 2013*

WHEN I WAS WITH THE AUSTRALIAN NATIONAL
Maritime Museum, we had a fairly good relationship
with one of the rare book dealers in Sydney, Horton
House, and one day they just gave me a call. I was at the office,
and the fellow said, "We've just had something come in, I think it
would be perfect for you. You know, it relates to the USA–Australian Maritime relationship, why don't you come in and have a look
at it?" So I went in, had a chat with him, and it was the narrative
of The Wreck of *Julia Ann*, which was published by Captain Pond,
about two years after the event. I had a look at it and immediately
just knew it would be perfect for a display. It dealt with Australia,
and California, Sydney particularly, during the gold rush period,
which is one of the core storylines within the gallery. . . .

After I had a look at the book, we acquired it for the collection
of the National Maritime museum, and I started doing a bit more
research on it. I thought about it, and wouldn't it be a very interesting project, to see if we could verify the history written down in
this book, with a maritime archaeological expedition to the actual
site? Over a period of about a year and a half, I discussed this with
the museum of Tahiti, and we were able to organize the necessary

permits to actually go out to the atoll, and see if we could find the sight. It was a joint expedition, with a group of maritime archae-ologists from French Polynesia, the US, and Australia. . . .

In the process of assembling the project, I actually went back to people that I went to University with, people I had worked with in the field for probably about ten years already. It was an international project, myself and a conservator from the National Maritime museum, Dr. Shelly Smith, and two other people from the United States, and local archaeologists from French Polynesia. We chartered a sailing vessel, it took three days to get out to the site, and for the first three or four days we actually worked from the outside, the deep water, in towards the reef. . . .

After those first few days, we actually made contact with a family who were caretakers on the island, Rene Taputo. He and his family knew exactly where the shipwreck was, so from his encamp-ment, he took us across the open water in the lagoon, and we were able to locate the ship's anchor, and the windlass, the first day we were on the top of the reef. We never expected to have that sort of information. We knew there was a local family there, but these sorts of things, generally you spend weeks and weeks looking, and find it on the last day. Here, we found it on the first.

This atoll [Scilly Island] is the furthest island in French Poly-nesia. It's a three day sail from Papeete, and there is just nothing around. The reef comes out of incredibly deep water, and there's just literally, in the dark, there's no warning that anything is there. In calm water you wouldn't even see the reef. So I can understand what happened to Captain Pond that night. . . .

The reef structure is a classic atoll, it's an ancient volcano that submerged below the water line. There are three small islands that project above high-tide, having palm trees on them, coconut palms. Aside from that, there's nothing to give any indication as to the danger that lies there. From one side of the reef to the other, it's about 10 miles across, and it goes from deep water, shoaling very quickly to the reef, and then across the reef-top it falls away again to very deep water, 80 meters deep. . . .

When we were taken out to the reef, we didn't really know what to expect, and to find the amount of material that we did was just amazing. The ship's anchor, the windlass, there were pieces of the rigging, would have been attached to both the mast as well as the side of the vessel. It all made sense when you read the narrative of the shipwreck, about cutting away the mast to make sure that the ship stayed up on the reef, and then how the ship broke in two. What we were finding were the remains of the bow of the ship, the anchor and the windlass. We knew that the stern of the ship had gone up high on the reef, and this was a question that we thought long and hard about. To me, there must have been something happen after the shipwreck, that the bough had separated from the stern, and this had shifted some distance along the reef. Now I knew from previous experience that this is possible, but it raised the question, where was the stern of the vessel? Now the answer to that question I actually didn't come across until about three years later, doing further research on the project. A local schooner captain, Captain Ruxton, actually came across the wreck of the *Julia Ann*, about a year later, and he noted in his ship's log, a little map of the island, and where he saw the ship, which is out on the south-west corner, probably about three miles away. So, in the wrecking process, the ship dropped its cargo of coal, and the buoyancy of the timbers in the bow of the ship allowed it to float and be pushed along that distance, before it finally got thrown up on the top of the reef. . . .

We had ten days to undertake the whole project. We spent the first four on the outside of the reef, with the efforts in the deeper water, working on scuba, as well as towed searches. It was really in the shallow water, knee-deep, waist-deep water, that we did most of our work. We used global positioning system, GPS, to plot in the scatter of material on the reef, and we took a few samples, copper fastenings, copper sheathing, and some coal, that would be diagnostic material to help us prove that this was indeed the wreck of the *Julia Ann*. We brought that material back to Sydney, we went into our labs, and did some analysis on it, and we feel incredibly confident that this is from the *Julia Ann*. We also went back and did historical research. The windlass that we found was patented in 1853, a year before the ship was actually constructed, so this was cutting-edge technology for the day. . . .

When people hear about shipwrecks, they automatically think

treasure. In fact, the wreck of the *Julia Ann* has a little bit of that as well. The captain left behind the gold that he had made from selling his cargo in Sydney, and took the important things, his timepiece, his sextant, and he told his crew to save his passengers rather than his gold. When we were actually on the reef, we thought we might find some remnants of that, but we never did. Possibly because that was in the stern of the vessel, and we found the bow. But going back to Captain Ruxton, he actually noted in his journal, that he recovered a small iron strong box, and in fact he came to a bit of a terrible demise. After he found the wreck of the *Julia Ann*, he took a trip to Sydney, and was spending money like the proverbial sailor, and on the way back, he actually fell overboard and was drowned, lost at sea, but in his possession there was a very large amount of gold sovereigns and half sovereigns. I think he actually found the strong box that the Saints had taken along with them as they emigrated to the United States; it wasn't Captain Pond's gold, but it was the church members'. . . .

The story of the wreck of the *Julia Ann*, in itself, isn't unique. During that period of time, thousands and thousands of ships leaving San Francisco, going to Sydney, were lost at sea every year. I think what's interesting about this *Julia Ann* is that we've been able to prove the written history with the archaeology, and the network of people who are still, even today, connected to that story. We were able to do an exhibition at the National Maritime museum in Sydney, in the Church Museum in Salt Lake City, and in the Maritime Museum in Long Beach, [California]. The people that came to this exhibition, many of them were members of the Church, and actually descendants of the people who were on board the *Julia Ann*, and even today we get inquiries, three or four a year, from people who can trace their history back to this event.

The story of the *Julia Ann* is unique in the way that the people were rescued. It goes against all logic. The winds at that time of year were contrary to the direction in which the captain set off, and reading the narrative that he wrote, there was obviously a close relationship between he and the leader of the Saints. I think that dialogue was very important, the vision that was, or the dream that they had, and how that affected both he and the shipwrecked survivors.

In reading the account, I think what really impressed me was the faith that people had in their dream, in their vision. Even Captain Pond. This went against all of his experience, everything he thought he should do, and in making his decision, he went back and called upon the head of that group, and he was short one crew member, and he asked this person, do you believe in what you saw? And he said, "Yes." I think it's that commitment that is unique, and really does hold a truth that made the difference in whether these people got off the island or not.

It's interesting that after everyone was rescued, they took very different paths in their lives. . . . After this event, Captain Pond stayed in San Francisco for a period of time I think through sheer exhaustion and possibly a bit of a breakdown from the event, but eventually went back to Sydney, closed off his business affairs, and basically retired to the east coast of the United States. Captain Coffin never went to sea again, but unfortunately the rest of the crew participated in a voyage and they were never heard from again. Lost at sea, and it would be interesting to follow up that event and see if we could find out a little bit more about what happened there.

At the end of this project, I've really been left with more questions than answers. The written history has been proven by the archaeology that we were able to do, but the historical research that came afterwards has really raised more questions than it's answered. The opportunity to go back, to find the spot that Captain Ruxton drew on his map, to find the actual spot on the reef where the stern of the vessel lay, would all be a worthwhile investigation, and possibly someday that might happen. Even if that doesn't, the network of people who are still connected to this event, to the wreck of the *Julia Ann*, continues to be a very active research project with new people contacting the museum, contacting me, every year. I think it binds people together who, through their ancestry, were related to this event.

Shipwrecks during this period happened more frequently than I think people realize. In fact, rescues were carried out very frequently. The records of ship captains being wrecked off the Australian coast, making their way back on their own through their ship's boats, or through other vessels that picked them up, are quite frequent. I think what is unique about this is the remoteness of the location where the *Julia Ann* wrecked. . . . To get his crew and his passengers to safety, only having lost those few people in the actual wrecking event, is an amazing feat in the history.

I found the account interesting in how they actually survived for those eight weeks on the island. As Captain Pond said, they divided up into family groups, they relied on each other. The crew, the passengers, everyone was basically in this together. They were able to capture turtles. It was nesting season at that time of year, so they had turtles for meat, they caught sharks for fish, there were coconuts on the island, so they had some vegetables, but it would have been a very meager existence, supplemented by supplies that they salvaged from the shipwreck.

I find the actual voyage that the captain and the crew took in the rowboat an absolute incredible feat of seamanship. To be out in the open ocean for three days, with only basic navigation equipment, going through storms. How he actually made his way from that atoll to Bora Bora is just a sheer testament to his navigational skills and the will that that team had, in making sure that there was a rescue for the people left behind.

I find the link between the Elder's dream and the actual voyage that was taken to be an incredible part of this story. That three days' sailing, rowing . . . to Bora Bora, I think, holds a special message. The dream and the events that took place after that has something to tell us . . . as an illustration of the faith and divine intervention, if you will. . . .

The story of the *Julia Ann*, and especially the voyage from the atoll to Bora Bora, has been used to illustrate people's faith in their religion and the influence of divine providence; in people relying not only on their own skills, but on something beyond that, in times of need. . . .

It's interesting in this event, when you read the narrative of the wreck of the *Julia Ann*. The captain wasn't worried about his gold and the money in the safe. He realized that in order to save himself, his crew, and his passengers, he needed his navigation instruments. This was something that ship captains would always fall back and rely on. They knew in this sort of situation, that you had to have some way to get yourself off the island, and to save yourself. Gold wasn't going to do you much good on a deserted island. . . . Finding your way at sea during that period of history relied on knowing what time of day it was, and to determine your location, you had to know where the sun was, or the stars. So you needed your octant, [which] later became a sextant.

In 1855, in order to find your way at sea, you needed to have a chronometer, an octant, and a book of calculations, to figure out where, in terms of latitude and longitude, you were at any time of day or night. It's proven, from what Captain Pond said, was that the location of this island was actually not charted properly on the maps of the day. . . .

It's interesting when you read the account of the *Julia Ann*. You can surmise what Captain Pond was actually thinking. At this time of year, there's a monsoon wind that blows from the east to the west. So his experience told him the only hope of rescue was to go with the winds, which was 1500 miles to the west, but in fact through intervention, or a fluke of nature, the winds turned contrary to what normally happens at that time of year, and he was able to go east, and three days later landed on Bora Bora.

The story of the wreck of the *Julia Ann*, I think, has special significance in that it tells the story of a group of very dissimilar people who came to rely on each other and survived almost insurmountable circumstances. That the story is still being told and is still generating interest and personal connections even today, I think, is unique among the stories of Australian–American maritime history.

Elder Peter Meurs

*Member of the Quorum of the Seventy of The Church of Jesus Christ of
Latter-day Saints in the Pacific Region
Perth, Australia, January 22, 2013*

THE DOCTRINE OF THE GATHERING IS A FASCI-
nating time of the Church. Nineteenth century—the
Church has just been restored to the earth, and the pioneers have travelled across to Utah and established the Church
in Salt Lake City. Remarkably, missionaries have been sent out
to . . . Australia and many other parts of the world. As early as
1850 there is missionary activity in Australia. . . . At that time, and
right through the nineteenth century, in fact, all of the saints were
invited to go to Utah, to go to Salt Lake City, to join with the other
saints there and build up the Church. That was a vital and important part of the establishment of the Church, to build a center of
strength, and also go to a place where they could ultimately receive
temple ordinances and receive the fulness of the gospel of Jesus
Christ. I still marvel at the fact [that] the early Church used its
resources to send out missionaries to places like Australia and that
so many responded to the call to go to Zion, playing a great part in
establishing the Church. It is an exciting part of our history that
we had pioneers that participated in that great event. . . .

As early as 1853, there are only ten missionaries in Australia.

These innovative missionaries establish a periodical called *Zion's Watchmen*. . . . This periodical helps inform and teach new members the doctrine of the gospel, but also promotes the gathering to Zion. It became one of the key tools that the missionaries were using to help encourage the Saints to go. The other thing that really helped was those that had already arrived in Zion, writing back to their families, and their friends, and telling them how wonderful it was to be with the saints. . . . They arrive, they feel the spirit, they love being there, and they write back home and talk about how wonderful it is to be in Salt Lake City and in Utah. . . . Some of those letters were published in *Zion's Watchman* and had a greater impact as a result. . . .

Today we don't gather to Salt Lake City, but we still build Zion . . . where we live. In my life time I've seen temples built across this country [Australia]. When I was married, we went to Hamilton, New Zealand—that was the closest temple. . . . Since then, with President Hinckley's vision of temples dotting the earth, we've seen temples built in five cities in Australia. We even have one in Perth, which President Hinckley called the end of the earth. . . . My parents joined the Church in 1958, and there was just one mission across southern Australia. Now we have missions and we have very strong stakes of Zion with multi-generational leaders. It's just wonderful to see how the gospel has progressed since those pioneers in the 1850s through today.

I really love the story of the *Julia Ann*. . . . Of over 500 voyages [in the nineteenth century] as part of the gathering . . . there was only [one] shipwreck. . . . Of the fifty-six people on board the *Julia Ann*, twenty-eight were Latter-day Saints. That all but five survived is a great miracle. . . . They get off the vessel and survive for sixty days on an uninhabited island in the Pacific with very little food. Then they were ultimately rescued; you can see the Lord's hand in every aspect of the story. It's incredible to me how he gets involved in the details of our lives and helps us in such an incredible way. One of the little stories that I love is where they needed some flint to light a fire on the island. They searched and couldn't find flint until they found a bucket which had some flint in it; later we found out it had been left there by a fisherman several years ago. How does that happen if the Lord's hand isn't involved? Incredible.

Marjorie Newton

Author of Southern Cross Saints: The Mormons in Australia
Sydney, Australia, January 24, 2013

THE LDS CHURCH IN SYDNEY IS COMMONLY regarded as beginning in 1851, and for Sydney this is true, but there were a couple of earlier attempts by immigrants from England . . . and Scotland. . . . One, Andrew Anderson, . . . managed to organize a branch where he was working. They both came as assisted immigrants. But the official opening of the Australian Mission occurred in 1851 as part of a larger project when Parley P. Pratt was assigned by Brigham Young to preside over the Pacific Mission, over the whole Pacific, which ranged from, theoretically, Japan and the west coast of America right down to South America and Australia and New Zealand. . . Parley P. Pratt was assigned nine missionaries to cover this enormous area. They traveled to California, and there he recruited another early missionary of the Church, Charles Wesley Wandell, who had done a great deal of missionary work and had been a leader in missionary work in New York and [was] now living in California. . . . That gave him [Pratt] ten [missionaries]. . . . He assigned Charles Wesley Wandell to accompany John Murdock, who had already been assigned to preside over a mission to Australia. . . . They traveled on the

Petrel, one of the many [vessels] taking gold seekers from California to New South Wales, and they arrived at the end of October 1851. . . .

One little detail that always intrigues me . . . is the official date of the beginning of the Australasian Mission [as] it was known then because it comprised New Zealand as well. . . . It's always given in Church records as beginning on the 30th of October 1851 when this vessel arrived. . . . They take that date from the journal of John Murdock, who was the mission president . . . but he wasn't a well-educated man and he had no concept of time zones, and although this preceded the international dateline, it still had the same effect. . . . All the Sydney newspapers and shipping records and Charles Wandell's own journal all specify that they arrived on the 31st of October. . . . They began work and they baptized a few converts before Christmas, and then Murdock set off to go to Melbourne and left Wandell there [in Sydney], and early in January 1852, Wandell was able to organize the first branch of the Church in Sydney. . . .

Murdock was elderly and suffering from ill health, and he returned home after only seven months. . . . Charles Wandell was the mission president and . . . [in March 1853] he was about to leave Sydney with a party of converts to gather to Zion. There were branches in both Sydney and Melbourne, and there were converts in the Hunter Valley and other places. . . . It took so long for news to come from America to Australia that he hadn't heard anything about events over there. . . . They were . . . about to sail in their vessel when another party of missionaries with a new mission president arrived in Sydney Harbour. Unfortunately, they had smallpox on board. One of the missionaries . . . had brought it on board and . . . the whole vessel was quarantined. . . . They . . . only allowed Wandell [to go] out in a boat and talk from the boat to [new] President Farnham on the deck of his ship. . . . That was really the only contact they had . . . before sailing themselves.

The new mission president, Augustus Farnham, was very vigorous and a very good president. He encouraged the work. . . . Elder Farnham had . . . as many missionaries to work with as Parley P. Pratt had been given to work with [for] the whole Pacific Rim. But

that still wasn't very many considering the size of Australia. . . .
It was many, many years before the presiding brethren in Utah
really comprehended the size of Australia. It is geographically the
same size as mainland continental USA—if you superimpose a
map of Australia of the same scale on a map of the United States,
it's roughly the same size. . . . They had to travel large distances
between the independent colonies—there was no legal or political connection between them, they were just six separate British
colonies in each of those areas—it was a very daunting task. . . .
But the work was progressing and the number of converts was
growing. . . .

One of the most important things that Farnham did was to
establish a mission newspaper . . . to publish the Church's case
because the local papers that were being published in the colony
were inclined to publish only scandalous stories of polygamy in
Utah. . . . He started a paper which continued throughout his
mission, and it is very valuable for the history it contains as well as
publishing talks by Brigham Young and others of the apostles in
Salt Lake City. He included a history of each branch in the mission and minutes of conferences. . . . The mission newspaper was
called *Zion's Watchman* and . . . one of the main emphases of it was
the request for the Saints to gather to Zion. Brigham Young sent a
letter to Augustus Farnham, the mission president, saying to come,
that they needed strong men to come to the Valley. . . . This was
repeated by various other letters and articles that were sent. . . . It
has been said that it was as much a requirement to gather in those
days as it was to be baptized and confirmed. . . .

I was always taught as a child that the Church didn't grow
and flourish here in Australia because . . . the people . . . were too
apathetic and . . . wouldn't accept the gospel. But I don't think
that that was the story. . . . As fast as they made converts . . . those
who were very faithful and could raise the means left the Australian mission and went to Utah. . . . This meant that the branches
remained small right throughout the nineteenth century until the
First Presidency began to change that policy because by that time
Zion was well established in Salt Lake City. . . . They now wanted
the converts to stay in their homelands and build up the Church

there. . . . This was very hard for people to do because they wanted to receive their temple ordinances . . . [and] there was no way that they could afford enough to take them to Utah to one of the temples there and then return. . . . They could only afford one way and so they tended to stay there. . . . It was this that to a large extent weakened the mission . . . The other thing was the enormous distances that had to be covered. In England at the same time the railroads were being built from the 1850s, and there were canals. . . . It was not too difficult to walk from one side of England to another. John McCarthy, one of the early converts here [Australia] who was set apart as a traveling missionary . . . [tried] to walk to Melbourne to fill an assignment to preach there. And it just couldn't be done at that time. The mission presidents right up until the 1920s usually traveled by boat when they wanted to visit from their headquarters in Sydney, so if they wanted to visit the branches in the other colonies they went by sea around the coast. . . .

The gathering from Europe . . . seems much more impressive, but . . . the [journey] from Australia was three times as expensive and at least twice the distance that the converts in Europe had to face. . . . When you compare the figures . . . over the nineteenth century, . . . despite the enormous distances [and] the very few missionaries in Australia, the actual number of converts per missionary is almost exactly the same as in the European mission. . . .

The missionaries here didn't have a very easy time. The New South Wales Conference (District) was made up of the Sydney Branch and three branches in the Hunter Valley in New South Wales. The colonies in New South Wales were . . . vastly different from each other. . . . Sydney was founded as a convict settlement—a penal settlement—in 1788 and was accepting convicts from England till the 1840s. At the same time, there'd been a big rush of free immigrants, and by the 1850s Sydney was a quite a thriving, bustling metropolis and was trying very hard to live down its convict beginnings. . . . There . . . were half a dozen or so convicts among the converts, and there were tradesmen, there was a shoemaker, there were various other tradesmen among the converts in Sydney. . . . Most of those in the Hunter Valley were either farmers or agricultural laborers. We only had one convert in the Australia Mission who could be regarded as high in the social register, and that was Martha Maria Humphreys. . . . She was a member of the illustrious Wentworth family and she was . . . drowned on her voyage to gather with the Saints . . . on the *Julia Ann*. . . .

The mission presidents did their best. They sent missionaries out into the nearby settlements in Sydney. . . . At this time they baptized the Chittenden family in the Camden area, and this family was actually found and converted by James Graham and John Eldredge, who were the missionaries who returned with the *Julia Ann* company. . . . They [Chittendens] actually moved to Goulburn, and they couldn't afford to gather in the 1850s. . . . The parents went in the 1870s, and their married daughters remained in Sydney and were the actual stalwarts of the branch when the missionaries began to return in the 1890s and the Sydney Branch was resurrected, as it were, and is still functioning today as the Greenwich Ward.

Missionary methods in . . . the Australian colonies in the 1850s were very different [from] those that the missionaries . . . use today. When John Murdock and Charles Wandell arrived on Friday, the 31st of October, the very following Sunday they went to the old race course in Sydney where people would assemble on Sundays to hear stump post speakers (stump speakers). People could . . . talk and gather a crowd on whatever subject they wanted. . . . Today it is Hyde Park and we can almost pick the exact spot where Murdock stood to preach. . . . It's . . . overlooked by a high-rise building which houses one ward of the Hyde Park Australia Stake today. . . . Murdock and Wandell preached there for a while. Murdock went off to Melbourne, Charles Wandell kept it up, but they did attract some of their very first converts at those meetings on the race course at . . . the old race course. . . . They organized the Sydney Branch early in January . . . the fourth of January 1852— and they held regular meetings. They rented rooms [at] . . . the top of King Street opposite St. James Courthouse and St. James church today. . . . They had meetings several times on Sunday. They held choir practice one night of the week. They had meetings . . . in the members' homes where they would invite their relatives and friends. . . . These were really the main ways that the gospel spread.

For a while, enemies of the Church, both in Australia and New Zealand, tried to make out for several decades that the missionaries . . . were baptizing women and taking them home for their harems in Salt Lake City. The membership records were faithfully kept, and the records all show that there were actually more men baptized than women . . . in most branches, and the largest proportion of the converts were families. The converts weren't single women looking for husbands or being recruited as plural wives for the missionaries. In fact very, very few . . . Australian converts, male or female, ended up in plural marriages in Utah . . . . By and large it was families who gathered. . . .

By 1852, when the Sydney Branch of the . . . LDS Church was organized, Sydney was quite a thriving metropolis. There were very mixed social groups there. There were still . . . people who were formerly convicts. There were their freeborn children who had now grown up and had families of their own. And above all, there were immigrants from the old country. . . . The vast majority were English and Scottish and Irish. . . . The whole idea of the establishment of this penal settlement . . . founded . . . in January 1788 [was] . . . to be self-sufficient. But most of the convicts, right through the convict period, were not from agricultural backgrounds; they were petty criminals . . . often from the slums of the big cities of England. The general myth which endured for a long time in Australia was that they'd all been sent out for stealing a loaf of bread or poaching a rabbit . . . to feed their starving families. . . . Most of them had prior convictions, not all, but many of them had prior convictions for larceny and theft and so on and were sent here virtually to get rid of them from overcrowded English prisons after they could no longer send them to America after the War of Independence. . . . There weren't enough that were able to work as farmers [or] farm laborers . . . [who] knew how to raise crops and tend animals. . . . There was an immediate need for free settlers from farming backgrounds. . . . The British government set up a program of recruiting farm laborers who would like to immigrate to New South Wales, and they [the government] would give them assisted passages or pay for their passages. They were called "bounty immigrants" at first, . . . "assisted immigrants" later. . . .

The big majority of the Mormon converts came from this group. . . . There were some that were convicts or children of convicts or even children of the some of the Marines or soldiers that stayed here, who didn't go [home to England] with their ships or with the regiments that replaced the original Marines. . . . The . . . majority were . . . drawn from the free settlers . . . such as Edmund and Eliza Harris. . . . Eliza was drowned in the wreck of the *Julia Ann* . . . she had certainly been baptized in England, and . . . on their immigration record, the Harrises described themselves as Latter-Day Saints. . . . Andrew Anderson was baptized in Edinburgh by Orson Pratt in 1840. When he arrived in New South Wales, he was described on his immigration record as a Presbyterian dissenter, which was probably the closest that the immigration officials could get to because they probably wouldn't have known much about The Church of Jesus Christ of Latter-Day Saints here in the colony at that time. . . .

Meg Rasmussen

Great-granddaughter of Captain B. F. Pond
Her family cabin outside Seattle, Washington, April 22, 2013

I PROBABLY HEARD ABOUT THE BARK JULIA ANN . . . when I was a young teenager. I love history, I love adventure. . . . I found out about the wreck of the *Julia Ann* from my grandfather, because he had a copy of the autobiography of his dad. . . . The whole idea of a ship and a captain in the 1800s being one of my relatives was pretty fascinating.

Once I got into high school and spent more time with my grandfather, he talked more about his family and the *Julia Ann* and the other ships that the captain owned [and] . . . we had the portrait that B. F. Pond's sister painted of the wreck. . . . The painting got passed through the family. . . . The family is all interested . . . in the story of their great-grandfather. We were told a lot about his life—he was a California forty-niner gold chaser, and then he started investing in ships. . . .

Benjamin Franklin's sister [Winifred] received letters from Benjamin from San Francisco after the wreck. . . . She was fascinated with that; she was a budding artist at the time. . . . She just imagined from his letters and from all of the interest that she had, she painted it out of her own imagination. Evidently when B. F. got back to New Jersey or wherever they were, he said, "Wow," because she had never seen an actual picture. She did a great job replaying the wreck with that portrait.

Captain Pond . . . was deeply religious. . . . Everything I know about Captain Pond came from his book and from my grandfather, his son. He's very religious, very deep in his faith, and very adventuresome. . . . He was extremely social, very friendly. . . . He was very successful in anything he tried.

He opened the trade lines between San Francisco and Australia. . . . He was very famous in San Francisco and in Sydney for doing that. Then he started bringing the Mormon pilgrims back from Australia to come here to go to Salt Lake. . . . Because of his religious faith, I'm sure he liked the idea of helping. Then, that voyage on the way back, they hit that reef and his life changed forever.

When I think about the wreck of the *Julia Ann* and the fact that most people on the ship at the time were preparing for bed, or already in bed, and I think about the shock, I relate it a little bit to the earthquakes I've been through. It just shakes up the whole world.

I would bet [the] captain was very courageous. I would have to believe that he was the last one off. Then, to get back in a hand-made boat with ten other people and leave that island where it was sort of safe and go out into the ocean again. . . . That's leadership at its best. . . . Captain Pond would believe he was captain until he couldn't be captain anymore . . . keeping everyone calm, organizing them into groups, putting the people together that could get along, helping them find out what they were going to eat and what they were going to do, and then proceeding to build that . . . boat—to get off the island so that he could save them. . . . I just believe that he never lost control. . . . Captain Pond had a calm demeanor, very present in everything he was doing. So they all trusted that if he said, "We're going on this boat, and we're going to go find help," that's what was going to happen. . . . That's the person you want to be with if you're having a problem. . . . The reality of that situation with the bark *Julia Ann* was so dire that . . . the wrong person leading that group the people would not have made it. . . . Divine providence put them on his ship. . . .

Captain Pond . . . was a man of great faith. He was not judg-
mental; he didn't think that everybody had to be thinking the same
way he was, but the Mormon people that were with him had great
faith as well, and if they believe that God was guiding them during
this time; I would have to say that they were getting help. There's
just too many things that happened that humans can't explain, and
Captain Pond would have believed the same thing, and I'm sure
that's why he told the elder not to share bad stories—that just
adds to the grief of the situation. But if he had something positive
and believed it himself by getting on that boat, that couldn't be a
bad thing. Someone was guiding them, and it was obviously the
Lord. . . .

I know Captain Pond was an avid reader. . . . That's one of the
traits I inherited as well. History was always important. God and
country were important. I'm sure he read every word of every book
he had and always had that stuff in his brain. He would quote
different stories. I would have to think that he drew on some of
that knowledge, even though it's fictional, to get himself through
these situations. The mutinies and the wreck; you just got to have
a special calm demeanor and a lot of faith in God to get through
that kind of stuff. . . . Thinking . . . about all of the Pond people
that I've been told about—I'd have to say I'm proud.

John Silverwood

Coauthor of Black Wave: A Family's Adventure at Sea and the
Disaster that Saved Them
San Diego Harbor, California, January 29, 2013

WHY DID WE HIT THE REEF? IT'S A COMBINA-
tion of events, but I would start with the fact that we
had a problem with the hardware on the boat that I'd
never experienced before. There's a stainless steel pin; it's an inch
in diameter and it holds the boom of the boat . . . close against the
mast. . . . And that whole pin shattered. And when it shattered, the
boom dropped, and it was making a horrendous noise, so Ben and
Jean, Amelia and I went up there to fix it. The boom weighs . . .
three hundred pounds, the sail weighs about another three hundred pounds, so . . . we needed a lot of muscle just to maneuver the
boom to get it to the point where I could stick a new pin in. . . . As
part of that process . . . I turned the autopilot off. . . . We were just
drifting; I wasn't really thinking about was the fact that the wind
was coming out of the southeast. . . . I was holding myself seven
and a half miles off the south shore of Manuae. But the wind was
blowing me towards land while we were drifting. We were never
able to fix the problem after wrestling with the boom for probably
an hour, so we just tied the boom off and we continued forward on
just the genoa, which is the head sail up on the bow of the boat,

because we still had plenty of wind. We had about eighteen knots of wind, so we were making five knots with just the genoa and it was getting dark. . . because it was the 25th of June [2005], one of the shortest days of the year. . . .

The Pacific's . . . got a very big swell. The swell that we had while we were out there that night as we approached the reef in Manuae was about fifteen feet. Now you think like a fifteen-foot, flat-sided wave, a very steep wave. That isn't what I'm talking about: you just go up, up, up, and finally down, down, down, to the point where you don't even realize that the boat's going up and down fifteen feet because the crests are separated by a quarter of a mile. There's a wave train that mimics the tops of those waves and the wave train is running beneath the sea. But the sea, right off the shelf, right off the wall of Manuae, Scilly Atoll—it's 4,990 feet deep there. It's 4,990 feet for miles and miles and miles. The wave-train has no problem, but when that same wave-train encounters the wall of coral that is Manuae and that coral extends for two hundred fifty feet, the wave-train goes from whatever that wave's speed is to zero by hitting that wall. . . . Those waves have nowhere to go. So instead of being fifteen feet they hump up, they become much higher, and they break with violence. . . .

You know, the very first time I started to even comprehend the force of the sea that was running underneath us was right as I was running towards the bow. Ben had slapped a knife in my hand and I was going up to cut the sheet off, the genoa sheet, and let that sail run free, because the sail was pulling us further up onto the reef. As I was running up the whole boat was picked up and thrown down and I almost fell over just running that short distance. That's when I realized what kind of a problem we were really in. . . . By the time I had go into the salon [again] . . . pots and pans from the galley [are] all being thrown forward on this wall of water that's just exploding through a hole in the hull that didn't even exist thirty seconds before.

Where does the hole come from? Well, the hole comes from the fact that the entire boat is being picked up and then thrown back down on the reef. And when it was thrown back down on the reef, a coral had come right through the bottom of the boat. There's a progressive disorientation that happens to you when you've got sound like that, when you've got a series of detonations, explosions, and just the roar of the sea in the background, the wind that's screaming through the rigging. . . . [Ben and I had] gone up on the bow after we'd struck the reef; we inflated our life raft and tied it down. We came back into the main salon. The main salon was kinda chaotic. My wife and my daughter Amelia were controlled to a point. They were in what used to be the galley. They're up to their armpits in water. They're taking fruit juice and that kind of thing at that time [and] throwing that stuff in the cloth bags. We're going to haul that up onto the deck and use it to supplement the supplies that we've already got built into the life raft.

In the middle of that, a wave just broke over the entire boat. . . . It was unbelievable. . . . It was a black night to begin with, but then . . . it got surreal. I told Ben that we had to go back up and tie that raft down better. . . . When I say I told Ben to go back up, in that situation, what it means is you take the other person's head, and you hold it close and you yell into their ear, "Ben, we're going back up on deck!" That's the only way that you can comprehend. You either do that or you use sign language. . . . It's impossible to hear [with] the grating of the boat being drug across the coral simultaneous with the impact of a wave breaking on top. . . . Our boat was actually spun through almost 720 degrees, spun around by the surf over the night by being picked up and thrown back down time and again. . . .

From the moment that we hit the reef, there was something that I always had to do, whether it was running up and cutting off the sheet that freed up the genoa, or coming back, throwing both engines in reverse trying to back the boat off, jumping into the salon, and looking at my wife Jean who's got these two helpless kids that are clutching her legs screaming, "I don't want to die!" I have no time to comfort them. That part of life was chaotic, but I was still trying to reestablish order. I jumped down into the radio room, calling out on my SSB, my single side band radio, the long distance radio, and all I can get is a couple of French guys voices, out there in the ether somewhere. Jean can't get out on the Iridium phone. Ben's trying to get out on the VHF. We've exhausted all of our means of communication and I finally end up hitting the button on the EPIRB. That's the last resort, Emergency Position Indicating Radio Beacon, a signal that's going up to a satellite. . . .

We hadn't been on the reef more than ten or eleven minutes, and Ben and I were up on the bow and we'd inflated the life raft. You never think that you're going to pull the tether on a life raft, but when you're in a situation like we were, you want to hear . . . the music of the compressed air being released and that raft inflating. So, we hear that music and then in the next second the lights go out. The water level inside the boat had flooded the battery banks and there was no more light, there was no more radio, there was no more nothing. We were alone. All communication was cut off, the only thing that we had coming out of our vessel anymore was the EPIRB, that one signal, this one little red light that was blinking.

Ben and I . . . go back out to tie the raft down, and the mast on *Emerald Jane*'s eighty feet— . . . like an eight-story building—. . . comes down on top of my leg. It cuts my leg off. Blood is going everywhere over the deck and as chaotic as the situation was prior to that time, it's now morphed into a life and death situation. . . . That's where the madness really began. The boat was still being picked up and thrown onto the reef, but now I'm under the mast; I can't get out. There's close to three thousand pounds of aluminum mast and rigging lying on top of me. The mast is eighty feet long, and the boat is thirty feet wide: if you subtract thirty from eighty, there's fifty feet of this aluminum hollow tube that's laying out on either side of us, and when the wave comes in, it picks the mast up and it drops it back down on my leg every time. It's shocking how painful that is. The same wave, because I'm trapped on the deck, comes two or three feet in depth over me and I'm under water. I can't breathe. I have to wait for the wave to recede before I can breathe again, and I'm bleeding to death. That's chaos. . . .

In the middle of that madness, at sea like that, it's unimaginable and your disorientation is complete. You have no idea where you are. You can't see the stars. You can't hear any other person speak. You're looking for safe harbor, you're looking for respite, you're looking for some way to make it stop. There is no land.

There's only reef. Some of the reef is above the tide, and some of it's below. And exactly like . . . Captain Pond on the *Julia Ann*, when they came to know that there was part of the reef that was above the tide, that there was an objective: they sent a guy and he swam in—my son Ben, he swam in. He swam in and he found the dried part of the reef, not even knowing that it existed because all of our flash lights were already dead. He went in over the objections of his mother. . . . We can't even see him anymore because it's black. . . . He rides the surf in and what he finds there is a piece of reef maybe the size of . . . a bed mattress. And it's maybe eighteen inches above the water line. It's still being washed over from time to time by larger surf but it's that part of the surf that really doesn't have any punch anymore. He knows it's good so . . . he leaves our can of flares and he leaves . . . that little Slurpee sized thing that's sending a signal up to a satellite and back down to the Coast Guard. . . .

I'll never forget the first time that I read . . . the Mormon . . . first person accounts of what it was like when the *Julia Ann* hit that reef. It just cut right to my heart. It was like my daughter was speaking. It was like I was there again. It was frightening to me, but at the same time it was a really great validation because we're sitting here on this story, and we don't know how to tell it. People look at us and they say, "That can't be true. How could that have happened, you couldn't have lived." And there it is: *Julia Ann*. . . . I've had time to reflect on the ties that bind us: my family and the crew and passengers on the *Julia Ann* on that night of October 4th. October 4th, my wife Jean and I, that's our anniversary. It's also the night that the *Julia Ann* hit the reef. The common bond of the anguish screaming of children and how clearly that was represented to me in . . . the Mormon accounts that were preserved, and . . . it brings back the ringing in my ears. My ears were ringing with that panic screaming on my children's part and there was nothing I could do about it. They were my compatriots . . . my fellow passengers. . . . Our situations were identical. Once a boat's disabled there's no remedy; you're at the mercy of the sea. And God made the sea, so you're at the mercy of God. . . .

The *Julia Ann* crew, Captain Pond, the passengers, what do

they have to do to reach a real safe haven? Because they know that the reef is going to flood again. At low tide you can stand up, you can walk around, but the tide's coming back in and you're going to drown. So they've got to get their patchwork boat together and then they've got to make that same trek, that same twelve miles that we did. . . . Captain Pond and company, they have to get there simply because otherwise, if you don't get off that reef, you're going to be wiped off just like the chalk on a board. . . . There was nothing left of *Emerald Jane*, our boat, the following day. It was all a mile below the ocean. . . . They had to traverse that lagoon and we had to traverse that lagoon. And we wound up going by wooden boat.

The only reason we were rescued was because the French jet kept over-flying those guys . . . and wiggling their wings. It even went to the point of turning around and coming back and dropping smoke flares, but the Polynesian guys. . . don't get it. The French guy in the search jet . . . writes a message out and rolls it up, shoves it in an orange soda bottle, screws the top on, and then these guys fly low and slow, right over that hut on stilts, and splash that bottle in the water. One of the Polynesian kids swims out and . . . brings it in to his dad, his dad opens the bottle, reads the message, goes, "Oh, wow! That's what they were trying to tell us! Come on, guys, we got to go!" . . . He gets three of his big Polynesian sons and then they take an hour and a half to get across over to that reef to get us. . . .

God is the reason I'm not dead. It's not coincidence that strung fifty-seven different events together and somehow I'm still alive. . . . I think he was preparing me for this whole thing because every night when I was on watch out in the South Pacific I would be on my knees on deck for an hour at a time with my arms outstretched, I was embracing the heavens, and I was praying to God out loud. I was being strengthened that way and I needed all the strength that God gave me. Because the events—they were tough. It was really tough. And you know, I wasn't up to . . . the challenge that God had given me. I fell into a real trough of despair as the mast was being dropped back on my leg repetitively and all I could think of was the fact that I had brought my wife and my kids out

178

here and that I was going to die and that they were going to die one after another behind me and it was me that had brought them out to this God-forsaken reef. There was nothing that I could do about it. I was really depressed for a long time and at that point in time, God gave me the faith. . . . I was concerned about my family. . . . I prayed repeatedly the same prayer. I asked God that in return for my suffering that he save the life of my wife Jean and all four of our kids. . . . It became like a mantra. Over and over again but there was no question that by that chain of words, by that spoken word, that God bound me to life—like an anchor in a boat, God's the chain. . . . He held my spirit on this planet. He didn't let go.

I was thrust into a position where I found out what true love really was. I was thrown into a position where I had to find in my heart, in my soul, what my true love for my maker, for my Father, for God was. And likewise, my daughter Amelia gave me an opportunity to see what the love of child is for her father in ways that I could never have imagined. Amelia stood in a tide pool holding the lines that were connected to the life raft in which I was lying—she held those lines like that from about three o'clock in the morning until five thirty. She was up to her armpits in water. She was freezing. The bottom of the life raft was all sliced up and the blood from my legs was lacing that sea water liberally with my blood; there [were] a lot of sharks on a reef and Amelia knew that. She was scared but she held her ground. That's real love. Then she slipped into the raft because she had to warm me up. . . . What kind of thing is she sliding into? She's sliding into my vomit, my pee, my blood; not really appetizing, but that's what true love does—I needed it and she gave it to me. . . .

I meet well-meaning people that . . . want to know if there was anything positive that came out of this tragedy. . . . I ask them, "What's the definition of a tragedy?" Because to me a tragedy is where the negatives—the unfortunate things, the horror—outweighs any positive good, and I say, "I can't answer your question if you want to classify what happened to us as a tragedy," because it isn't a tragedy when the good far outweighs the bad. Simple things like the reaffirmation of my faith and the faith of my children, the faith of my wife, in a loving God that saves us from ourselves. There's no way for me to put words on something like my son, at sixteen years of age, instantly becoming a man and taking care of his mom and taking care of his three siblings at great risk to himself. . . . Personally, why is it more positive? I lost my leg, right? What did I gain though? When I have the memory—a memory that will never leave me—of each one of my children and my wife battling not just to save me but to save each other and coming to that strength through a concrete and a tested belief in God, to reflect on the fact that it was through that and the miraculous intercession of God that we lived—what's that memory worth? Those are the things that I'll hold dear to my heart the day I die and every day in between. Every day I carry those memories with me and those aren't just positive memories. They are glowing examples of faith in action. So, there was no tragedy. There was a revelation. It was growth; it wasn't retreat.

Marifrances Trivelli

Director of the Los Angeles Maritime Museum
Los Angeles Maritime Museum, San Pedro, California, July 5, 2013

I F YOU WERE COMING INTO CALIFORNIA IN THE 1850s, you most likely did not sail directly into San Pedro; it was just a shallow mud flat, so there was no place for larger ships to deposit you on the shore. You had to get a lighter, smaller vessel, or make some kind of overland arrangements, but it wasn't a port the way San Francisco, or even San Diego, would be, where you could sail right in. . . .

It's interesting to note that when we think about what Richard Henry Dana's reaction was visiting San Pedro in the 1830s, how desolate it was, and how devoid of any aesthetic, he even called it the "hell" of California. Then you have Mormon migration from Australia two decades later, and you have Alonzo Colton wishing back the fleshpots of Sydney. He cannot wait to leave San Pedro; it had no appeal, even two decades later. . . .

You can imagine the contrast and the great shock for these Mormon migrants who are planning to arrive in California and think of the mental picture they must have had of what San Francisco was like in the 1850s. You have clipper ships clogging the harbor, gold rush excitement, lots of people, lots of opportunity, and instead they end up in San Pedro—just a mud flat, very desolate, not at all what they'd imagined. Then they want to ask themselves, why are they even here? And the answer was that they were en route to San Bernardino. . . .

The Mormons who arrived here in LA harbor in the mid-nineteenth century had contact with Phineas Banning. Phineas Banning is known as the father of the harbor. He was an entrepreneur, he was from Wilmington, Delaware, and he arrived in San Pedro, and he saw the same thing that other well-known people have seen—a mud flat, not a whole lot going on. But instead of wishing to get out right away, Phineas Banning saw possibilities. Through his vision, the harbor was dredged; a railroad was [built] connecting then Los Angeles and Wilmington. He even helped facilitate the Mormon migration. . . .

Who could have imagined what this harbor would be like, one hundred fifty years after the Mormon migration when you think about all of the engineering changes and the population changes. I think this harbor would be unrecognizable today, not just to Phineas Banning, but to the Mormon immigrants as well.

Gérald Tulasne

Lawyer
Papeete, Tahiti, January 26, 2013
Translated from French

I N 1842–1843, . . . THERE WERE VERY FEW WHITE
people in Polynesia and Tahiti. There were approximately sixty
to seventy westerners, both Europeans and Americans, and
among these westerners, there must have been at the very most
twenty to thirty Frenchmen. In reality, it was a few Frenchmen,
with Americans, Englishmen, and Germans, that created the first
lodge. This was the year of the protectorate in Tahiti, when France
took charge of the Kingdom of Tahiti, which was independent
but under French influence. Therefore, the Freemasons who came
from the exterior were soldiers from the French navy, or Americans, Englishmen, and Germans who had just settled here. They
wanted to create a Masonic lodge because they had been initiated
in the United States, for the most part in California, and one had
to be previously initiated to create a lodge here. Thus, they established a lodge, and in the mind of the French, it was a marker of the
beginning of the French Protectorate. Furthermore, . . . they had
the idea to create a lodge in late 1842 and they officially instituted

it, the Upper Tahiti Lodge, in March of 1843. Looking at history, French settlement took place in 1842 and the acceptance of the French Protectorate (which had been decided in late 1842) took place in March 1843. Thus, the dates correspond exactly.

I think that the Masonic lodge consisted of a lot of navigators, highly-ranked officers in the French navy, and so there was a sort of sea-going brotherhood. . . . This assistance was twofold. Firstly, to clothe those individuals involved in the shipwreck once they arrived in Tahiti. The lodge took care of clothing and feeding them for about a month, according to a witness in one of the documents I have, and then established a subscription with the representative of the United States to procure the money for the people to continue on to the United States. This was done in two phases. In the first phase, they clothed and fed the passengers, and in the second phase, they helped them continue their journey to the United States. This was the twofold assistance provided by the Masonic lodge.

The purpose of the Freemasons at this time was to be an initiatory school, the first goal of which was to improve the individual and society. Therefore assistance, even to strangers, is part of this philosophy.

When the survivors arrived in Tahiti, there were two groups. There was the American group, which sought and received help from the American Consul, and the English, which found themselves alone. They went to see the English Consul, but he refused to help them because they were on an American ship. Thus, one group of survivors was in Tahiti without any assistance. It is likely at this time that the Masonic lodge intervened. Remember that in this lodge, there were Frenchmen, Americans, and Englishmen, and this is without a doubt the reason why the Masonic lodge could not leave these survivors without any help. So, they formalized the assistance with food and clothing, and then the Masonic lodge began a subscription among the population to raise money so that the Englishmen and the Americans could be repatriated to California by ship.

In rereading John Penfold's historical text of this story that he experienced himself as a survivor, we see that the group of survivors stayed in Tahiti for four months. After four months, they decided whether they would continue on their way to Australia or, leave for San Francisco. It would seem that the United States' Consul and the Masonic lodge worked together to gather money in dollars to pay the captain of a schooner so that all of the survivors could leave for San Francisco as part of a new voyage. This is all we know from contemporary witnesses.

Thomas Magee would have been a Freemason at this time and, consequentially, he could have very possibly come in contact with the Masons once he arrived in Tahiti, because we know that there were many Englishmen and Americans who were members of this lodge, including Adams, Darling, Philidore Danican, Hardy, Eleanor Segar, Clark, Taylor, Mark, and Farlow. Therefore, it was very possible to be recognized in the Masonic community; the tie between the survivors and the Masonic lodge was established by Mr. Thomas Magee. We cannot verify this hypothesis, but it is within the realm of possibility, in which case it is even better because we see that the Masonic lodge helped not only Thomas Magee and his family, but the entire group of survivors.

Courtesy of Yann Hubert - GRAN, 2006

Robert Veccella

Head Maritime Archaeologist in Tahiti who assisted
with the Julia Ann *excavation*
Papeete, Tahiti, January 26, 2013

W E WENT TO SCILLY IN 1996 TO FIND THE wreck of the *Julia Ann* at the request of Paul Hundley from the Sydney Maritime Museum. . . . The operation was expanded by a team of Americans. On the site, we, the naval archaeology research group, were there to take care of all of the administrative aspects, as well as the technical preparation from the on-site mission. This team consisted of nine people: Hundley, the curator of the Sydney Maritime Museum; Sue Bassett, also a curator at the Sydney Maritime Museum; Shelly Smith, the director of the Newport Maritime Museum; and two American archaeologists, Jack Hunter and Rick Sweet, who represented the American interests. There were three of us on our side . . . : Max Guiroud, our association's spokesperson who came specially from France; Jean-Pierre Carlotti, a colleague who worked in our association at the time; and myself. The last, yet most important person, was the manager and pilot of our boat, Francois Maillol, the nephew of Jacques Maillol, the famous free diver. With this team, we embarked on a ten-day journey. The purpose of this mission was to find the traces of the *Julia Ann*, which was shipwrecked . . . . The goal was to find the vestiges of this wreck.

One thing must be made clear: the atolls of French Polynesia are essentially coral atolls. The problem is that when a wreck sinks over a reef, it is rapidly destroyed by the shipwreck itself, and what remains does not hold up very well. This is not the case when the ship sinks in areas of silt. What we found were essentially heavy pieces: anchors, chains, ballast, ballast stones, coal, and copper plating, because the ship was reinforced with an outer layer of copper. . . . This wreck was completely dispersed; we found the pieces over an approximately three hundred to four hundred meter distance. One must not imagine that the wreck of the *Julia Ann* was one on which we could really explore and excavate. . . .

There are two essential reasons [for which we could not find more of the wreck]. First, the configuration of the island does not allow the discovery of many things because the island is basically vertical. Whatever falls will fall rapidly; that is, if a boat runs aground, there is a risk of sinking. That's the first thing. Secondly, we know that the boat split in half. Therefore, one part stayed where it fell, and the other part came up on the reef. Each year when the cyclones came, this area was very exposed, so with all the cyclones there could have been, the wreckage that remained on the site was completely exposed. We must remember that this ship was made of wood, so the wood on the reef would have been completely displaced, or at least the floating pieces would have been carried to the other side of the island, where they disappeared.

It is possible to find other vestiges; that is undeniable. We went to Scilly for only ten days—that's not a lot of time. Furthermore, during the first two days, we were not able to access the atoll because of the swell. . . . It is also possible that the shipwrecked passengers salvaged pieces of the ship and put them somewhere on the atoll. Therefore, it would be possible to recover other vestiges on land. It is also possible that other vestiges remain on the oceanside. Another mission is still foreseeable to find other vestiges.

The difficulty of navigation in the Pacific comes from the fact that, at the time, there were no maps. Even on the maps that existed, the atolls and islands were placed a little randomly. In any case, all we have to do is look at what happens today—practically every year there are boats that run aground in Polynesia, even though we have GPS, maps, etc. At the time, this entire area was called the Dangerous Archipelago because in the middle of the night, an atoll cannot be seen. The *Julia Ann* made its route with a lot of sails and often during the night, which should not have been done. They saw the atoll very, very late, just at the last moment when they were upon it. During a storm at night, one cannot see this danger. Thus French Polynesia, notably the lower islands, is very dangerous because there is no way to signal these atolls. There is a lack of knowledge of these atolls.

There were so few deaths—only five—in this shipwreck. . . . That's barely ten percent of the total number of passengers. That's somewhat of a miracle. When we arrived at the site in 1996, we could not pass the coral barrier; it was extremely dangerous. The people had a lot of luck to survive the shipwreck and then stay on the atoll for two months with so little means of survival. They were quite lucky in their misfortune since this atoll had a potentially fruitful food source. There were animals, especially birds. They ate a lot of birds, and turtles as well. They were also able to live because they dug in the sand and found an aquifer with fresh water, just slightly brackish. This, however, was what allowed them to hold on for two months. If not for this . . . they would not have been able to live, especially because there were children with them. I think that life must have been very, very hard for them. Even more difficult was the heat, because once the cyclone passed, they had to stay for weeks and weeks with an enormously intense sun and very little protection.

The shipwreck of the *Julia Ann* could have a different reading according to the angle from which you look at it. This story could be read for the local history of French Polynesia. It could be read much more globally from the angle of immigration in the Pacific, since there were . . . Mormons on the ship [going] from Australia to Salt Lake City. This migration was in contrast with what was normally done, because, at the time, immigration usually came from the United States moving toward Australia. Thus, there must be a meaning for the shipwreck in the context of the history of immigration in the Pacific. The third story that appears to be interesting is the story of the survival of this people who stayed on the atoll for two months. At one point, there was a team who left to seek rescue. That is really a very interesting story in terms of the human capacity for survival in different conditions. Thus, this story can be read in different ways, which could interest people with completely different problems.

Clint Warby

Great-great-grandson of James and Mary Warby
West Jordan, Utah, December 28, 2012

MY GREAT-GREAT-GRANDFATHER [JAMES WARBY] came from Australia on the first voyage of the *Julia Ann*. . . . We . . . trace our ancestors by going to the places where they were and doing some of the things that they might have done. . . . We know that the missionaries who came into that region [were] William Hyde and his companion John McCarthy. They had come to a place now known as Raymond Terrace. My great-great-grandfather is coming home from work; he's a farm laborer. He sees them on the street corner; they have a conversation. They invite him to come to a cottage meeting that night. He goes home and tells his wife, and she says, "We're going." There are four little ones that tag along with their parents, and we believe that right there my great-great-grandmother Mary Blanch Warby decides to join the Church. She's baptized by John McCarthy. Grandfather is baptized later in June, by William Hyde.

Then tragedy strikes. There are . . . three children that died within a two-week period, and it's our belief that William Hyde offers great counsel to them that tells them that they need to go to Zion to get to the temple and . . . have those children sealed to them. That's uppermost in their mind. . . . The William's River branch, along with . . . other folks from the Hunter River region . . . get together . . . I think there are sixty-three members . . . and they go down to the harbor at Newcastle. . . . William Hyde makes arrangements for the *Julia Ann* to take them to Zion. . . . .This branch comes together and supports my family . . . with a new, two-week-old baby, Sarah, and little John, the only survivor. . . . They've [the Warbys] made preparations; they come to Newcastle and they load all the provisions, what little they have, onto the boat. It's March of 1854, the first voyage of *Julia Ann* off to America, off to Zion. . . .

With the baptism of my great-great-grandparents and the association that they have with the members of the branch and with the missionaries teaching them and telling them that they need to come to Zion, it's important for them to realize the eternal blessings that will be theirs if they do make that decision. . . . As they are taught the gospel in Australia by the missionaries, and the Plan of Salvation, it becomes very apparent to them with the loss of four little ones . . . that the only work that they could do that would seal them together as a forever family would be in Zion and in sacred places that have been dedicated to that purpose. When they do come to Utah, they come to a place in Salt Lake where that is performed. Eventually in St. George [Utah], another temple . . . is built, and so they then realize the fulfillment of that promise that was given to them that if they did come they would be a family forever. . . .

There were other prominent families that came with them. One of which is the Stapley family, and from that came . . . Delbert L. Stapley, a member of the Quorum of the Twelve. There are literally thousands upon thousands of descendants of our family and of other families that have been blessed because they did gather to Zion with that first voyage. Because of that first voyage, and because there was a good experience from all of the people that went on that first voyage, there was this great need now to encourage others that were still in Australia to get on the boat again and to come to America, and to be able to enjoy the blessings that they had received. . . .

They came as free settlers—they were encouraged by the

government to come. At that point Australia was a very harsh country. There [were] some climate issues. It rains a lot down there, and today there's still flooding. . . . It was difficult . . . to earn a living and to start from scratch, and they knew [they would go] if there was an opportunity . . . elsewhere where they would enjoy the blessings of the gospel as well as being able to enjoy producing goods and services that would be able to take care of their families. There was an economic push to try and make things a little better in their lives. There was an opportunity to be some of the first set- tlers. . . . There's a certain element in people's lives that they want to be first, that they would like to . . . be the pioneers, that they want to have the world open up to them and be able to build upon the foundation that they've put together, the legacy that they're leaving to their ancestors. . . .

From the history accounts, we know that the first voyage of the *Julia Ann* was rather successful. There was a place where the winds didn't blow, but eventually that all changed, and they got to California. What really impressed the captain, Captain Pond, was the demeanor of the people that were on board. These were people who were happy. They were excited about getting to Zion. As they're on the ship things work out well, and so the captain is very, very impressed with these Mormons that are coming all the way from Australia to the United States. These are great pas- sengers, and I think he sees that if there are more to come, that's perhaps an opportunity for him to make some money. . . .

It was marvelous for them to make that decision that would make all the difference in the world for all their descendants and for those who come. . . . Since they went to Zion and eventually to Utah, there was much more opportunity for the gospel to be spread throughout the entire earth, from missionaries and from people who served the Lord in various capacities and in various ways. Even though the Church struggled for a while without these people there [in Australia], the Church itself is much better and much greater because these people made the sacrifice to come to Zion.

ENDNOTES

1. Richard L. Bushman, "Mormon History Inside Out," *Fides et Historia* 43, no.2 (Summer/Fall 2011), 8. Herein Bushman further notes, "I think we should encourage the pursuit of interests that grow out of the personal. The ideal antiseptic inquiry, scrubbed of everything subjective, is no longer the goal. . . . We aim to talk about the world, not just about ourselves, but we should recognize that our individual conversations with the world may in the end yield the most compelling truths."

2. My dissertation was eventually published. See Fred E. Woods, *Water and Storm Polemics Against Baalism in the Deuteronomic History*, in *American University Studies; Series VII: Theology and Religion*, vol. 150 (New York: Peter Lang Publications, 1994).

3. A notable exception is Conway B. Sonne, who pioneered the study of Mormon maritime migration with two great works: *Saints on the Seas: A Maritime History of Mormon Migration 1830–1890* (Salt Lake City: University of Utah Press, 1983), and *Ships, Saints, and Mariners: A Maritime Encyclopedia of Mormon Migration 1830–1890* (Salt Lake City: University of Utah Press, 1987).

4. This website is located at http://mormonmigration.lib.byu.edu/ and is sponsored by the Brigham Young University Harold B. Lee Library.

5. Conway B. Sonne, *Saints on the High Seas: A Maritime History of Mormon Migration 1830–1890* (Salt Lake City: University of Utah Press, 1983), 139, notes that during the years 1847–1853 alone, there were 59 disasters among ships carrying immigrants across the Atlantic. An online list entitled "Pacific Ocean Shipwrecks" records about one hundred shipwrecks in the Pacific Ocean during the 19th and early 20th centuries coming to and from Australia, although the *Julia Ann* is not mentioned; see http://oceans1.customer.netspace.net.au/pacific-wrecks.html, accessed June 24, 2013.

6. Historians who have written articles on this topic are Russell T. Clement, "The Shipwreck of the *Julia Ann*," unpublished paper presented at the Mormon Historical Association Conference, May 10–13, 1984; John Devitry-Smith, "The Wreck of the *Julia Ann*," *BYU Studies* 29, no.

2 (Spring 1989):5–29 and a later revised piece of this same article in *Coming to Zion*, eds. James B. Allen and John W. Welch (Provo: Brigham Young University, 1997), 224–60. Marjorie Newton also included a few pages on this subject in *Southern Cross Saints: The Mormons in Australia* (Laie, Hawaii: The Institute for Polynesian Studies, 1991), 145–48.

7. The Latter-day Saints' Article of Faith #10 states, "We believe in the literal gathering of Israel and in the restoration of the Ten Tribes."

8. Wallace Stegner, *The Gathering of Zion: The Story of the Mormon Trail* (New York: McGraw Hill Book Company, 1964), 8.

9. Joseph Smith, Jr., *Teachings of the Prophet Joseph Smith*, ed., Joseph Fielding Smith, (Salt Lake City: Deseret Book, 1972), 307–8.

10. The full title of this LDS book of scripture is *The Doctrine and Covenants of the Church of Jesus Christ of Latter-day Saints* (Salt Lake City: The Church of Jesus Christ of Latter-day Saints, 1981) and consists of revelations given to Joseph Smith Jr. and several other LDS modern-day prophets. It is cited hereafter as D&C.

11. The D&C also defines Zion as a spiritual condition: "This is Zion—the pure in heart" (D&C 97:21). This same definition is attested in another book of LDS scripture known as the Pearl of Great Price, which explains that a people of Zion are "of one heart and one mind" who dwell "in righteousness" with "no poor among them" (Moses 7:18). Hymns with the very same theme continue to be sung in Latter-day Saint congregations. See, for example, in the LDS hymnal (Salt Lake City: The Church of Jesus Christ of Latter-day Saints, 1985) the hymns, "Israel, Israel, God is Calling" (Richard Smyth, no. 7) and "Ye Elders of Israel" (Cyrus H. Wheelock, no. 319). However, the emphasis for modern-day Latter-day Saints is directed toward a spiritual condition, rather than a physical journey. As recent as 1999, the Church First Presidency has discouraged international converts from immigrating to the United States. See "Remain in homelands, members counseled," *Church News*, December 11, 1999, 7.

12. D&C 29:7–8. The tribulation and desolation here spoken of has reference to a millennial doom that was perceived as being nigh at hand. On this topic, see Grant Underwood, *The Millenarian World of Early Mormonism* (Urbana: University of Illinois, 1993).

13. Latter-day Saints believe that "two separate Jerusalems, the old and the new, will serve as headquarters of the millennial Kingdom of God from which Jesus will rule. Old Jerusalem will be built up by Judah. The New Jerusalem, also to be known as Zion (D&C 45:66–67), will be built up in Jackson County, Missouri." See D. Kelly Ogden, "Jerusalem," ed. Daniel H. Ludlow, *Encyclopedia of Mormonism* (New York: Macmillan Publishing Company, 1992), 2:723.

14. D&C 101:1–2 also explains that another reason the Jackson County LDS community was driven out was "in consequence of their transgressions."

15. Joseph Smith, *History of the Church of Jesus Christ of Latter-day Saints*, ed., B. H. Roberts, Rev. ed., (Salt Lake City: *Deseret News*, 1965), 3:175. Hereafter cited as *HC*.

16. M. Hamlin Cannon, "Migration of English Mormons to America," *American Historical Review* 52, no. 3 (April 1947): 441, asserts that 4,733 British Saints gathered to Nauvoo from 1840–1846. Andrew Jenson, "Church Emigration," *Contributor* 12, no.12 (October 1891): 441–450, provides a list of the chartered voyages. This was reproduced and supplemented with additional independent voyages in Fred E. Woods, *Gathering to Nauvoo* (American Fork, Utah: Covenant Communications, Inc., 2002), 153–170.

17. In D&C 20:2–3, Joseph Smith and Oliver Cowdery were designated by revelation as the first and second elders of the LDS Church. The priesthood keys mentioned here refer to the right to direct the work of gathering. LDS believe that the ancient prophets restored these keys to Joseph Smith, including the prophet Moses.

18. James B. Allen and Glen M. Leonard, *The Story of the Latter-day Saints*, 2nd ed., (Salt Lake City: Deseret Book, 1992), 127, notes that the other missionaries were Willard Richards, a dear friend of Heber C. Kimball, as well as four Canadian missionaries: Elders Fielding, Goodson, Russell, and Snyder.

19. *HC* 2:492

20. Orson F. Whitney, *Life of Heber C. Kimball* (Salt Lake City: Bookcraft, 1967), 130.

21. James B. Allen, Ronald K. Esplin, and David J. Whittaker, *Men with a Mission 1837–1841: The Quorum of the Twelve Apostles in the British Isles* (Salt Lake City: Desert Book, 1992), 53. Apostles Kimball and Hyde left England on April 20, 1838.

22. For more information on the mission of the Twelve to the British Isles, see James B. Allen and Malcom R. Thorp, "The Mission of the Twelve to England, 1840–41: Mormon Apostles and the Working Classes," *BYU Studies* 15 (Summer 1975): 499–526; James B. Allen, Ronald K. Esplin and David J. Whittaker, *Men With a Mission*.

23. *HC* 4:119. By this time the total membership of the Church in the British Isles was reported as 1,671, including 132 priesthood leaders. See Orson F. Whitney, *Life of Heber C. Kimball* (Salt Lake City: Bookcraft, 1967), 278.

24. Journal of John Murdock, April, 1852, 93, CHL.

25. Laurie F. Maffly-Kipp and Reid L. Neilson, eds., "Nineteenth-Century Mormonism and the Pacific Basin Frontier," in *Proclamation to the People: Nineteenth-Century Mormonism and the Pacific Basin Frontier*, (Salt Lake City: University of Utah Press, 2008), 5.

26. "Elders from Zion who have labored in the Australasian Mission," Australasian Mission Manuscript History, (hereafter cited as AMMH), Salt Lake City, Church History Library (hereafter cited as CHL) lists the following names of twelve elders called between 1851 and 1854: "John Murdock, C. W. Wandell, A. Farnham, Wm. Hyde, J. W. Fleming, Burr Frost, Ab. P. Dowdle, James Graham, John S. Eldredge, J. Norton, John Hyde, Paul Smith." Of this number, John Hyde, who was ill on the passage over, died less than five months after arriving in Australia, apparently of cancer. See "Australia. —Death of Elder John Hyde," *Millennial Star* 16, no. 10 (March 11, 1854), 155, which details his valiant life and death on August 26, 1853. Robert Owens is also listed as being called in the year 1854, but he did not receive his appointment until October 10, 1854, seven months after the first voyage of the *Julia Ann* had departed from Australia.

27. For a biographical sketch on Barratt, see Appendix C: Biographical Register.

28. George Albert Smith, "My Journal," *Instructor* 82 (September 14, 1947): 417. See also *HC* 4:154 which confirms that "William Barrett, aged 17, was ordained an Elder in Hanley, Staffordshire, England, by Elders George A. Smith and Alfred Cordon, and took leave for South Australia, being the first Elder who went on a mission to that country."

29. *HC* 4:343.

30. Alfred Cordon, "Reminiscences and Journal, 1839–68," CHL, 37. On the eve of Barratt reaching Australia, statistics for New South Wales reveal that about nine percent of Protestants and eleven percent of Catholics were attending church meetings. One article noted, "The number of Protestants at any one time attending divine worship, at the commencement of 1839, cannot, it is feared, be estimated at more than 11,000. Of these, the number attending the ministrations of the clergy of the Church of England was about 7,000, the number attending the ministrations of the clergy of the Presbyterian church about 2,000, the number attached to the Wesleyan connexion 1,450, those attending the Independent congregation 300, the Baptist 300, and the Quakers about 50.* This estimate is formed with respect to the number attending divine worship in 1839 ; at that time the general population of the colony had been increased from 77,096 (the number in 1836) to about 102,000. . . . The number of Roman Catholics attending divine worship, in 1836, was not estimated at more than 2,450 ;* the Roman Catholic portion of the community being at the same time 21,898. The number

of persons of that profession, and of their congregations in 1839, is unknown." See Robert Montgomery Martin, ed., "Religious Wants of the Colonies," in *Colonial Magazine and Commercial-Maritime Journal* 2, no. 6 (May–August 1840): 196–97.

31. John Devitry-Smith, "William James Barratt: The First Mormon 'Down Under,'" *BYU Studies* 28, no. 3 (Summer 1988): 61.

32. The Wellington district is 225 miles northwest of Sydney. Marjorie Newton, *Southern Cross Saints: The Mormons in Australia* (Laie, Hawaii: The Institute for Polynesian Studies, 1991), 24–25. In an article titled "Abroad" in the Nauvoo periodical *Times and Seasons* 6, no. 13 (July 15, 1845), 975, reported: "There is a church in New South Wales, Australia, of eleven members, raised up by Elder Andrew Anderson." For a biographical sketch of Anderson, see Appendix C: Biographical Register.

33. Andrew Anderson, *Times and Seasons* vol. 6, no. 14 (August 1, 1845), 989–990. Anderson later reported that a few people he had baptized years ago were scattered and had grown very cold.

34. Letter of Andrew Anderson to Charles Wesley Wandell, May 17, 1852, in Australasian Mission General Minutes, 1851–1891 (hereafter cited as AMGM), 63, CHL, deposited with the Church in Salt Lake City in 1859 by Wandell. The minutes of a Church conference held in Sydney (July 6, 1852), 72–73, reveals that Anderson did indeed attend and presented his license to preach, which had been given him nine years earlier by Elder Orson Pratt in Edinburgh, Scotland. Elder Anderson "gave in his Report, stating that some years ago he had baptized a few members, who are very much scattered abroad; and who have grown very cold in the work, and asked counsel What to do with them? The President recommended that they renew their covenants, if they wish still to be considered as members of the church."

Three days after Anderson wrote his letter noted above, on May 20, 1852, Wandell received another letter from Edmund and Eliza Harris, who were living in East Maitland, Australia, at the time. They had also been previously baptized and congratulated Wandell on "the spirited and able manner in which [he had] advocated the cause." (AMGM, 64–65). Wandell told them that he would be sending a young missionary named John McCarthy to visit them. (AMGM, 65–66).

35. David Goodman, *Seeking: Victoria and California in the 1850s* (Stanford, CA: Stanford University Press, 1994), xxiii.

36. Stuart Macintyre, *A Concise History of Australia* (Cambridge, UK: Cambridge University Press, 2004), 86.

37. In a letter to Asa Calkin, president of the European Mission, Thomas Ford explained his feelings in dealing with the impact of the Australian

quest for gold in the mid-nineteenth century: "Gold is the god of this people. To obtain it, no sacrifice is considered too great, nor toil too arduous; but the truth they will not have, though carried to their doors." See *Millennial Star* 21, no. 19 (May 7, 1859), 304–305.

38. John Murdock to the First Presidency, January 22, 1852, Journal of John Murdock, 69, CHL. For a biographical sketch of Murdock, see Appendix C: Biographical Register.

39. Andrew Jenson, "Australian Mission," *Encyclopedic History of the Church of Jesus Christ of Latter-day Saints* (Salt Lake City: *Deseret News* Publishing, 1941), 35–36, recognized the early part-time LDS missionary labors of Barratt (1840) and Anderson (1842), yet noted, "The real opening of the Australian Mission marks the arrival at Sydney, Oct. 30, 1851, of Elders John Murdock and Chas. W. Wandell." The discrepancy of dates can be accounted for by the international dateline. See Marjorie Newton's interview in Appendix E for her comments about the dateline. For a biographical sketch of Wandell, see Appendix C: Biographical Register.

40. AMGM, 1–2, CHL.

41. Journal of John Murdock, "Report of my mission to Australia, addressed to the Conference held in G. S. L. City April 1853," 110.

42. Newton, *Southern Cross Saints*, 28–29, notes that the old race course was actually Hyde Park, which was a Methodist meeting place. Further (p. 230), "the last race meeting in Hyde Park was held in 1824, but the name lingered."

43. Journal of John Murdock, November 1, 1851, 67.

44. Charles Wesley Wandell to Parley P. Pratt, January 1, 1852, AMGM, 3, CHL.

45. Journal of John Murdock, "Report of my mission to Australia, addressed to the Conference held in G. S. L. City April 1853," January 5, 1852, 111. Wandell to Pratt, January 1852, AMGM further noted, 4, "On the 15th of December [1851], I baptized four persons on the the 21st two persons, and yesterday, the 31st, two persons; making thirteen (13) persons in all; and I have appointed next Sunday to organize ourselves into a Branch. On Sunday, Jan 4th, we were organized into a Branch." At the end of the month in another letter to Parley P. Pratt, January 28, 1852, AMGM, 6, Wandell reported, "I am still baptizing—I have baptized sixteen (16) in all, and more are ready. The brethren are poor as to worldly goods, but in the scale of intelligence they will compare possibly, with other Branches of the Church. We have union and peace in our midst, and the brethren rejoice in the truth. . . . These Colonies are greatly misunderstood and underrated by both England and America. They are numerous and extensive, and the great majority of the

inhabitants are industrious and reported honest. I consider the moral condition of this city far in advance of San Francisco, and nearly, equal to that of the Atlantic cities of the United States."

Just a few months after the Sydney Branch was established, the Sydney correspondent for *The* [Melbourne] *Argus* in an article titled, "Sydney," *The Argus* (May 4, 1852), 2, appears to reflect a positive opinion of the Mormons, as Wandell did of the Australian colonies at this time. The correspondent reported, "I fell in recently with a collection of hymns printed for the sect known to the world as the Mormons, but calling itself, 'The Church of Jesus Christ of Latter Day Saints.' Seeing that this had been got out at a Sydney printing office, I made further inquiries, and found, somewhat to my surprise, not only that a Mormon mission had established itself in Sydney, but that it had made considerable although quiet progress. We have, I understand, a missionary here from the new and flourishing state of the Mormons in the valley of the Great Salt Lake, the State of Deseret, who holds from his own body the rank of Bishop." [He is probably referring to John Murdock, who was ordained a bishop in Nauvoo in 1842; see Andrew Jenson, "Murdock, John" *LDS Biographical Encyclopedia* vol. 2 (Salt Lake City: Western Epics, 1971), 362–4.] The correspondent also stated, "It is by no means improbable that a good deal of the emigration to California may be attributed to the exertions of this missionary and his coadjutors, for as Deseret is at no great, distance from the Californian frontier San Francisco would afford the readiest approach from Sydney to the 'promised land.' It is the object of the Mormons to gather the whole sect, as far as practicable, within the fold at head quarters, for, in the first place, this gathering has been enjoined upon them by their founder, and, in the second place, there is the present object of gathering together a sufficient population to demand admission into the American Union as a Sovereign State. This extention of the Mormon Missions to Australia, is a matter worthy of much thought. In England, they have made enormous progress of late years, and large bodies of emigrants leave the British ports annually for the Valley of the Great Salt Lake. There is a degree of steadiness, industry, and perseverance in the people of this sect, and of quiet energy in their missionaries, which gives them a strong influence."

46. John Murdock to the First Presidency, Journal of John Murdock, January 22, 1852, 75, CHL.

47. Stuart Macintyre, "In Thrall to Progress, 1851–1888," *A Concise History of Australia*, 114. Murdock noted shortly after his arrival in Australia, "Sydney is a city of 80,000 inhabitance, and has from forty to fifty meeting houses in it of different sects" (Journal of John Murdock, late fall

of 1851, 67–68. Murdock's figure probably includes the suburbs of the Sydney region as well. The population of Australia as a whole in 1850 was estimated at about 405,000 and had blossomed to over 1,145,000 by 1860. See Jan Lahmeyer, "Australia: Historical Demographic Data for the Whole Country," http://www.populstat.info/Oceania/australc. htm, accessed May 4, 2013).

48. Mark Peel and Christina Twomey, "New Australias: 1829–49," *A History of Australia* (New York: Palgrave Macmillan, 2011), 54–55. Barbara A. West with Frances T. Murphy, "Gold Rush and Governments," *A Brief History of Australia* (New York: Checkmark Books, 2010), 65, observed, "The many social and economic changes wrought on Australian society in the 1850s had both immediate and long-term political ramifications. The most immediate occurred in December 1852, when the British authorities decided to end all convict transportation to Australia's east coast. This decision was made partly in response to pressure brought to bear by free settlers and Australian-born leaders who wanted to see their country prosper as a real colony rather than the final resting place of Britain's criminal class. The other factor in the decision, however, was gold. With thousands of middle-class migrants paying for their passage to the gold fields of New South Wales and Victoria, it made little sense to spend governmental funds to ship criminals to a place where they could potentially become millionaires at the end of their sentences."

49. Journal of John Murdock, "Report of my mission to Australia, addressed to the Conference held in G. S. L. City April 1853," 110, CHL. However, these Mormon missionaries were not treated as harshly as the Chinese, who, speaking a different language, apparently appeared to be even further removed from what the Australians may have viewed as normalcy. Stuart Macintyre, *A Concise History of Australia*, 102, notes, "The Chinese encountered the greatest hostility. For more than a century they were the largest non-European national group in Australia, distinctive in appearance, language, religion and customs. From their arrival on the multinational diggings in the early 1850s, they were singled out for criticism."

50. Journal of John Murdock, late fall 1851, 70. Marjorie Newton, *Southern Cross Saints*, 55, notes that door-to-door tracting with pamphlets in Australia began in 1851, was still being used throughout the twentieth century.

51. Journal of John Murdock, March 1, 1852, 77.

52. Charles W. Wandell to President S. [Stephen] W. Richards, December 20, 1852, "The Australian Mission," *Millennial Star* 15, no. 14 (April 2, 1853), 220–21.

53. "General Intelligence," *Zion's Watchman* 1, nos. 18–19 (September 16, 1854), 151.

54. Augustus Farnham to President Franklin D. Richards, May 31, 1855, "Foreign Correspondence. New South Wales," *Millennial Star* 17, no. 37 (September 15, 1855), 590. This same year, John McCarthy, "Quarterly Conference of the Australasian Mission . . . 1855," *Zion's Watchman* 2, no. 3 (June 18, 1855), 42, wrote, "I have visited the Williams' River and Hinton; I got an opening to preach at Hinton and baptized four, but since then the door has closed, for the landlords warned their tenants that if they opened their doors for the Mormons, their farms would be taken from them."

55. Charles Wesley Wandell to the editors, "The Mormons," *Sydney Morning Herald* (May 15, 1852), 4, evidences Wandell's keen ability to write as he responds in defense of Mormonism to an article titled "The Mormon Delusion," which was published two days earlier in the *Sydney Morning Herald* (May 13, 1852), 2.

56. Letter of Charles Wesley Wandell to the First Presidency, May 1852, AMGM, 62.

57. Andrew Jenson, in AMMH, introductory information.

58. Geoffrey Blainey, *The Tyranny of Distance: How Distance Shaped Australia's History* (Melbourne: Sun Books, 1966), viii.

59. Augustus Farnham to President Franklin D. Richards, May 31, 1855, "Foreign Correspondence. New South Wales," *Millennial Star* 17, no. 37 (September 22, 1855), 590–92. For a biographical sketch of Farnham, see Appendix C: Biographical Register.

60. Josiah W. Fleming to President Richards, June 16, 1854, "Foreign Correspondence. Australia," *Millennial Star* 17, no. 1 (January 6, 1855), 11–12. Marjorie Newton, *Southern Cross Saints*, 164–65, observed that for the year 1855, there were only six full-time missionaries in the entire Australasian Mission, which is nearly as large as all of North America. With Australia's population of 793,260 at the time, this ratio was 1:132,210. However, she notes that when compared with the British Mission, which had thirty-eight missionaries and a population of 18.5 million during the 1850s, the Australasian Mission had a much better ratio of missionaries than what was had in the British Mission. This calculation does not take into consideration the other local part-time missionaries who were serving in Australia, nor those serving in the British Isles. Augustus Farnham wrote a letter to Elder Franklin D. Richards, dated January 26, 1855, *Millennial Star* 17, no. 18 (May 5, 1855), 283–284, which stated that there were then "thirty Elders in these lands, who labour as circumstances and opportunities permit." Therefore, there were really six times as many missionaries when we

take into account those local Australian elders who were laboring part-time as determined by circumstance and opportunity.

61. Concerning this proclamation, which was titled "Proclamation! To the People of the Coasts and Islands of the Pacific (Ocean), of Every Nation, Kindred and Tongue," Elder Parley P. Pratt, president of the Pacific Mission, wrote in the late summer of 1851, "During my stay in San Francisco I wrote a proclamation of the gospel addressed to the people of the coasts and islands of the Pacific, which was afterwards published by Elder Wandell in Australia." See *Autobiography of Parley P. Pratt*, 3rd rev. ed. (Salt Lake City: Deseret Book, 1938), 387. The following year, this entire tract was published in two parts in the *Millennial Star* 14, no. 30 (September 18, 1852), 465–70, and 14, no. 31 (September 25, 1852), 481–85. Two years later, Australia was also under the supervision of "the 'European Mission' [which] was founded by the union of all the missionary districts, conferences, and branches of the church in European countries, as also all such subdivisions in Africa, Australia and India, under one presiding authority in June, 1854, when Elder Franklin D. Richards" arrived in England. See B. H. Roberts, *A Comprehensive History of the Church of Jesus Chris of Latter-day Saints: Century I*, 4:241, note 5. For a biographical sketch of Pratt, see Appendix C: Biographical Register.

62. Journal of John Murdock, late fall 1851, 67, 71. "A Voice of Warning" is the well-known tract published by Elder Parley P. Pratt. The full title of the work referred to by Orson Pratt is *A Interesting Account of Several Remarkable Visions, and the Late Discovery of Ancient American Records*, (Edinburgh: Ballantyne and Hughes, 1840). According to R. Lanier Britsch, *Unto the Islands of the Sea: A History of the Latter-day Saints in the Pacific* (Salt Lake City: Deseret Book, 1986), 197, also printed was "a clip-and-paste booklet by Charles W. Wandell titled *History of the Persecutions!! Endured by the Church of Jesus Christ of Latter-day Saints, in America* (64 pages; 2000 copies); a tract by Wandell replying to some local anti-Mormon literature, titled *Reply to Shall We Believe in Mormon?*"

   Wandell's title to his tract may have been influenced by an earlier work titled *History of the Persecution of the Saints*. The Joseph Smith Papers Project includes a letter written by Joseph Smith on March 10, 1839, from Liberty Jail requesting the Saints and especially Bishop Edward Partridge to document the "suffering and abuses" experienced in Missouri. In response, Partridge wrote a detailed eyewitness account that was published serially in the Church's newspaper, the *Times and Seasons*. The series, titled "A History, of the Persecution, of the Church of Jesus Christ, of Latter Day Saints, in Missouri," also drew on previously published accounts of the Saints' hardships, including writings by

Sidney Rigdon and Parley P. Pratt." See "Letter to Church and Edward Partridge, 20 March 1839," http://josephsmithpapers.org, accessed May 10, 2013.

In a letter from Charles W. Wandell to President Franklin D. Richards, written in San Francisco on August 30, 1851, "Mission to Australia," *Millennial Star* 13, no. 22 (November 15, 1851), 349–50, Wandell made the following request: "I wish you to send me one or more copies of the Book of Mormon, Book of Covenants, Voice of Warning, and, in fact, a copy of every thing that you think will be useful to me in a strange country [Australia]. Send me as many copies of the Voice of Warning and Book of Mormon as you think proper." Nearly two years later, Augustus Farnham wrote a letter to President S. W. Richards, dated July 25, 1853, "Australian Mission," *Millenial Star* 15, no. 47 (November 19, 1853), 766–67, with a similar request: "We wish you to forward us more of O. Pratt's works complete and bound, 200 more Hymn Books, 100 Books of Mormon, 100 Doctrine and Covenants, more Voice of Warning, and Spencer's Letters, 100 O. Pratt work on Celestial Marriage."

Orson Pratt, an LDS apostle as well as a gifted writer, publicly announced the practice of plural marriage in a discourse titled "Celestial Marriage," on August 29, 1852. He also published information on Celestial Marriage in an eight-part series (January–August 1853) of an LDS periodical he edited titled *The Seer*, which was published in Washington, D.C. from 1853–1854. See http://en.wikisource.org/wiki/Author:Orson_Pratt.

Farnham referenced "Spencer's Letters," a work by Elder Orson Spencer, which is the book *Letters exhibiting the most prominent doctrines of the Church of Jesus Christ of Latter-day Saints by Orson Spencer*, in reply to the Rev. William Crowell (Liverpool: Orson Spencer, 1848). It was written by Spencer when he was the president of the British Mission and editor of the *Millennial Star* (1847–48) to Crowell who was the editor of the newspaper *Christian Watchman*, in Boston, MA. This work is 245 pages long and was placed in the capstone of the Salt Lake Temple. The competent Spencer had a keen intellect and was the head of the University of Nauvoo and the first chancellor of the University of Deseret (Salt Lake City) in 1950. See this entire work digitally at http://ia700404.us.archive.org/21/items/lettersexhibitin-03spen/lettersexhibitin03spen.pdf. For more biographical information on Orson Spencer, see *Encyclopedia of Latter-day Saint History*, 1173–1174; Andrew Jenson, "Spencer, Orson," *LDS Biographical Encyclopedia*, 1:337–39; and http://en.wikipedia.org/wiki/Orson_Spencer.

Regarding this LDS literature referred to above, John Jones,

"A Sketch of the History of the Work of the Lord in the Australian Colonies," *Zion's Watchman* 1, nos. 32–33 (April 12, 1855), 265, notes, "There has been about 24,000 tracts published and distributed in these colonies, besides some thousands that have been distributed that were sent from England. There has also been received from England several hundred pounds worth of books, and there is not now a supply of the standard works in the office." Peter Crawley, "The First Australian Mormon Imprints," *Gradalis Review* 2 (Fall 1973) 1:43, notes, "The importance of these tracts goes far beyond the Australian mission. . . . They are the earliest publications associated with that enormous effort in the early 1850's that spread the Mormon missions beyond North America and Western Europe, harbingers of publications that within the half-decade would come from San Francisco, Cape Town, Madras, and Calcutta." Regarding the books noted above, *Zion's Watchman* 1, nos. 30–31 (March 15, 1855), 248, offered the following literature for sale in addition to the English edition of the Standard Works of the Church: "Voice of Warning, Spencer's Letters, Joseph the Prophet, Government of God, Pearl of Great Price, Divine Authenticity of the Book of Mormon, Divine Authority of Joseph Smith, Hymn Books, Millinnial Star, Books of Mormon in German & French."

63. "Foreign Intelligence—Australia," *Millennial Star* 16, no. 16 (April 22, 1854), 249. The first editor of the *Millennial Star* was Elder Parley P. Pratt. Among other things, Pratt indicated in his prospectus, issued May 27, 1840, that the purpose of the periodical was to spread the truth, gather Israel, and be as a star of light for the faithful to prepare for the second coming of Jesus Christ. For more information, see, Alan K. Parrish, "Beginnings of the *Millennial Star*: Journal of the Mission to Great Britain," in *Regional Studies in LDS Church History: British Isles*, ed. Donald Q. Cannon, (Provo, Utah: Department of Church History and Doctrine, Brigham Young University, 1990), 135–39.

64. "Foreign Intelligence—Australia," *Millennial Star* 16, no. 16 (April 22, 1854): 249. See also Andrew Jensen, "*Zion's Watchman*," *Encyclopedic History*, 976, notes a total of twenty issues published.

　　See also Andrew Jenson, "Farnham, Augustus," *Latter-day Saint Biographical Encyclopedia* (Salt Lake City: Andrew Jensen Memorial Association, 1936), 4:307; and Allen D. Roberts, "More of Utah's Unknown Pioneer Architects: Their Lives and Works," *Sunstone* 1, no. 3 (1967), 51.

65. *Zion's Watchman* 1, no. 1 (August 13, 1852), 1. Just over a year later, there is evidence that the mission presidency felt this LDS Australian periodical had been successful. "An Epistle of the Presidency of the

Australian Mission," *Zion's Watchman* vol. 1, nos. 20–21 (October 14, 1854), 153, noted that the influence of *Zion's Watchman* had "been felt, not only among the Saints, but also throughout every ramification of society . . . it has thus been read by all classes in these colonies, and has thus been instrumental of much good."

66. "Preface," *Zion's Watchman*, i.

67. Marjorie Newton, *Southern Cross Saints*, 29–30, points out that when ten new Mormon missionaries disembarked in Sydney in the early spring of 1853, the ship that transported them also carried copies of San Francisco newspapers which reported the public announcement of polygamy, reprinted and sent out by the *Sydney Morning Herald* the following day. On the same weekend that plural marriage was publicly announced (August 28–29, 1852), 106 missionaries were called to foreign countries, including these ten men who went to Australia.

68. "A Sermon on plurality of wives. . . ," *Zion's Watchman* 1, nos. 2–3, (September 24, 1853), 9; see also vol.1, nos. 4–5 (November 12, 1853), 33. Concerning the practice of polygamy, Marjorie Newton, *Southern Cross Saints*, 99, notes, "Plural marriage was never officially practiced by the leaders, missionaries or members of the Mormon Church in Australia. . . . Even if the missionaries in Australia had not taught that plural marriages could be performed only by the First Presidency in America, it would probably have been difficult for Mormon males in Australia to find enough unattached women." Further, (p.104) "the doctrine of plural marriage was taught to the Australian members from the arrival of Augustus Farnham and the second group of American missionaries in April 1853, not as something to be practised in Australia, but as a ceremony which could only be performed by the First Presidency in America." Newton (p.105) points out that "very few of the Australian converts entered plural marriage once settled in Utah. . . . Only twelve male converts in Australia are known to have taken plural wives in Utah and only fourteen females from Australia are known to have been married to men with more than one living wife."

69. "A Reply to the 'Christian Herald' on the Plurality of Wives," and "Celestial Marriage in Deseret," *Zion's Watchman* 1, nos. 4–5, (November 12, 1853), 25–35, 50–52, 66–67, 76–85.

70. "Defence of Polygamy. By a Lady of Utah, in a Letter to Her Sister in New Hampshire" reprinted from the *Millennial Star* in *Zion's Watchman* 1, nos. 22–23, (November 15, 1854), 171–80.

71. Andrew Jenson, "Australian Mission," *Encyclopedic History*, 36.

72. "Elders from Zion who have Labored in the Australasian Mission," AMMH, CHL. "Progress of Mormonism," *The Argus* (April 16, 1853), 9, lists the names of the ten missionaries as previously noted. An article

titled "Mormonism," *Sydney Morning Herald* (April 2, 1853), 5, noted that "we find that a number of missionaries from the Mormons, or, as they style themselves the 'Church of Jesus Christ of the Latter-day Saints,' have arrived in the Pacific from California. We published in yesterday's *Herald* an article from a San Francisco paper, containing several extracts from the *Deseret News*, a Mormon paper, and giving also a list of the missionaries who were to be sent forth to various parts of the world to carry on the work of 'conversion.' Eighteen of these, it would seem, are destined to labour in Australia, and among them are some names which have made a considerable figure in the history of this extraordinary sect. We have no information as to the relative rank and authority of these missionaries among themselves, except that they are generally designated as 'elders.' The general, we believe the invariable, aim of the Mormon agents is not simply to propagate their doctrines among the people to whom they are sent, but also to forward their proselytes, with all possible speed, to the head quarters of the sect at Salt Lake city, and its vicinity, in the country generally known as 'Deseret,' its Mormon appellation. They come here, therefore, not merely to get converts, but to promote an emigration to the country of the Faithful. . . . There is one point arising out of the extracts already referred to, which it would be wrong to pass over in silence. . . . The principle allegation in support of these charges was, that the Mormons held what was termed the Spiritual Wife Doctrine: that one of the faithful, even if married, might lawfully contract a marriage with a spiritual wife. . . . Downright polygamy . . . made manifest in a special revelation to the late Joseph Smith, the Prophet of the Mormon faith." AMGM, April 11, 1853, 171, also reported, "The announcement of their arrival was accompanied by an extract from the *Deseret News*paper, which admitted the practice of polygamy as a part of the doctrine of the Church. This caused a great excitement in the town."

Two weeks later, a letter titled "Mormonism. *To the Editor of The Argus*," *The Argus* (April 16, 1853), 9, presented evidence that the arrival of the incoming Mormon elders was viewed as significant and met with both acceptance as well as hostility: "Sir, The letter of your 'Own Correspondent,' from Sydney, dated April 2d, 1853, and published in your paper of April 8th, says:— 'Perhaps the most important event for some time past is the arrival, on Tuesday, of a batch of Mormon missionaries, by the Pacific.' And again, in the same letter, he says, 'Mormonism, then, in 1853 is not a thing to be despised; nor is the arrival of its missionaries in Australia an event to be considered unimportant.' If all this be true, then perhaps a few remarks on the subject may not be out of time and place. I wish to correct an idea expressed by your correspondent in regard to the persecution of Mormons in the State of Illinois.

The Mormons, believing that everything on earth belongs to God, and that they are God's chosen people, and consequently that they have the best right to those things, and, acting in accordance with this belief, help themselves to anything they wish, in the neighborhood of their sojourn, and path of their exodus. This, with their plurality of wives, impostures, and other disagreeable peculiarities, make them bad neighbors for any moral and intelligent community. Religious persecution does not exist in the United States, and the Mormons were driven from Nauvoo for their crimes, and not for their religion."

73. For more information on the *Envelope*, see Conway B. Sonne, *Ships, Saints, and Mariners: A Maritime Encyclopedia of Mormon Migration, 1830–1890* (Salt Lake City: University of Utah Press, 1987), 72.

74. AMGM, 171, notes that Wandell and the incoming missionaries were just barely able to make contact: "A brief conversation was permitted, which was the only personal interview, that Elder Wandell could get with them previous to his leaving the Colonies."

75. Journal of Burr Frost, November 19, 1853. However, Frost also notes that "after some conversation he concluded to further investigate the work which he agreed to do." For a biographical sketch of Frost, see Appendix C: Biographical Register.

76. William Hyde to Augustus Farnham, *Zion's Watchman* 1, nos. 10–11 (March 4, 1854), 73.

77. Brigham Young to Augustus Farnham, *Zion's Watchman* 1, nos. 12–13 (May 6, 1854), 89–90.

78. Brigham Young to Augustus Farnham, January 31, 1855, *Zion's Watchman* 2, no. 3 (June 18, 1855), 43.

79. Yet as noted above, Marjorie Newton, *Southern Cross Saints*, 164–65, points out that when the population of Great Britain and Australia is compared, the Australasian Mission, though with few full-time missionaries, actually had a better ratio of missionaries than the British Mission.

80. Marjorie Newton, *Southern Cross Saints*, 140–41.

81. Frost arrived in Australia at the end of March 1853 along with nine other elders, but they had to stay on their vessel, the *Pacific*, for a number of days due to an out break of smallpox which also came upon several of them. See Burr Frost Journal, March 30–April 9, 1853, CHL, for narrative regarding the quarantine and arrival in Sydney. William Hyde, a member of this group, wrote to President S. [Stephen] W. Richards, November 7, 1853, "The Australian Mission," *Millennial Star* 16, no. 9 (March 4, 1854), 141–42, explaining, "Soon after our landing

in Sydney . . . on the 9th of April, we assembled ourselves in a suitable room, where, in secret, we offered up our prayers and our thanks
to God. . . . After a suitable time was spent in council assembled, each
Elder's field of labour was assigned him, and after blessing each other
somewhat after the same order as the sons of Mosiah did, we separated,
each for his respective portion of the colony, being full of good desires,
and fully determined to use all diligence to bring the people to a knowledge of the truth."

Frost was given the charge to tend to the gold fields. On September 18, 1853, in the tent of Brother Francis Evens at the Bendigo gold
fields, Frost noted that he organized a small branch of a half dozen
members. Upon a motion by one of the miners, Frost and the group
agreed to call it the "Gold Diggers Branch," and [Wm.] Cooke was
appointed as the presiding elder of the branch. (See Burr Frost Journal,
September 18, 1853). Several days later, Elder Frost noted, "Having frequently spoken upon the principles of tithing the Brethren concluded
to send some means to the church." (See Burr Frost Journal, September
22, 1853, wherein the names of the brethren and the amount of tithing
they paid, as well as other donations to use for the Church in gold). At
the end of the following month, Frost noted that he "posted a letter to
Bendigo with instructions for the Brethren to stay at the mines if they
wished to do well for themselves and the Kingdom of God." (See Burr
Frost Journal, October 31, 1853). In early December 1853, a branch of
the Church was also organized in Newcastle made up mostly of Welsh
Saints who had immigrated to Australia in order to work in the coal
mines within that region. See John Jones, "A Sketch of the History of
the Work of the Lord in the Australian Colonies," *Zion's Watchman* 1,
nos. 32–33 (April 12, 1855), 264. William Hyde, "The Australian Mission," November 7, 1853, *Millennial Star* 16, no. 9 (March 4, 1854), 142,
reported to President Samuel W. Richards, via letter dated November
7, 1853, that this Welsh group was fourteen in number and had come
to Newcastle in order to get funds to immigrate to Utah. Upon seeing
their low spiritual condition in such a worldly enviornment, Hyde
thought it best to revive them through re-baptism. Hyde then advised
Richards, "If there are heads of families among the Saints in Wales, who
are very anxious that their sons and daughters should take the shortest
cut to hell, my advice to them is, that they come stringing along, a few
families at a time, to Australia, and then, in all probability, they can have
the consolation, in the end, of finding themselves safely landed in the
same warm climate, as a reward for pursuing so unwise a course."

82. Jane Benson, "History of John Perkins and His Wife," 1–3, Harold

B. Lee Library, L. Tom Perry Special Collections, Provo, Utah. For a biographical sketch of Perkins, see Appendix C: Biographical Register. Latter-day Saints believe that the Book of Mormon is a scriptural record kept by prophets in the ancient Americas from about 600 BC to 421 AD and serves as a second witness to the ministry and resurrection of Jesus Christ.

83. Journal of John Perkins, February 11, 1854, CHL.

84. Ibid., February 12, 1854.

85. Ibid., February 15, 1854.

86. Ibid., February 16, 1854.

87. Ibid., February 17, 1854.

88. Ibid., February 19, 1854.

89. See for example, Journal of John Perkins, March 24, 30, 1854; April 18, 1854, CHL. A teacher is a priesthood office in the LDS Church. One of the duties of a teacher is to take care of the Church members, including visiting the house of each member. See D&C 20:53–57.

90. Brigham Young to Augustus Farnham, October 31, 1853, *Zion's Watchman* 1, nos. 12–13 (May 6, 1854), 90.

91. Brigham Young to Augustus Farnham, January 31, 1855 (CHL), also published in *Zion's Watchman* 2, no. 3 (June 18, 1855), 43.

92. "Address of P. P. Pratt on the Occasion of Laying the Foundation Stones of the Temple, on April 6, 1853," *Zion's Watchman* 2, no. 2 (June 15, 1855), 24. The Doctrine and Covenants had already published a revelation given a dozen years earlier when the Nauvoo Temple commenced: "Let all my Saints come from afar. . . . Come ye, with all your gold, and your silver, and your precious stones . . . and build a house to my name, for the Most High to dwell therein" (D&C 124:25–27).

93. Augustus Farnham and Josiah W. Fleming, "Second Epistle of the Presidency of the Australasian Mission," *Zion's Watchman* 2, no. 3 (June 18 [15], 1855), 36, 39.

94. Marjorie Newton, "The Gathering of the Australian Saints in the 1850s," in *Proclamation to the People: Nineteenth-century Mormonism and the Pacific Basin Frontier*, eds. Laurie F. Maffly-Kipp and Reid L. Neilson (Salt Lake City: University of Utah Press, 2008), 188. In this same article, Newton (p.185) points out that at the time the gathering was being taught by Mormon missionaries in Australia, "the tide [of immigration] was flowing into the country." Thus, "the Australian Mormon emigration went *against* the larger population trend." Newton, in an earlier work, *Southern Cross Saints*, 140, noted that the cost incurred by this emigration was high: "For most Australian Saints, gathering

to Zion involved a *second* emigration. The great majority of them had already immigrated to the Australian colonies from the British Isles." For information on immigrating from Great Britain to Australia in the nineteenth century, see Robin Haines, *Life and Death in the Age of Sail: The passage to Australia* (Sydney: University of New South Wales Press Ltd., 2003); Andrew Hassam, *Sailing to Australia: Shipboard diaries by nineteenth-century British emigrants* (Manchester: Manchester University Press, 1994); Don Charlwood, *The Long Farewell* (Victoria: Allen Lane, a division of Penguin Books, 1981); and Michael K. Stammers, *The Passage Makers* (Brighton, Sussex: Teredo Books Ltd., 1978).

95. Augustus Farnham to Franklin D. Richards, September 18, 1854, *Millennial Star* 16, no. 30 (December 16, 1854), 798–99.

96. Augustus Farnham to Franklin D. Richards, January 26, 1855, "Foreign Correspondence. Australia," *Millennial Star* 17, no. 18 (May 5, 1855), 283–84. It is also quite possible that information concerning the productivity of the land of Zion influenced the Australian Saints and other foreign converts to gather to Utah. For example, one article titled "Profitable Farming," *Zion's Watchman* 2, no. 1 (May 15, 1855), 15, noted a rich harvest of beets, potatoes, onions, cabbage, and cucumbers for pickles coming forth.

97. See P.A.M. Taylor, *Expectations Westward: The Mormons and the Emigration of their British Converts in the Nineteenth Century* (Ithaca, NY: Cornell University Press, 1966), 151–54, for a view of why British Saints gathered to Zion in the nineteenth century. For a comparison between the British and Australian gathering, see Marjorie Newton, "The Gathering of the Australian Saints in the 1850s," in *Proclamation to the People: Nineteenth-Century Mormonism and the Pacific Basin Frontier,* eds. Laurie F. Maffly-Kipp and Reid L. Neilson (Salt Lake City: University of Utah Press, 2008), 187–95. The *"Mormon Migration"* website, compiled and edited by Fred E. Woods contains over one thousand first-person Mormon immigrant accounts for the years 1840–1890, which strongly support this thesis of the motive in gathering to America during the nineteenth century as being primarily spiritual. See http://mormonmigration.lib.byu.edu/

98. Thomas C. Stayner was born June 22, 1802, in Brentwood, Essex, England, and his wife was named Elizabeth Pill.

99. Thomas C. Stayner to Josiah Fleming (June 18, 1854) including excerpt from Stayner children to their father Thomas C. Stayner (October 28, 1853), "Original Correspondence," *Zion's Watchman* 1, nos. 16–17 (August 5, 1854), 125. Optimistic statements gleaned from the *Millennial Star* and republished in *Zion's Watchman* probably also had an influence on the desire for the Australians to gather. For example, "Editorial," *Zion's Watchman* 1 [2], no. 4 (October 27, 1855), 64, notes,

"Universal peace and prosperity prevail among the saints in Utah." Apparently Captain Thomas C. Stayner gave heed to the plea of his children and joined them in Zion; evidence reveals his burial in the Salt Lake Cemetery soon after his death on October 7, 1869. See his gravestone pictured at "Thomas Colley Stayner," findagrave.com, accessed June 18, 2013. Stayner had joined the LDS Church in England and had a connection with Charles Wandell as early as 1852. AMGM, 9, notes, "On the 5th of January 1852, Captain Stayner of the Barque Tamar visited Elder Wandell and invited him on board of his vessel. He is a brother, and being just from England, and having a small supply of tracts with him, as also some bound volumes, which he kindly gave for the benefit of the mission, he was a very great assistance to the cause. He, his wife, and daughter will not soon be forgotten by the Saints in Sydney."

100. Jane Charters Robinson Hindley, "Journals 1855–1905," vol. 1, Feb. 16, 1855, 3, CHL. See "Liverpool to Philadelphia on the *Siddons*," mormonmigration.lib.byu.edu, accessed June 4, 2013.

101. Conway B. Sonne, *Ships, Saints, and Mariners: A Maritime Encyclopedia of Mormon Migration 1830–1890* (Salt Lake City: University of Utah Press, 1987), 124. Sonne's research also reveals that there were far more sailing vessels built in Maine which carried Latter-day Saints to America than in any other eastern state, or anywhere else for that matter. See Sonne, *Saints on the High Seas*, (Salt Lake City: University of Utah Press, 1983), Appendix 3, 161–165. Pond and his business partner, Captain Staples, purchased the *Julia Ann* in San Francisco during the fall of 1852. Pond writes, "The bark ' *Julia Ann*' was in the harbor for sale, a new vessel, recently arrived from Boston on her first voyage, with passengers, never having carried a cargo, clipper built and staunch, of about 350 tons register, just the vessel we required. We purchased her for $10,000., a much less price than her cost in Boston, and it was considered a great bargain for us." See *Autobiography of B. F. Pond*. Written at the request of his Wife and Children. (Tenafly, New Jersey, June 15, 1895), United States National Archives, Washington, D.C., typescript, National Archives, Washington D.C., 135. A bark or barque is a sailing vessel that has three or more masts. See "Barque," http://en.wikipedia.org/wiki/Barque, accessed June 11, 2013.

102. For a biographical sketch of Pond, see Appendix C: Biographical Register. Apparently the lives of Captains Davis and Pond and the Australian Saints were spared thanks to a conspiracy being thwarted by a Dr. Downs, who revealed a secret plan to take over this voyage of the *Julia Ann*. According to Pond, Dr. Downs made him swear on a Bible that he would never reveal the conspiracy plan of killing the captain and taking possession of the vessel as conceived by nine men who had recently

"'stuck up' the Government escort en route from the Ballerat [gold] diggings to Melbourne." Pond noted, "My own life, and probably that of many on the *Julia Ann* were undoubtedly saved by the loyalty of the ship's doctor" (See *Autobiography of B. F. Pond*, 166–170).

103. "The Hunter [River] Region, more commonly known as the Hunter Valley, is a region of New South Wales, Australia, extending from approximately 120 km (75 mi) to 310 km (193 mi) north of Sydney. It contains the Hunter River and its tributaries with highland areas to the north and south." See "Hunter Region," http://en.wikipedia.org/wiki/Hunter_Region, accessed July 11, 2013.

104. "General Intelligence," *Zion's Watchman* 1, nos. 10–11 (March 4, 1854), 85–86.

105. According to Marjorie Newton, *Southern Cross Saints*, 136–37, between the years 1853–1859, 449 Saints gathered to Zion on eight different voyages and disembarked at either San Pedro or San Francisco (on at Honolulu). The first voyage was led by Charles Wandell, accompanied by twenty-nine other Saints. The name of the vessel was the *Envelope*, which left Sydney on April 6, 1853, and arrived in San Francisco on July 8. For a list of the known Mormon passengers on this voyage, see Marjorie Newton, *Southern Cross Saints*, 223. In a letter from Charles Wandell to S. W. Richards, March 29, 1852, AMGM, 170, Wandell notes that there were nineteen adults and ten children to sail on this voyage. The Minutes further note, 172, "On April 6th, the 22nd anniversary of the organization of the Church, Elder Wandell sailed for San Francisco, in the Barque 'Envelope,' accompanied by 29 saints and children," which should probably be taken to mean 29 Saints, including children.

106. For a biographical sketch of Hyde, see Appendix C: Biographical Register.

107. Pond probably refers to this same event of meeting Hyde wherein he notes, "I also made the acquaintance of a mormon elder, who was in Australia as missionary, proselyting for his church, who engaged my entire second cabin accommodations and several cabin staterooms for his recruits, immigrants to Utah, Salt Lake City, of the LatterDay Saints." (See *Autobiography of B. F. Pond*, 166).

108. Brigham Young to Augustus Farnham, August 19, 1854, *Zion's Watchman* 1, nos. 28–29 (February 15, 1855), 217. President Young gave counsel on how immigration assistance for the poor in Australia should be carried out: "I have understood that some of the brethren in Australia, donated means to help the poor to emigrate with Elder Hyde, with the expectation that such donations would be credited to them on the books of the Perpetual Emigration Fund [PEF]. The motives that

prompted this course I presume were good; and were the Fund much larger than it now is, and the poor saints in the British Isles far less numerous than they now are, and still further, were not the facilities for outfitting far greater in Australia, than in any other place where there are poor saints to be gathered,—still all who have assisted or may assist the saints to gather from Australia, with a view to being credited on the books of the Fund, will be so credited whenever the amount advanced by any individuals actually paid into the Fund."

The following year, the "Second Epistle of the Presidency of the Australasian Mission," *Zion's Watchman* 2, no. 3 (June 18, 1855), 37, advised those who wished to immigrate to Utah: "Let them not therefore forget the poor, but let them do all they can . . . if you do this, the posterity of the poor in generations yet to come, will rise up to bless you. . . . We now counsel all saints who have the means to commence to arrange their business, and order their circumstances, so that they may be prepared to gather to Zion in or about April, 1856."

The genesis for the PEF in Australia was initiated by Charles Wesley Wandell in a spring 1852 conference held in Sydney. See AMGM, 45. In that meeting Wandell said, "Brethren if this mission prospers, we shall, by next February, want to send a company of Saints to Zion. . . . I think it will be wisdom in us to establish a 'Perpetual Emigration Poor Fund.'" Some of the clauses of the said Fund included the following: "Clause 1st. That a fund be established by means of voluntary contributions, from the members, to be paid weekly: 2nd. That the said fund be called, the Perpetual Emigration Fund, of the Sydney Branch of the Church of Jesus Christ of Latter day Saints. 3d. That the object of said fund shall be, to assist the poor brethren and sisters to emigrate to Zion, and that it be applied to no other purpose: - 4th. That any brother or sister receiving assistance from said fund, shall enter into an agreement that as God shall prosper him or her, he or she will refund into the hands of the Officers of said fund, or the proper authorities of the Church, the amount advanced in their favor." See AMGM, 52.

109. Journal of William Hyde, February 13–15, 19; March 9–10, 1854.

110. Journal of William Hyde, March 22, 1854. Newcastle is about seventy miles northeast of Sydney.

111. Journal of William Hyde, March 26–27, 1854.

112. "General Intelligence," *Zion's Watchman* 1, nos. 10–11 (March 4, 1854), 86. For a list of the sixty-three Mormon passengers, see Marjorie Newton, *Southern Cross Saints*, 223–24. Diane Rich Parkinson, "The Maiden Voyage of the *JULIA ANN*," 1, unpublished paper in author's possession, notes that over half of the sixty-three passengers onboard

this passage were from the Bryant, Stapley, and Parkinson families. For a list of first-person Mormon immigrant accounts kept aboard this voyage, see http://mormonmigration.lib.byu.edu/Search/searchAll/keywords:Julia+Ann+1854.

113. "General Intelligence," *Zion's Watchman* 1, nos. 10–11 (March 4, 1854), 86. One reason why these Saints and other foreign converts wanted to leave Babylon (symbolic of the world) was because they felt the world would soon come to an end, but that gathered Saints would be generally preserved in Zion. Five months after the *Julia Ann* had embarked, an article titled, "Foreign Intelligence. *Australia.*," *Millennial Star* 16, no. 28 (July 15, 1854), 441 [450], reported, "We have received the *Zion's Watchman* of March 4, from which we learn that Elder William Hyde, with a company of 63 Saints from Hunter River District, was expecting soon to sail in the barque *Julia Ann.*" This is an indication of how slow the mail was at this time between Australia and Great Britain; the *Julia Ann* had already crossed the Pacific and had landed over a full month previous to the British Saints hearing about the embarking of this voyage.

114. Maitland is a city in the lower Hunter River District of New South Wales.

115. Journal of John Perkins, March 18, 1854, CHL. Missionary work in Maitland, New South Wales was opened by local missionaries John Jones and John McCarthy in the spring of 1852. According to a family tradition compiled by Stella B. Neilson, McCarthy rebelled against his Catholic teachings and was punished: "He was placed in a dungeon with skeletons; a horsehair coat, which had been dipped in lime was placed upon him, and the punishment was so severe from this treatment, that he carried flesh wounds from it for the rest of his life." He later managed to escape and after extensive travel in various places in the world, he settled down in Sydney, where he came into contact with Elder Charles Wandell, who baptized him a member of the Church on May 2, 1852. Shortly thereafter, at 22 years of age, "he was set apart as a traveling missionary, and in company with Elder John Jones, went to Maitland, New South Wales, a fine town on Hunter River, about 80 miles Northeast of Sydney." See "History of John McCarthy," comp. Stella B. Nielson, CHL, 1–2. For a biographical sketch on McCarthy see Appendix C: Biographical Register.

116. First called the Australian Mission (1851), but the name was changed to Australasian in 1854 when mission president Augustus Farnham opened New Zealand to missionary work. See Andrew Jenson, "Australian Mission," *Encyclopedic History of the Church of Jesus Christ of Latter-day Saints* (Salt Lake City: *Deseret News*, 1941), 35.

117. AMMH, March 22, 1854, CHL.

118. Journal of William Hyde, April 6, 1854, BYU Special Collections.

119. The Mormon Battalion was a volunteer unit made up of about 500 Latter-day Saints who were involved with the United States war with Mexico in 1846. See John F. Yurtinus, "Mormon Battalion," ed. Daniel H. Ludlow, *Encyclopedia of Mormonism* (New York: Macmillan Publishing Company, 1992), 2:933.

120. According to Diane Parkinson, "The Maiden Voyage of the *Julia Ann*," unpublished document in author's possession, 14, "Sister Allen" was Esther Allen, wife of Richard Allen, born in 1811 and died at the age of 43.

121. Concerning the death of Sister Esther Allen and the replenishing of supplies at the island of Huahine, oranges for exporting at Tahiti, and provisions in Honolulu, Pond wrote, "We put into the island of Huanea to bury a woman who had died, not from any malignant disease however, thence to Tahiti, where we took on board 90,000 oranges on ship's account. . . . We [also] put into Honolulu for supplies and fresh provisions. Thence sailed for San Baradino [Bernardino], Southern California to land our mormon passengers, thence to San Francisco. . . . Of the 90,000 oranges taken on board at Tahiti only 10,000 were delivered at San Francisco." (See *Autobiography of B. F. Pond*, 171–72).

122. The first mate on both voyages that carried Australian Latter-day Saints was Peter Martin Coffin. See Paul Hundley, "Captain Coffin and the *Julia Ann*," *Signals: The Quarterly Magazine of the Australian National Maritime Museum* no. 35 (June–August, 1996):9. For a biographical sketch of Coffin, see Appendix C: Biographical Register.

123. Conway B. Sonne, *Ships, Saints, and Mariners: A Maritime Encyclopedia of Mormon Migration 1830–1890* (Salt Lake City: University of Utah Press, 1987), 124; AMMH, March 22, 1854, CHL. In an article from the *Los Angeles Star*, "Arrival of Mormonites from Australia," reprinted in *Zion's Watchman* 1, nos. 20–21 (October 14, 1854), 167–68, the editor notes, "fifty Mormon converts arrived by the *Julia Ann*, disembarked at San Pedro, to join the Saints at San Bernardion. They number twenty-seven men and women, and twenty-three children—first fruits of Mormon missionary teaching in Australia. There must be very strong faith in these people; but their conduct accords with that [what] was related to us by others at San Bernardino. We are told, among the fifty are four women who left their husbands and children, and husbands who left wives and families, believing their salvation depends upon their joining the body of the Church. In that company there was one man who left his wife and all the property he had with her, and she is preparing to follow him in the next company, and as to the women one of them was a widow, whose husband was drowned at Adelaide, the other was an unfortunate being, who had been tied in wedlock to a drunken

brutal husband who abused her so much that her constitution was so much destroyed, she never had a family to leave. Why are the world and especially Editors and persons so ready to speak evil of the Saints." This same article was also reprinted in the *Sydney Morning Herald*, "Arrival of Mormonites from Australia," (September 27, 1854), 4.

124. Journal of Alonzo Colton, August 15, 1856, 18, CHL.

125. William Hyde to President Augustus Farnham, July 1, 1854, "Original Correspondence," *Zion's Watchman* 1, nos. 22–23 (November 15, 1854), 184. Herein Hyde notes, "On Monday, the 12th of June, we dropped anchor in the harbour of San Pedro. On my arrival, I found that the old firm of Douglass & Co. had changed hands, and is at present under the name of Alexander and Banning, who in every respect are gentlemen, and are now agents for our people." The catalytic gentlemen referred to are David W. Alexander and Phineas Banning. They formed a partnership with a short duration as Alexander sold his interest in 1855. Yet his brother George went on to form a successful freight and stage business with Phineas and Wm. T. B. Sanford. Among other things, David was involved with real estate and also served twice as sheriff of Los Angeles. See "David W. Alexander," http://en.wikipedia.org/wiki/David_W._Alexander, accessed June 4, 2013; see also H. D. Barrows, "Don David W. Alexander," *Annual Publication of the Historical Society of Southern California and Pioneer Register* (Los Angeles: California Voice Print), 43–45.

The adventurous, ambitious Phineas Banning arrived in California at the age of twenty-one. He became a very successful entrepreneur, also becoming known as the "Father of the Port of Los Angeles." See "Phineas Bannaing," http://en.wikipedia.org/wiki/Phineas_Banning, accessed June 4, 2012. Banning's freight business yielded millions of dollars in commerce each year as it ran from Los Angeles to Salt Lake City during the mid-nineteenth century. For more details on contact between the Banning freighting company and the Mormons, see Fred E. Woods, *A Gamble in the Desert: The Mormon Mission in Las Vegas (1855–1857)* (Salt Lake City: Mormon Historic Sites Foundation, 2005), 111–113. On the life of Phineas Banning in general, see Maymie Krythe, *Port Admiral: Phineas Banning 1830–1885* (San Francisco: California Historical Society, 1957), which specifically references his relationship with the Mormons (pp. 58, 72, 75, 78 and 151).

126. William Hyde to President Augustus Farnham, June 12, 1854, "Original Correspondence," *Zion's Watchman* 1, nos. 20–21 (October 14, 1854), 157–58.

127. AMMH, June 13, 1854, CHL. Nine months later, *Zion's Watchman* 1, nos. 24–25 (December 15, 1854), 185–91, also issued the First Presidency's

Eleventh General Epistle (written April 10, 1854), which noted, "The Saints in Australia, India, and all countries bordering upon the Pacific, are instructed to gather to California, where they will be directed in their future movements by the Presidency of the Church in that country."

128. "During the 1850s, San Bernardino was the most populous LDS settlement outside of Utah and also the largest Euro-American community in Southern California. Brigham Young sent more than four hundred colonists there in 1851 to extend the Mormon corridor all the way from southern Utah to the Pacific Ocean. That July the settlers established the San Bernardino Stake, the first in California." See Reid L. Neilson and Laurie F. Maffly-Kipp, "Nineteenth-Century Mormonism and the Pacific Basin Frontier," in *Proclamation to the People: Nineteenth-Century Mormonism and the Pacific Basin Frontier* eds., Laurie F. Maffly-Kipp and Reid L. Neilson (Salt Lake City: University of Utah Press, 2008), 6. However, St. Louis would have been San Bernardino's rival for the most Latter-day Saints outside of Utah in the 1850s. For more information on this topic, see Fred E. Woods and Thomas Farmer, *When the Saints Came Marching In: A History of the Latter-day Saints in St. Louis* (Salt Lake City: Millennial Press, 2009).

129. Milton R. Hunter, "The Mormon Corridor," *Pacific Historical Review* 1, no. 1 (1932), 181, explains the establishment of the Mormon Corridor as "the founding of a contiguous line of Mormon settlements from a good seaport to Salt Lake City and also the connecting of those towns by a highway over which immigrants could be conveyed with ease and safety."

130. Brigham Young, Latter-day Saint Journal History, LDS Church Archives, hereafter cited as JH, March 9, 1849. The following year, he made clear his desire to establish colonies from Salt Lake City to the Pacific Ocean to assist these immigrants. See Brigham Young, JH, October 27, 1850. However, the Saints continued to use New Orleans for several years, but the route would change by early 1855. In response to the threatening epidemic of yellow fever and cholera, which had already struck a fatal blow to thousands traveling up the Mississippi River, Brigham Young on August 2, 1854, sent a letter from Salt Lake City to Elder Franklin D. Richards, who was in charge of immigration from Liverpool to the United States. Young (who as President of the Church oversaw all aspects of Mormon migration by land and sea) counseled, "You are aware of the sickness liable to assail our unacclimated brethren on the Mississippi river, hence I wish you to ship no more to New Orleans, but ship to Philadelphia, Boston, and New York, giving preference in the order named." See *Millennial Star* 16, no. 43 (October 28, 1854), 684.

131. Brigham Young, "Fifth General Epistle," *Millennial Star* 13, no. 14 (July 15, 1851), 214.

132. Brigham Young, "Fifth General Epistle," *Millennial Star* 13, no. 14 (July 15, 1851), 213.

133. Leonard J. Arrington, *Great Basin Kingdom: An Economic History of the Latter-day Saints 1830–1890* (Lincoln: University of Nebraska Press, 1958), 88. San Bernardino, though no longer a predominantly LDS community, now has over 200,000 residents of varied faiths. See "San Bernardino, California," http://en.wikipedia.org/wiki/San_bernardino, accessed June 4, 2013. Since 2003, the Redlands California Temple of the Church of Jesus Christ of Latter-day Saints now sits on the original land purchased by the Mormons in 1851, which is frequented by thousands of Latter-day Saints in the San Bernardino region. See "Redlands California Temple," http://www.ldschurchtemples.com/redlands, accessed June 4, 2013.

134. Brigham Young, Heber C. Kimball, Jedediah M. Grant, "Eleventh General Epistle of the Presidency of The Church of Jesus Christ of Latter-day Saint," first published in the *Deseret News*, April 13, 1854 and later in the *Zion's Watchman* 1, nos. 24–25 (December 15, 1854), 186.

135. Edward Leo Lyman, *San Bernardino: The Rise and Fall of a California Community* (Salt Lake City: Signature Books, 1996), 296, lists three Hawaiian women who gathered to San Bernardino in the mid-nineteenth century with their *haole* husbands. He also notes that Sandwich Islands missionary Nathan Tanner had even purchased a ship in 1854 to carry Polynesian converts to California. However, financial challenges made the plan impossible; there is evidence that the Polynesian experience in California was difficult because of cultural and climatic conditions. Another problem was the lack of cooperation by the Hawaiian government, which would not allow emigration.

136. See Newton, *Southern Cross Saints*, 223–26, for a list of Australian Mormon ships and passengers who voyaged to California in the 1850s. It should also be noted that some Saints chose to stay permanently in San Bernardino rather than migrate farther north to Utah.

137. "Letter from Elders A. Lyman and C. C. Rich," *Millennial Star* 14, no. 5 (March 1, 1852), 75–76.

138. "Sixth General Epistle," *Millennial Star* 14, no. 2 (January 15, 1852), 24. Only three voyages were known to have brought Latter-day Saints into the port of San Pedro, California, during this period. All three voyages carried Australian converts, which, including returning missionaries, totaled only 162 Saints. (See Newton, *Southern Cross Saints*, 223–26, for a list of Australian Mormon ships and passengers who voyaged to California in the 1850s.) One group of sixty-three Australian converts came on the first voyage of the *Julia Ann* in 1854, the year before the Las Vegas Mission was established; one Australian company of seventy-one Saints came on the *Lucas* just after the Mission closed.

(See "Sydney to San Pedro on the *Lucas*," http://mormonmigration.lib. byu.edu, accessed June 4, 2013.) The only voyage that occurred during the time of Mormon occupation in Las Vegas arrived in San Pedro on August 15, 1856, with about 120 Saints on board the *Jenny Ford*. (See "Sydney to San Pedro on the *Jenny Ford*," http://mormonmigration. lib.byu.edu, accessed June 4, 2013). There is evidence that at least some members of this company did not leave the nearby Mormon colony of San Bernardino until the following spring when the Las Vegas Mission had just closed. (See *Church Almanac 1997–1998* (Salt Lake City: *Deseret News*, 1998), 161–62, for a list of these three LDS Australian voyages.) Adelaide Whiteley Ridges, Autobiographical Sketch, LDS Church Archives, 3–4, notes that her Australian Mormon family immigrated to America aboard the *Jenny Ford* in 1856, but did not leave for Utah until the spring of 1857. She and her husband Joseph H. Ridges worked in Los Angeles for several months to raise funds for their family to complete their journey to the Salt Lake Valley. Joseph was a gifted craftsman who built a pipe organ which Augustus Farnham suggested he take to Utah. Ridges, obedient to this counsel, dismantled the organ and had it transported across the Pacific in the hold of the *Jenny Ford* and then by mule teams to Salt Lake City, arriving on June 12, 1857. See Newton, *Southern Cross Saints*, 150.

139. Arrington, *Great Basin Kingdom*, 86.

140. Edward Leo Lyman, *San Bernardino: The Rise and Fall of a California Community* (Salt Lake City: Signature Books, 1996), 35.

141. "The Mormons in San Bernardino," cited from the *Daily Alta California*, in *Zions's Watchman* 1, nos. 18–19 (September 16, 1854), 150–151.

142. Newton, *Southern Cross Saints*, 153. For a biographical sketch of Warby and his wife Mary, see Appendix C: Biographical Register.

143. "Extract of a Letter from James Warby, Formerly of the Williams River Branch," August 28, 1854, *Zion's Watchman* 2, no. 2 (June 15, 1855), 31–32.

144. *Zion's Watchman* 1, nos. 20–21, (October 14, 1854), 158.

145. *Zion's Watchman* 1, nos. 20–21, (October 14, 1854), 158–59. However, there is evidence that this was not the first time Pond had been an eyewitness of the Saints. His autobiography (p. 31) reveals that when Pond left his New York home to go west, he later encountered the Mormons in Illinois: "As I neared Nauvoo, I learned by experience that before inquiring the road to the hated city of the 'Latter-day Saints', I must begin by roundly abusing the Mormons, for there was such an intense feeling among the people of Hancock County against them, and which culminated before many months subsequently in driving them from the State to make a new settlement, and found a prosperous city, 'Salt Lake

City' in the far, far West—that at night, on my first day's walk from Carthage, I found myself ten miles further from Nauvoo than when I started in the morning, having been purposely directed the wrong road on the supposition that I was a Mormon pilgrim. . . . I spent about a week in Nauvoo, but failed to meet Joe Smith, the Mormon prophet and founder of the sect, as he was then in hiding [1842], to escape the serving of a writ for murder which had been sworn out against him."

146. Journal of William Hyde, March 26, 1854, 78.

147. Journal of William Hyde, April 23, 1854, 79.

148. 148 For more information on the *Tarquinia*, see Conway B. Sonne *Ships, Saints, and Mariners: A Maritime Encyclopedia of Mormon Migration 1830–1890* (Salt Lake City: University of Utah Press, 1987), 185–6.

149. X.Y. Z., "To the Editor," *The Argus* (April 20, 1855), 6. This letter may have been actually written by a local Latter-day Saint who used this pseudonym, or simply an admirer who, like a modern-day Nicodemus, did not want to be connected too closely with the Mormons.

150. "The Flight of the Mormons," *The* [Melbourne] *Argus* (April 27, 1855), 6. Less than three months later, in another article titled "South Australia, *The* [Melbourne] *Argus* (July 18, 1855), 6, another antagonistic article, noted, "A Mormon preacher, who was holding forth at Hindmarsh, in the open air . . . was saluted by a shower of stones and other missiles by some indignant listeners, and the magistrate dealt so leniently with one man, who was proved to have thrown stones, as to fine him only a schilling, without costs, saying that wherever there was street preaching there must be disturbances. Several persons, chiefly women, have left this colony for the Salt Lake, but the number of saints in the province is small,—not above forty."

151. Burr Frost to President Augustus Farnham, April 26, 1855, "Original Correspondence," *Zion's Watchman* 2, no. 1 (May 15, 1855), 10. It was further reported in "Editorial and General Intelligence," *Zion's Watchman* 2, no. 1 (May 15, 1855), 13, that "a perfect union existed" among this gathered group of seventy-two Saints. The editorial also noted, "There are many Saints remaining in Victoria, who are making every effort to gather out as soon as circumstances will permit. The prospects are good for a much wider spread of the Gospel through that colony."

152. August Farnham to President Franklin D. Richards, May 31, 1855, "Foreign Correspondence. New South Wales," *Millennial Star* 17, no. 37 (September 15, 1855), 590–92. On the passenger list, Edward Meyer is noted as the master of the *Tarquinia*. The name of Burr Frost is the first passenger listed with the notation that he is 39 years old and a merchant. A total of seventy-nine names are written, not seventy-two, as previously noted above: forty-eight adult males, eleven adult females,

eight male children, and twelve female children, all between the ages of 1 and 14. See "Passengers' List" for the *Tarquinia*, April 27, 1855, Outward Passenger Lists (January–May 1855), VPRS 3506, reel 10, Victoria Archives Center, Melbourne.

Note that the Saints then took passage on to Honolulu on the ship *Williamatic* and eventually came to San Bernardino, via San Pedro. One secondary account recounts the travel of the Jose family, who were passengers on the *Tarquinia*: "Elder Frost, following instructions from Brigham Young to form a company to go to Salt Lake City, gathered Saints at Melbourne where he found that many had 'made a shipwreck of the faith' on the [gold] diggings." (See Corlyn Holbrook Adams, *The Jose Family Utah By Way Of Australia* (Wolfe City, TX: Hennington Publishing, 1995), 2, Family History Library, Salt Lake City.)

153. AMMH, April 27, 1855, CHL. Most of the Saints who embarked on the *Tarquinia* eventually made their way to California on various passages, and it is known that some of this group voyaged to San Francisco aboard the *Williamantic* and then traveled down to San Bernardino, where other Australian Saints had gathered.

154. According to Pond, a *buster* is "the name given to an exceedingly dangerous wind, peculiar to the east coast of Australia. It comes without warning, no premonition of its approach before it is upon you." (See *Autobiography of B. F. Pond*, 180).

155. In addition to coal, Pond also transported a variety of goods aboard the second voyage of the *Julia Ann*, including 50 picks, 50 axes, 100 brooms, and 6 barber chairs. See B. F. Pond Papers, box 1036 (Frank Pond), series no. 5, "papers relating to the *Julia Ann*, c.1855–August 22, 1856," ANMM, which also contain valuable materials pertaining to Pond's experience with the *Julia Ann*. (The B. F. Pond Papers, box 1035, belonging to Meg Rasmussen, also contain valuable material on Pond's experience with the *Julia Ann* correspondence). The lucrative trade of goods crossing the Pacific from Australia to San Francisco commenced with the California gold rush. According to Malcolm J. Rohrbough, "We Will Make Our Fortunes—No Doubt of It: The World Wide Rush to California," in *Riches for all: The California Gold Rush and the World*, ed. Kenneth H. Owens, (Lincoln: University of Nebraska Press, 2002), 59, the news of California gold reached Sydney by the close of 1848 and Australia would first offer their goods, rather than hopeful miners. "In part this difference reflected distance; in part it reflected the deliberate policy of Australia's editors and colonial leaders to minimize emigration. . . . But ship owners . . . saw in the news from California a glowing opportunity." Rohrbough adds that despite the distance, by the spring of 1849 the Australian merchants were some of the first to make their start into "a trans-Pacific gold rush trade." On the heels of the rush

came Captain B. F. Pond and his partners, who focused on bringing the mineral of Australian coal to San Francisco rather than trying to take California gold out of the ground. In the end, it would be the merchants who offered goods rather than the miners who would prove most profitable and at this time coal was a precious commodity as it provided the central source of primary energy for both transportation and industry in manufacturing regions from the eighteenth to mid-twentieth centuries. See "History of Coal Mining," http://en.wikipedia.org/, accessed June 8, 2013. According to Kieran Hosty, curator for the Australian National Maritime Museum, "The coal trade out of Sydney. . . . Started in the early 1800s. [By] 1803 Australia was exporting coal to places like India, quite surprisingly, and also back to England and to the United States. The coal supplies here were quite abundant and they were easily obtained from a place called Newcastle, only seventy or so miles north of Sydney." (See interview of Kieran Hosty noted above, Appendix E).

156. *Autobiography of Captain B. F. Pond*, 182, 188; John Devitry-Smith, "The Wreck of the *Julia Ann*," in *Coming to Zion*, eds. James B. Allen and John W. Welch, (Provo, Utah: *BYU Studies*, 1997), 226–27, after summarizing the damage to the *Julia Ann*, notes, "It is obvious from later statements by Church leaders that even after the wreck they were unaware that the *Julia Ann* was not in perfect condition." By the end of the year, President Young, in the "Fourteenth General Epistle of the First Presidency," December 10, 1856, in James R. Clark, *Messages of the First Presidency* (Salt Lake City: Bookcraft Inc., 1965), 2:195, first notes that church leadership had been under the impression that the *Julia Ann* "was good and new" and then warned the Saints in Australia and elsewhere "not to permit an over anxiety to emigrate and gather with the Saints to make them careless or indifferent to the kind and condition of the vessel in which they embark, nor to the character of the officers and crew on board. This is the second instance of vessels, sailing from that mission with Saints on board, not reaching their destination."

157. Augustus Farnham and Josiah Flemming, "Second Epistle of the Presidency of the Australasian Mission," *Zion's Watchman* 2, no. 3 (June 18 [15], 1855), 36, 39.

158. Brigham Young to Augustus Farnham, January 31, 1855, *Zion's Watchman* 2, no. 3 (June 18 [15], 1855), 43.

159. For a biographical sketch of Graham, see Appendix C: Biographical Register.

160. For a biographical sketch of Eldredge, see Appendix C: Biographical Register.

161. For a biographical sketch of McCarthy, see Appendix C: Biographical Register.

162. Zion's *Watchman* 2, no. 3 (June 18 [15], 1855), 45. There is evidence that the *Julia Ann* had been back in Sydney for at least five weeks. The Diary of John Perkins, August 1, 1855, CHL, notes, "the *Julia Ann* is come back to Sydney again. She has a cargo of flour this time. There is another company of Saints Expected to go in her this time." The Saints who voyaged on the *Julia Ann* were from the New South Wales region. A letter from Augustus Farnham to President Franklin D. Richards, May 31, 1855, *Millennial Star* 17, no. 37 (September 15, 1855), 591, just three months before this voyage would embark, observed, "In New South Wales, the work is more prosperous than in the other colonies. The Saints are more numerous, and the calls for help more frequent and urgent."

163. Diary of John Perkins, September 3–7, 1855.

164. See Appendix B for a list of the each of the passengers and crew. See also the list of Mormon passengers aboard the *Julia Ann*, in Newton, *Southern Cross Saints*, 224. For known *Julia Ann* first-person voyage accounts, see http://mormonmigration.lib.byu.edu. See also Appendix C: Biographical Register for bio-sketches on all passengers and crew.

165. Andrew Jenson, "The *Julia Ann* Wreck," *Deseret Weekly News* (May 14, 1898), 697. For a biographic sketch of Penfold, see Appendix C: Biographic Registry.

166. Andrew Anderson to Augustus Farnham, February 22, 1856, recorded in the Diary of Augustus Farnham, copies in the CHL, notes, "a little after you left we gathered between the poop and sterage house to sing, we sang or attempted to sing 'The Gallant Ship Is under Weigh,' which seemed to me ridicuously done, more like a funeral hymn than on the occasion it was." This letter was also published in *Zion's Watchman* 2, no. 5 (May 24, 1856), 76. "The gallant ship is under weigh" was written on the tenth anniversary of the Church, April 6, 1840, by W.W. Phelps (*HC* 4:103).

167. Captain Benjamin F. Pond, *Narrative of the Wreck of the Barque "Julia Ann"* (New York: Francis & Loutrel, 1858), 14. Andrew Jenson, "The *Julia Ann* Wreck," *Deseret Weekly News* (May 14, 1898), 698, add that this rough weather "caused considerable sea sickness."

168. John McCarthy to George Q. Cannon, first published April 25, 1856, in the *Western Standard*, an LDS periodical in San Francisco, with Cannon as editor. Republished in *Deseret News* 6, no. 17 (July 2, 1856), 130. Jenson, "The *Julia Ann* Wreck," 698, notes, "The Scilly Islands consist of a number of very low islets or motus, lying on a coral reef which measures about fifteen miles in circumference. The eastermost motu is in latitude 16 deg. 28 min. south: longitude 154 deg. 30 min. west. It is also about 185 miles west of Riaiatea and 300 miles west northwest of Tahiti. Besides the circular reef composing the island a hidden reef extends westward for many miles. It was on this reef that the *Julia*

Ann was wrecked. The whole island system constitutes a very danger-ous locality for navigators." The Scilly Islands are an atoll also known as Manuae which was discovered by Samuel Wallis, a British navigator in 1767. "A small village was established there at the time, the remains of which can still be found on the northern part of the main island. . . . There is no evidence that the islands were ever permanently inhabited prior to the shipwreck. . . . Beginning in 1952, the islands were regu-larly visited by copra merchants. During the 1960s, these casual visi-tors began capturing large numbers of sea turtles until their activities were legally restricted in 1971." See "Manuae (Society Islands)," http://en.wikipedia.org/, accessed May 11, 2013.

In 2005, John and Jean Silverwood, along with their four children, hit the very same reef the *Julia Ann* did aboard their 55-foot catamaran after sailing for two years from their home in San Diego. John lost one of his legs, but all of the family members miraculously survived. Their riveting story at sea and their rescue is told by John and Jean Silverwood in *Black Wave: A Family's Adventure at Sea and the Disaster that Saved Them* (New York: Random House, 2008). On page 151–180, a compari-son is specifically made between the Silverwood accident and the wreck of the *Julia Ann*. On p.180 of their text it is noted, "For the survivors of the *Julia Ann*, the dawn light revealed a distant line of palm trees on the horizon—the sun would rise right through the trees, as it had for us. In that 150 years the view had not changed. For them as for us, it meant hope after a desperate night."

169. Charles Logie, *Deseret Weekly News* (April 23, 1898), 591.

170. Journal of James Graham, "Graham Family Notebook," 3, (CHL). The difference in the dates given as October 3 and October 4 can be explained by the International Date Line.

171. Andrew Anderson to Augustus Farnham, recorded in the Diary of Augustus Farnham, copies in CHL, also published in *Zion's Watchman* 2, no. 5 (May 24, 1856), 76.

172. For a biographic sketch of Spangenberg, see Appendix C: Biographical Register.

173. Esther Spangenberg, "Particulars of the Wreck of the Bark *Julia Ann*," *San Francisco Daily Herald* (March 11, 1856), 2. This is Captain Pond's first officer, Peter M. Coffin. For a biographic sketch of Coffin, see Appendix C: Biographical Register.

174. Esther Spangenberg, "Particulars of the Wreck of the Bark *Julia Ann*," *San Francisco Daily Herald* (March 11, 1856), 2. This article was also republished in the *Western Standard* (March 15, 1856), 2 and in Pond's *Narrative* as noted below.

175. Captain Benjamin F. Pond, *Narrative of the Wreck of the Barque "Julia Ann,"* (New York: Francis & Lourtrel Stationers and Steam Job Printers, 1858), 15.

176. For a biographic sketch on Rosa Logie, see Appendix C: Biographical Register.

177. For a biographic sketch on Charles Logie, see Appendix C: Biographical Register.

178. John McCarthy to George Q. Cannon, April 25, 1856, *Western Standard*. Republished in *Deseret News [Weekly]* 6, no. 17 (July 2, 1856), 130. Laura Clara Logie Timpson, "A Brief History of the Lives of Charles Joseph Gordon Logie & Rosa Clara Friedlander Logie," 1965, typescript in possession of the Shauna Johnson, 2, notes that when Rosa reached San Francisco and related her account to Elder George Q. Cannon, he gave her a pewter teapot as a token of her bravery.

179. Esther Spangenberg, "Particulars of the Wreck of the Bark *Julia Ann*," *The Daily Herald* (March 11, 1856). Details from Spangenberg's account were republished in the *Western Standard* (March 15, 1856), 2.

180. "The Wreck of the Bark *Julia Ann*," January 28, 1856 letter to the *San Francisco Herald* editors by one of the passengers on the *Julia Ann*, *San Francisco Daily Herald* (April 16, 1856), 1.

181. Captain B. F. Pond, "Incidents of the Wreck (Extracts from a letter written by Capt. Pond)" to his nephew, in *Narrative of the Wreck of the Barque "Julia Ann*," 28.

182. Peter Penfold to Charles Penfold, *Zion's Watchman* 2, no. 5 (May 24, 1856), 77–78. Just before she drowned, Martha Humphreys asked her fellow Saints to "protect her children and convey them safely to Great Salt Lake City, for her earthly career was run." See *History of John McCarthy*, 11. For biographical sketches of Martha Humphreys, Mary Humphreys, Eliza Harris, and Marian Harris, see Appendix C: Biographical Register.

183. Autobiography of Capt. B. F. Pond, 206.

184. John McCarthy to George Q. Cannon, April 25, 1856, *Western Standard*. Republished in *Deseret News [Weekly]* 6, no. 17 (July 2, 1856), 130.

185. *Autobiography of B. F. Pond*, 213.

186. *Western Standard* (March 15, 1856), 2. Esther Spangenberg, "Particulars of the Wreck," in B. F. Pond, *Narrative of the Wreck*, 9, echoed these same sentiments of both Captain Pond as well as his crew: "Next to God, our thanks are due to Captain Pond, his officers and crew, for their noble exertions in our behalf. They fearlessly risked their lives in endeavoring to do all in their power to save the passengers. For one moment neither the

Captain or his officers ever lost their presence of mind. Had they done so, the loss of life would have been great." Concerning the loss of the captain's money, of this occurrence Pond himself, in "Incidents of the Wreck," in *Narrative of the Wreck,* 26–27, wrote: "When the ship first struck, Mr. Owens, (my second officer) came to me and enquired whether I had not considerable gold on board? I told him I had. He then offered, with my consent, to make an effort to save a portion of it. He went into my state room and opened the iron safe, in which I had three gold watches, some rings, and other jewelry, and $15,000 in English sovereigns. I took out two bags of gold, containing about $8,000 or $9,000, and gave them to him. I was in great haste, for the sea was breaking over the ship and my presence was very necessary on deck. I thought it very doubtful whether we should save our lives, and therefore considered the gold of but little importance; but as I was closing the safe I happened to see a roll of Sterling Exchange for $10,000 lying before me, utterly forgotten. I picked it up, and stuffed it into my pocket; also my favorite watch cased in gold of my own digging in the mountains of California. It was well that I put them in my *pantaloons* pocket, for when I left the ship I considered my chance so very dubious that I threw off all my clothes, excepting my pants, thinking nothing of gold or valuables; and thus this large amount of money was eventually saved."

Another interesting note is that at this time Owens was probably making a hundred dollars or less a month—Peter Coffin as first mate was making a hundred dollars a month, and Owens as second mate was likely making less—yet he still forsook the money on behalf of saving a child. See also "Ships articles and crew lists, 1854–1856, 1861–1862, 1883, 1886, 1892" U.S. Custom List, San Francisco, microfilm # 0,976,995.

Evidence also reveals that the "Australian General Assurance [Insurance] Company" paid Captain Pond about £2500 for the ruined craft and lost coal, so some small part of his losses were recouped. See "Papers of Captain B.F. Pond," in possession of Pond's great-grand-daughter Meg Rasmussen. As far as the remains of any lost money on the *Julia Ann* is concerned, according to the log of Captain Ruxton and a small map drawn in the log, Ruxton and his crew came upon the remains of the *Julia Ann* wreck on December 21, 1855, wherein the log notes: "Noon observed the wreck of the vessel on the reef, what seemed to be a stern frame with one quarter of a large vessel at some distance from this, and higher up on the reef, saw another piece which had the appearance of . . . a vessel's bottom. Two very conspicuous objects, one having the appearance of a staff and flag. continued to attempt landing until 2 p.m., and finding it impossible in consequence of the tremendous surf." See log book of the *Rob Roy* (Captain Ruxton), Paul Hundley personal papers (in possession of author) culled from the State Library of New South Wales (Mitchell Library), Pacific Manuscripts Bureau microfilm, United States Consular correspondence, Tahiti, 1855. Deposition at the inquest into the death of Captain Ruxton of the schooner *Rob Roy*. In an interview with Paul Hundley by Martin Andersen in Doha, Qatar, June 7, 2013, Hundley, who played a key role in excavaing the wrecked *Julia Ann*, reported that Captain Ruxton "actually noted in his journal, that he recovered a small iron strong box, and in fact he came to a bit of a terrible demise. After he found the wreck of the *Julia Ann*, he took a trip to Sydney, and was spending money like the proverbial sailor, and on the way back, he actually fell overboard and was drowned, lost at sea, but in his possession there was a very large amount of gold sovereigns, and half sovereigns." Hundley also conjectured, "I think he actually found the strong box that the Saints had taken along with them as they emigrated to the United States, it wasn't Captain Pond's gold, but it was the [LDS] church members'."

In any case, further evidence reveals that Ruxton had indeed come into some wealth after coming across the wreck of the *Julia Ann*. A "Notice," which appeared in *The Polynesian* 8, no. 44 (March 7, 1857), 1, told of the recent demise of Captain Ruxton, former captain of the *Rob Roy*. It indicated that Ruxton "had taken from the barque *Julia Ann*, wrecked at the Scilly Islands, the sum of 310 ½ sovereigns." However, Ruxton had maintained that he only took 42 ½ sovereigns, and he was suspected of embezzlement. Therefore, an inquest was ordered to look into these allegations. Evidence revealed that Ruxton was involved with elaborate expenditures at Sydney and was found with 69 sovereigns, other goods and jewelry on his person at the time of his death. As a result, the Commissioner of H.I.M. made the decision that the public should know about this issue, "so that all interested parties . . . [could] present their claims upon the succession of said Ruxton, delivered into the hands of the British Consul, who . . . [would] preserve it during one year from this date. Papeete, Dec. 19, 1856."

187. Pond, *Narrative of the Wreck of the Barque "Julia Ann,"* 17.

188. In his letter to Charles Penfold, February 17, 1856, *Zion's Watchman* 2, no. 5 (May 24, 1856), 78, Peter Penfold recalled, "We passed a dreadful night, sitting on some of the broken masts, up to the waist in water. At daylight we were all busily engaged picking up such provisions as could be found." John McCarthy adds, "With our bodies much lacerated by the sharp coral reef, and with a dreary waste of water without land in sight, our situation was pitiable." See letter by John McCarthy to George Q. Cannon, April 25, 1856, *Western Standard*. Republished in *Deseret News* [*Weekly*] 6, no. 17 (July 2, 1856), 130.

189. Pond, *Narrative of the Wreck of the Barque "Julia Ann,"* 18–19. McCarthy also confirms that the men went without anything to eat or drink for two days "under a burning tropical sun." Letter by John McCarthy to George Q. Cannon, April 25, 1856, *Western Standard*. Republished in *Deseret News* [*Weekly*] 6, no. 17 (July 2, 1855), 130. Another castaway recalled, "The morning sun found us cast a way on a desolet Island whare no living voice was to be herd but the roaring of the brackes and howling of the night birds. In this bewildred condishion we spent seven weeks with our bodeys almost naked, and our only subsistons was a littel fish and wild foul." "The Wreck of the Bark *Julia Ann*," January 28, 1856, letter to the *San Francisco Herald* editors by one of the passengers on the *Julia Ann*, *San Francisco Daily Herald* (April 16, 1856), 1.

190. Pond, *Narrative of the Wreck of the Barque "Julia Ann,"* 19.

191. Charles Logie, the *Deseret Weekly* (April 23, 1898), 591.

192. Letter by John McCarthy to George Q. Cannon, April 25, 1856, *Western Standard*. Republished in *Deseret News* [*Weekly*] 6, no. 17 (July 2, 1855), 130.

193. According to mariner Richard Henry Dana Jr., a quarter boat was "a boat hung at a vessel's quarter." See "Quarter boat," http://www.the-freedictionary.com/Quarter+boat, accessed July 11, 2013. The quarter or quarterdeck is the "raised deck behind the main mast of a sailing ship." See "Quarterdeck," http://en.wikipedia.org/wiki/Quarterdeck, accessed July 11, 2013.

194. McCarthy noted, "After we were all landed on the island, Captain Pond called all hands to order, and delivered a short address, stating that as we were cast away upon a desolate island, that a common brotherhood should be maintained, and that every man should hunt birds and fish for our common sustenance, to which proposition all assented." Letter by John McCarthy to George Q. Cannon, April 25, 1856, *Western Standard*. Re-published in *Deseret News* [*Weekly*] 6, no. 17 (July 2, 1855), 130.

195. "Manuae (Society Islands)," http://en.wikipedia.org/wiki/Manuae_ (Society_Islands), accessed July 13, 2013, notes that Manuae or the atoll known as Scilly is 217 miles west of Bora Bora and 342 miles west of Papeete.

196. Autobiography of B.F. Pond, 215.

197. Autobiography of B.F. Pond, 218. The theme of "divine providence" or "providence," seems to play a key role in Pond's Autobiography and is attested several times (pp. 34, 57, 136, 249). The genesis for this kind of verbiage probably springs from Pond's Christian upbringing, which is also very apparent in his writings. Several passages in his autobiography reveal his Christian base and belief. For example, Pond notes that his

father was one of a few "earnest Christian workers" who established the West Presbyterian Church in New York City (p.6). He also uses the words "Sprit Land" and "Heavenly Home," (p. 9) when referring to the place where some of the friends of his youth who have died have gathered to. Further, biblical language is evidenced by the statement, "Truly His ways are not our ways" (p. 185), wherein Pond appears to be a paraphrasing a portion of Isaiah 55:8. This same scriptural passage is again used wherein he writes, "'Thy ways are not our ways', mysterious are Thy leadings, setting at naught the best devised human plans" (p. 249). His belief is also manifest by his attending Sunday religious Church services during the time when most other miners did not bother, during his days mining in California (see for example page 85, 87, 102). Finally, after his retirement from the sea, Pond was involved with nurturing the faith of people at his cotton factory in Bloomvale, New Jersey, where he and his wife felt a responsibility to help generate religious services, including a Sunday school. Concerning this issue, Pond notes, "about forty from among the factory people were received into the Millbrook church on confession of their faith in Jesus Christ" (p. 258).

198. Pond, *Narrative of the Wreck of the Barque "Julia Ann,"* 20–24.

199. Esther Spangenberg, "Particulars of the Wreck," in B. F. Pond, *Narrative of the Wreck*, 11. The wreck of the *Julia Ann*, nor this daring rescue attempt, was the first or the last kind of harrowing maritime events for Pond. He began to witness storms on the water commencing on his first trip from home at the young age of nineteen while traveling on a canal from New York heading west. Pond writes, "After many rough sea experiences, I often amuse my friends by stating that my first shipwreck overtook me on the raging canal. . . . As the first night from Schenectady, a storm, reaching almost to the dignity of a hurricane, swept across our deck." (See *Autobiography of B. F. Pond*, 23.) The year after the *Julia Ann* wreck he also encountered both a fire and a near crash into the rocks while aboard a vessel as a passenger when he was traveling from San Francisco to Sydney, before returning home to New York. (See *Autobiography of B. F. Pond*, 233–236.)

200. "Papers of Captain B. F. Pond," original in possession of Pond's greatgranddaughter Meg Rasmussen. Captain Coffin was given strict instructions to give this letter to Pond's father if Coffin ever escaped the reef. "It was written on a leaf torn from an old account Book, found in a chest upon the reef with pen and ink, and after the decease of B. Pond was found carefully filed among his valuable papers." See "Papers of Captain B. F. Pond." Coffin delivered this letter by hand to Pond's parents in New York and dined with them. In a touching response letter from his father dated May 5, 1856, Dr. James Otis Pond wrote to his son Benjamin: "Capt. Coffin delivered a letter to me which purported

to have been written by you on Scilly Island, before your voyage to Bolo Bolo [Bora Bora]. I shall preserve this letter as a memento of filial affection, written under trying & disheartening circumstances. I consider the dealings of Providence but manifestations of love & kindness to us. Our afflictions temporary disasters & losses & especially, the preservation of our lives in the midst of dangers; when resulting in their legitamate design, all tend to insure rational reflection, to affix a more suitable value on the unstable possessions after which so many are striving; to bring us to a more suitable state of humility before our Heavenly Father; & to 'cast all our cares upon him, for he careth for us.'" See B. F. Pond papers in possession of Meg Rasmussen.

201. Letter by John McCarthy to George Q. Cannon, April 25, 1856, *Western Standard*. Republished in *Deseret News* [*Weekly*] 6, no. 17 (July 2, 1856), 130. McCarthy further noted, "After four days hard pulling through the squalls and calms, we succeeded in reaching Borabora, one of the Society Islands, a distance of about two hundred miles. The inhabitants treated us with much kindness, and fed us upon poi and breadfruit."

202. Two of the men on this ten-man crew were LDS: Charles Logie and Elder John McCarthy. In light of the winds complying on this life or death voyage, it is of interest that McCarthy was told in his patriarchal blessing under the hands of Isaac Morley, October 26, 1856, "the winds and waves will be obedient through Thy prayers of faith." See "Copy of Patriarchal Blessing give to John McCarthy," in "History of John McCarthy," comp. Stella B. Nielson, (CHL). One of the crew also described his experience: "At the experation of that time we lancht a small quarter bote and mand her with ten men to seek some land of inhabitance, I was one of that number that vulenteerd to accompany Capt Pond in the bote. After four days hard pulling we reacht the Island of Berobora [Bora Bora], a distance of 200 miles, the Inhabitance treated us with kindness The King Tapoa of that land, fited out too small schuner's to take the passenger, from the Island, I returned back in one of the botes to resque my fellow passengers from starvation, But to my great surpryze when I reach'd the Island the wair taken to Tahiti by Captain Leathon of the Emapaca, I then made the best of my way after them, but through dark misfortune and squaliley gails I reacht Tahiti on the 26th of Jan'y." See "The Wreck of the Bark *Julia Ann*," January 28, 1856, letter to the *San Francisco Herald* editors by one of the passengers on the *Julia Ann*, *San Francisco Daily Herald* (April 16, 1856), 1.

203. Captain B. F. Pond, "The Boat Voyage," in *Narrative of the Wreck*, 31–32.

204. This elder is thought to be Elder John McCarthy; he was one of only two Mormons who were part of the ten-man crew who rowed to Bora Bora. The other was Charles Logie. McCarthy had just been serving as a missionary in Australia before departure, and Logie, though a Church

member, was actually already part of the regular crew, but was not then called an elder. The fact that Pond referred to an "Elder" makes it probable that McCarthy had the dream or vision.

205. *Autobiography of B. F. Pond*, 221–222. John McCarthy, the presumed elder who had the vision or dream, went with two of the crew to the island of Maupiti, "where they met King Tapoa and obtained two small schooners, with which to return to the Island of Scilly and rescue their marooned companions. They found they were just 12 hours late in making the rescue, as Captain Pond, in the meantime had been successful in chartering a sailing vessel, the 'Emma Packer,' at Huahine." However, McCarthy made the best of the situation and returned to Maupiti, where he preached to King Tapoa, baptized the King's interpreter, Captain Delano, and found good favor among the natives. After a three-week period he then went to the island of Raiatea where he stayed for two weeks and also performed baptisms, as well as ordaining a man named Shaw to the office of elder. See "History of John McCarthy," comp. Stella B. Neilson, 8, (CHL).

206. Pocket Memorandum of B. F. Pond, "Papers of B. F. Pond," original in possession of Pond's great-granddaughter Meg Rasmussen.

207. For more information on the *Emma Packer*, see Conway B. Sonne, *Ships, Saints, and Mariners: A Maritime Encyclopedia of Mormon Migration 1830–1890*, 69–70.

208. Charles Logie, "Local and other Matters," April 23, 1898, *Deseret Weekly*, 591; John McCarthy to George Q. Cannon, April 25, 1856, *Western Standard*. Republished in *Deseret News* [*Weekly*] 6, no. 17 (July 2, 1856), 130. It appears that Pond went directly to Captain Latham of the *Emma Packer*, as this vessel was recommended to him by the British Consulate at Raiatea. See letter of Alex Chisholm, British Consul on Raiatea, to Captain Pond, "Papers of Captain B. F. Pond," November 23, 1855, in possession of great-granddaughter Meg Rasmussen. Despite Pond's public record, which dates leaving the Scilly Islands on December 3 (see *Narrative of the Wreck of the Barque "Julia Ann,"* 23, published in 1858, three years after the wreck), a letter dated December 21, 1855, written at Papaeete, Tahiti, to G. C. Miller, Esquire, from Robert H. Irvine, pilot for the British Consul at Raiatea and sent for the purpose of helping the survivors of the wreck, records "On the 23, Nov. a boat containing the Capt. and nine men arrived at Borrabora with the news of the loss of the vessel," which clarifies the date of Pond's departure from the Scilly Islands was earlier. Although Pond (papers of B. F. Pond, in possession of Meg Rasmussen) recorded privately that the date of departure with his crew of nine from the Scilly Islands was November 22nd, inasmuch as he also said it took them three days to reach Bora Bora, they must have

left on November 20th. Therefore, the survivors waited nearly another two weeks for their deliverance.

209. Shortly after the survivors of the *Julia Ann* were rescued, as previously noted, the wreckage of the vessel was apparently spotted; the log book of the schooner *Rob Roy*, whose master was Captain Ruxton, for December 21, 1855, notes: "Run down on Scilly Island, find it very low and uninhabited. on the N.E. side the land rises some ten or twelve feet, covered with low bush and pandanus trees all the rest is a low reef on which the sea breaks very high. . . . S. W. side Noon observed the wreck of a vessel on the reef, what seemed to be a stern frame with one quarter of a large vessel at some distance from this, and higher up on the reef, saw another piece which had the appearance of the ruins of a vessel's bottom." See Log book of the *Rob Roy* (Captain Ruxton), Paul Hundley personal papers in possession of author.

210. Letter of John S. Eldredge in *Deseret News* [Weekly] 6, no. 17 (July 2, 1856), 130. News of the wreck was also published in other major newspapers both in Australia as well as in America. See for example, "Total loss of the American Barque *Julia Ann*," *Sydney Morning Herald* (April 2, 1856), 6; "Letter Addressed by Captain Pond to the United States Consul at Tahiti," *New York Herald* (March 17, 1856), 2.

211. Letter by Captain H. Eldredge to Captain B. F. Pond, November 29, 1855, in possession of Meg Rasmussen.

212. Peter Penfold to Charles Penfold, February 17, 1856, in the diary of Augustus Farnham, copies in the CHL, 58–59; also published in *Zion's Watchman* 2, no. 5 (May 24, 1856), 78. The French newspaper, *Messenger de Tahiti* (December 23, 1855), published at Papeete, under the heading "Arrivals," notes the following: "[Dec.] 19. American Schooner Emma Packer. Captain Latham. 93 barrels, 7 man crew, 51 passengers from Huahine." (The author thanks Michael Hunter, BYU librarian, for this translation.)

213. One passenger noted, "I been a british subgect, as a matter of cors applye'd to the british Councel for protection. But what was my protectors ancer, No sir said he I can not assist, nor protect you, If you air [are] a british subgect you had no right to travel under American colours." See "The Wreck of the Bark *Julia Ann*," January 28, 1856, letter to the *San Francisco Herald* editors by one of the passengers on the *Julia Ann*, *San Francisco Daily Herald* (April 16, 1856), 1.

214. Peter Penfold to Australian Saints via Charles Penfold, February 17, 1856, *Zion's Watchman* 2, no. 5 (May 24, 1856), 78. See also the interview of Gérald Tulasne in Appendix E. However, it is evident in a letter to Pond from the British Consulate at Raiatea that they were saddened by the loss of the *Julia Ann* and that they were committed to finding a

vessel to help rescue the passengers. See letter of Alex Chisholm to B. F. Pond, "Papers of Captain B. F. Pond," November 23, 1855, in possession of great-granddaughter Meg Rasmussen. Alexander Chisholm was "born July, 1814, at Turriff, Aberdeenshire. Ch.m., Cresent Ch., Liverpool, Nov., 1834 (Kelly). Studied at Blackburn Academy. Appointed to *Tahiti*. Ordained, July 14, 1842 at Crescent Ch. Married ELIZABETH DAVIES, born Dec. 23, 1822, Ch.m. Oswestry (Reeve). Sailed, Aug. 11, 1842. Arrived at *Tahiti*, March 13, 1843. His appointment having been changed to *Samoa* he proceeded to that Group, and arrived at *Upolu*, April 1843, and settled in June at *Salailua*, Savaii, as arranged by the Samoan Committee, he was instructed to join the *Tahiti* Mission, and in Dec., 1846, left Samoa, and proceeded to that island, and settled at *Hitiaa*. In 1849 he removed to *Papara*, Tahiti. In Sept., 1852, in consequence of the arbitrary measures of the French authorities, he retired to *Raiatea*, where he continued to labour until April, 1860, when he proceeded with his family to England, and arrived Oct. 2. After his return to England he was chiefly engaged in carrying through the press a revised version of the *Tahitian Scriptures*. He died at Oswestry, May 29, 1862. Mrs. Chrisholm continued to reside at Oswestry." *Annotated Register of L.M.S. Missionaries 1796—1923*, register #172. (School of Oriental and African Studies Library, University of London), register # 452.

215. Peter Penfold to Charles Penfold, February 17, 1856, in the Diary of Augustus Farnham, copies in CHL, 58–59; also published in Zion's *Watchman* 2, no. 5 (May 24, 1856), 78. Herein, Penfold further explained that after going back to the English Consul, he agreed to feed them until the end of the following month, which proved sufficient until their deliverance from Tahiti. Gérald Tulasne, Un siècle de franc-maçonnerie à Tahiti. 1842–1940: Implantation, chroniques et portraits. Mémoire de maîtris, (Université de Polynésie française, 2004), 42, notes that an 1856 Masonic lodge log reveals that in this year G. Cuzent was the president of the Masonic fraternity in Tahiti. His first supervisor was a French trader named Joseph Cassaubon, with Adam John Darling, the son of an English protestant missionary, as his second advisor. Other Masonic lodge officers listed at this time are as follows: " *Secretary: Philippe Mangey: justice* Speaker: Fautrey under Commissioner Navy (?).* Treasurer: Philidor Danican colonial treasurer.* Deputy Speaker:. E Hardy, Lieutenant.* Chaplain: Eleanor Segar"

Gérald Tulasne also provided the author with information which noted that Peter Penfold later became the Grand Master at the Lexington Masonic lodge, no. 104 in El Monte, Los Angeles County, California.

Another *Julia Ann* passenger noted, "Permit me to return my sinceir thanks, to the Royal masonic body of gentlemen in Tahiti, for the

[they] administered to us kind hospitality in unison with the French military hoffisurs [officers], And I am also glad to testify that we resived much kindness from the American Councel, he is a gentleman an a man of honour, shuch kindness can not be forgot . . . while the stripes of Samuel can chastize the prosumptious foe; The second day I was in Tahiti, a gentelman by the name of Mr. Joseph Richmond, made me welcome to his table and also procured me a passage to California through the kind instrementiality of Capt Bisbey of the Fare-west, May the Spirit of unity joy plenty and prosperity upheld by the son's of freedom, croun their days for ever more. Gentelmen I have the honour to be your homble servant A PASSENGER." See "The Wreck of the Bark *Julia Ann*," January 28, 1856 letter to the *San Francisco Herald* editors by one of the passengers on the *Julia Ann*, *San Francisco Daily Herald* (April 16, 1856), 1.

216. Peter Penfold to the Australian Saints, via his father, Charles Penfold, Tahiti, February 17, 1856, *Zion's Watchman* 2, no. 5 (May 24, 1856), 78.

217. "Annual Conference of the Australasian Mission . . . April 6th 1856," *Zion's Watchman* 2, vol. 5 (May 24, 1856), 79. The Diary of John Perkins, March 25, 1856, reveals that President Farnham and other local Australian Saints must have known about the wreck by this date, as Perkins recorded, "Mrs. Bailey railed most bitter . . . & said that Brother Farnham was a false Prophet with respect to the *Julia Ann*." Bailey also seemed to be out of harmony with the local LDS congregation in Sydney at this time, as Perkins further noted, "She also said that some things in the Book of Doctrine and Covenants was such a devilish devised thing." On April 5, 1856, Perkins's diary notes, "There was also several other Subjects Brought before the Council (Viz) respecting the next company going out, the loss of the *Julia Ann*."

218. John Penfold to President Augustus Farnham, Tahiti, March 21, 1856, *Zion's Watchman* 2, no. 5 (May 24, 1856), 71.

219. "Special Conference of the Australiasian Mission . . . May 4th 1856, in *Zion's Watchman* 2, no. 5 (May 24, 1856), 49 [81].

220. "Editorial and General Intelligence," *Zion's Watchman* 2, no. 5 (May 24, 1856), 50 [82].

221. The cost of the voyage from Sydney to San Pedro for steerage was £23.10 for adults and £35 for cabin lodging. See AMMH, April 23, 1856. For a list of the passengers aboard the *Jenny Ford*, see Marjorie Newton, *Southern Cross Saints*, 225. Although it is estimated that 120 actually went on the voyage, Absalom P. Dowdle, who succeeded Farnham as mission president, reported to Franklin D. Richards in a letter, July 7, 1856, "Foreign Correspondence. New South Wales," *Millennial Star* 18,

no. 44 (November 1, 1856), 702, that the number of passengers on the *Jenny Ford* was "130, including children." In order to make sense of this apparent ambiguity, it should be noted that it is possible that some of the men worked as crew members, which would mean that they would be placed on the crew members list and not the passenger list. Also, some of those destined to go may not have actually embarked. A third possibility is that Dowdle may have simply been off on his numbering. For a list of the passengers and various first-person Mormon accounts kept on this voyage, search "Jenny Ford 1856" on http://mormonmigration.lib.byu.edu, accessed June 4, 2013.

222. For a biographical sketch of Fleming, see Appendix C: Biographical Register.

223. Letter of Josiah Fleming, AMMH, May 28, 1856, 2.

224. Diary of John Perkins, June 24 and 25, 1856.

225. "Journal of the Augustus Farnham Company," June 9, 1856, 17–19, copies in the CHL. See also "Journal of Augustus Farnham Immigrating Company," www.mormonmigration.lib.byu.edu, accessed July 22, 2013. Farnham had already been a Freemason for a dozen years. In an email to Fred E. Woods from Brady Winslow, May 7, 2013, Winslow wrote, "On April 5, 1844, during the meeting of Nauvoo Lodge when the new Masonic hall was dedicated, an 'Augustus A. Farnham' is listed as a 'member.' Typically, the designation of a person as a member in the minute book indicates that the individual listed had already been made a Master Mason by the lodge and was in attendance at that particular meeting." The author expresses thanks to Brady Winslow and Jay G. Burrup for bringing this source, Nauvoo Masonic Lodge Minute Book 1841–February 1846, April 5, 1844, CHL, to his attention. See also David John Buerger, "The Development of the Temple Endowment Ceremony," vol. 20 (Winter 1987), *Dialogue: A Journal of Mormon Thought*, 46, who notes, "During the Nauvoo period, [1839–1846] it is useful to note that in 1840, only 147 men in Illinois and 2,072 in the United States were Masons. . . . By the time of the exodus [1846] to Utah, approximately 1,366 Mormon males in Nauvoo had been initiated into the Masonic Order." On this topic of masonry and Mormonism, see also Mervin B. Hogan, "The Milieu of Mormonism and Freemasonry at Nauvoo: An Interpretation," *Transactions: The American Lodge of Research, Free and Accepted Masons* vol. 13 (1976):188–202; Matthew B. Brown, *Exploring the Connection Between Mormons and Masons* (American Fork, Utah: Covenant Communications, Inc., 2009).

226. "Journal of the Augustus Farnham Company," June 23, 1856, 51–54, copies in CHL. See also "Journal of Augustus Farnham Immigrating Company," www.mormonmigration.lib.byu.edu, accessed July 22, 2013. A baptismal record reveals that the name of this three week old infant

was Gabriel Marie Richard Magee who was born June 7, 1856 on Petite Pologne Street in Papeete, courtesy of Diane Benedetti, great-granddaughter of Richard and Eliza Magee.

227. "Register Book of the Names and Particulars of Distressed Subjects of Great Britain," Tahiti British Consulate Papers, Mitchell Library, Sydney, Australia, Paul Hundley personal papers, copy in author's possession. For a biographical sketch on Thomas Magee and his family, see Appendix C: Biographical Register.

228. Journal of Alonzo Colton, June 26, 1855, 10–11, CHL.

229. When interviewed, Gérald Tulasne, an attorney in Papeete who wrote a thesis on the history of freemasonry in Tahiti, noted that although it is not absolutely verifiable, he maintains that the author's hypothesis that Mr. Thomas Magee would contact the Freemasons upon arrival at Papeete was quite possible. Tulasne pointed out that at the time the passengers of the *Julia Ann* came to Tahiti, many English and Americans were part of the Lodge, in addition to the French. See Appendix E for the full interview. Interview in French (with interpreter) by Fred E. Woods with Gérald Tulasne, January 26, 2013, in Papeete, in Tahiti. From the letter that Farnham had dictated, it shows he too was a member of this global fraternity, which had a commitment to assist others in distress, especially those belonging to this order.

230. "The Wreck Passengers of the Bark *Julia Ann*," January 6, 1856, letter from Tahiti by Thomas Magee and other passengers to Captain Latham, via the editor of the *San Francisco Daily Herald* 16, no. 320 (April 16, 1856), 1. Although Gumric, Symmonds, and Clagger do not appear on the passenger list, they were possibly aboard the *Julia Ann*.

231. Wm. H. Kelley, U.S. Consul in Papeete to the Secretary of State, December 20, 1855, ANMM *Julia Ann* Reference Files; "Particulars of the Wreck of the Bark *Julia Anne*," *San Francisco Daily Herald* (March 11, 1856), 2.

232. Peter Penfold, *Zion's Watchman* 2, no. 5 (May 24, 1856), 78.

233. Biographical information of passengers on the 1855 voyage of the *Julia Ann*, compiled by Paul Hundley, in possession of the author; see also Appendix C for bio-sketches containing all available information on both Sarah Wilson and Captain Latham.

234. This paragraph above is both quoted and paraphrased from Paul Hundley in the ANMM *Julia Ann* Reference Files, in which Paul provided a brief overview of the background of the *Julia Ann* wreck for the maritime archaeological excavation he was involved with. Following the wreck, Captain Pond wrote to his brother Samuel M. Pond, telling of his safety. Captain Pond humorously writes, "I can assure you the postal arrangements on 'Scily island' of which I have been acting monarch for

the past few months are none of the best." On a more sobering note, Pond also indicates that he lost at least $10,000 and "had I arrived safely in San Francisco I could have closed up my business & returned to New York with the handsome sum of $30,000 in my pocket." See "Papers of B. F. Pond," original in possession of Pond's great-granddaughter Meg Rasmussen. Pond's health also suffered; he had a nervous breakdown, apparently from the stress he encountered largely from the *Julia Ann* loss of passengers and cargo and strain of saving the survivors, as evidenced by what occurred shortly after reaching San Francisco. He recalled, "I made my appearance three days after the arrival of the ship *Lucas* in San Francisco. . . . After conferring with my partner for a few days, and in a measure shifting the burden of a mass of business from my own to his broad shoulders, it seemed as though my nerves collapsed utterly. I was not conscious to what a terrible strain and tension they had been subjected to until the reaction came, leaving me physically and mentally for a week or two, well, if I may so express it, a vacuum. . . . They put me to bed, then administered glass after glass of hot whisky. It put me to sleep most effectually, and certainly I awoke after a season. . . . I very much desired to take a vacation, and make a visit to the Eastern states, but Mr. Wetherbee insisted on the necessity of my returning to Sydney to look after our insurance and other business." (See *Autobiography of B. F. Pond*, 231–232.)

235. See death notice of Thomas Magee in San Andreas Independent, March 31, 1860, 2–3. Courtesy of Diane Beneditti, a great-granddaughter of Thomas Magee. Thanks is expressed to Diane and also Susan Clemons (a great-great-granddaughter of Magee) who assisted with research on Thomas and Eliza Magee.

236. "Anderson, Andrew," *Early Members of the Reorganized Church of Jesus Christ of Latter Day Saints* 5 vols., comp. Susan Easton Black (Provo: BYU Religious Studies Center, 1993), 1:96, was born July 26, 1810 in Edinburgh, Scotland. "Andrew Anderson was baptized a member of the Reorganized Church of Jesus Christ of Latter Day Saints on 2 August 1868 by W. W. Blair. He was confirmed by Thos. Dungan. Andrew was ordained a priest on 26 September 1869 at Washington, Nevada, California, by W. W. Blair. He attended the Irvington, California Branch." He died January 1, 1891, in Petaluma, Sonoma County, California. "Penfold, Peter," *Early Members of the Reorganized Church*, 4:778, was born January 22, 1830. "Peter Penfold was baptized a member of the Reorganized Church of Jesus Christ of Latter Day Saints on 6 June 1864."

237. Jenson, "The *Julia Ann* Wreck," 698. In his journal, James Graham, "Graham Family Notebook," 18–19, (CHL), wrote, "Broather Penfold and Logie with Their families Embarked for san francisco California

A short time afterwards And finally Brother Anderson and his Family & the Last Members of the ship Wrecked Company Embarked And sailed from tahiti on the ship Georg W Kendall on May the 5, 1856." See also, Conway B. Sonne, *Saints on the Seas*, 79.

238. Jenson, "The *Julia Ann* Wreck," 698, notes, "Elders Graham and Eldredge returned with the schooner [*Emma Packer*] to Huahine, [to Papeete] where they remained a month and then sailed for Honolulu . . . per American schooner Navigator, which arrived at Lahaina Maui, March 12th. After remaining in the Sandwich islands a little over two weeks, they were enabled through the assistance of an Elder Evans and others to engage a passage for California, on board the Francis Palmer, which sailed from Honolulu April 1st. After twenty-three days' sailing they arrived safely in San Francisco, Cal., April 23, 1856." Gratitude is expressed to Chad Orton, archivist at the Church History Library, who sent the author an email (January 11, 2013) regarding Elders Graham and Eldridge: "The Hawaiian Mission Manuscript History (LR 3695 2, Box 1) for March 11, 1856, states: Tuesday, March 11 <Wednesday March 12>. Elders John Eldredge and Graham landed at Lahaina per ship 'Navigator' from Tahiti; from the ship '*Julia Ann*.' Silas S. Smith's journal entry for March 14, 1856 states: 'On landing at Lahaina we [He and the other Silas Smith] met Bro Hammond and family at the Beach ready to embark for San Franciso Here we also met Bros Graham and Eldridge from Australia.'" For more information on the *Francis A. Palmer*, see Conway B. Sonne, *Ships, Saints, and Mariners*, 77.

239. Peter Penfold, *Zion's Watchman* 2, no. 5 (May 24, 1856), 78.

240. Humphreys then added to the letter, "Mother why cannot you take the Same Step. I tell you, *Mormonism is truth, and the only truth. . . .* Believe me my dear Mother." Letter of Martha Humphreys to her mother, December 8, 1853, Mitchell Library, Sydney, Australia. For the background of this handwritten letter, see Marjorie Newton, "'Seduced Away': Early Mormon documents in Australia," *BYU Studies* 35, no. 3 (1995–96):149–65.

241. Thomas Magee and other passengers to editors of *San Francisco Herald*, "The Wreck of the Bark *Julia Ann*," January 28, 1856, *San Francisco Daily Herald* 6, no. 320, April 16, 1856, 1.

242. "Andrew Anderson," www.ourfamilyinfo.org, accessed July 22, 2013.

243. Anderson Family Group Record, courtesy of Marjorie Newton. Copy in possession of the author.

244. *Times and Seasons* 6, no 14 (Aug 1, 1845), 989–90.

245. "Register Book of the Names and Particulars of Distressed Subjects of Great Britain," Tahiti British Consulate Papers, Mitchell Library,

Sydney, Australia, copy in author's possession, courtesy of Paul Hundley.

246. *Times and Seasons*, vol 6, no 14 (Aug 1, 1845), 989–90.

247. Anderson Family Group Record, courtesy of Marjorie Newton, copy in possession of the author. "Passenger list of the September 1855 voyage of the *Julia Ann*," www.mormonmigration.lib.byu.edu, accessed June 7, 2013.

248. Anderson Family Group Record, courtesy of Marjorie Newton, copy in possession of the author.

249. Marjorie Newton, "Pioneering the Gospel in Australia," *Ensign* (October, 1986)

250. *Times and Seasons* 6, no 14 (Aug 1, 1845), 989–90.

251. "Register Book of the Names and Particulars of Distressed Subjects of Great Britain," Tahiti British Consulate Papers, Mitchell Library, Sydney, Australia, copy in author's possession, courtesy of Paul Hundley.

252. "Andrew Anderson," www.ourfamilyinfo.org, accessed July 22, 2013.

253. "Anderson, Andrew," *Early Members of the Reorganized Church of Jesus Christ of Latter Day Saints* 5 vols., comp. Susan Easton Black (Provo: BYU Religious Studies Center, 1993), 1:96

254. "Andrew Anderson," www.ourfamilyinfo.org, accessed July 22, 2013.

255. "Ships articles and crew lists, 1854–1856, 1861–1862, 1883, 1886, 1892" U.S. Custom List, San Francisco, microfilm # 0,976,995.

256. July 24, 1855, crew manifest from San Francisco to Sydney, ANMM *Julia Ann* Reference Files, copy in author's possession.

257. John Devitry-Smith, "William James Barratt: The First Mormon 'Down Under'" *BYU Studies* 28, no 3 (Summer 1988), 53–56.

258. HC 4:154

259. John Devitry-Smith, "William James Barratt: The First Mormon 'Down Under'" *BYU Studies* 28, no 3 (Summer 1988), 57–65.

260. See Paul Hundley personal papers, copy in author's possession.

261. "Ships articles and crew lists, 1854–1856, 1861–1862, 1883, 1886, 1892" U.S. Custom List, San Francisco, microfilm # 0,976,995; See also July 24, 1855 crew manifest from San Francisco to Sydney, ANMM *Julia Ann* Reference Files, copy in author's possession.

262. "Ships articles and crew lists, 1854–1856, 1861–1862, 1883, 1886, 1892" U.S. Custom List, San Francisco, microfilm # 0,976,995; See also July 24, 1855 crew manifest from San Francisco to Sydney, ANMM *Julia Ann* Reference Files, copy in author's possession.

263. Edgartown, MA, Town and Vital Records, 1620–1988, 28; www.ancestry.com.

264. "Married," *Nantucket Inquirer* 38, no. 309 (September 23, 1826), 3.

265. "Notice," *New Bedford Mercury* 33, no. 14 (September 27, 1839), 3.

266. *New-Bedford Mercury* 40, no. 16 (November 20, 1846), 3.

267. Paul Hundley, "Captain Coffin and the *Julia Ann*," *Signals: The Quarterly Magazine of the Australian National Maritime Museum* no. 35 (June–August, 1996):9.

268. *Autobiography of Captain B. F. Pond*, 216.

269. Paul Hundley, "Captain Coffin and the *Julia Ann*," 11.

270. Autobiography of Captain B. F. Pond, 230.

271. "List of Letters," *New York Herald* (August 15, 1856), 7.

272. Personal papers of Paul Hundley, copy in author's possession.

273. "Ships articles and crew lists, 1854–1856, 1861–1862, 1883, 1886, 1892" U.S. Custom List, San Francisco, microfilm # 0,976,995; See also July 24, 1855 crew manifest from San Francisco to Sydney, ANMM *Julia Ann* Reference Files, copy in author's possession.

274. "Ships articles and crew lists, 1854–1856, 1861–1862, 1883, 1886, 1892" U.S. Custom List, San Francisco, microfilm # 0,976,995; see also July 24, 1855 crew manifest from San Francisco to Sydney, ANMM *Julia Ann* Reference Files, copy in author's possession.

275. "Ships articles and crew lists, 1854–1856, 1861–1862, 1883, 1886, 1892" U.S. Custom List, San Francisco, microfilm # 0,976,995; see also July 24, 1855 crew manifest from San Francisco to Sydney, ANMM *Julia Ann* Reference Files, copy in author's possession.

276. "John Sunderlin Eldredge," www.findagrave.com, accessed July 26, 2013.

277. Culled from a typescript which stated, "Chapter Nine John Sunderlin Eldredge. . ." comp. Welma (Hoggard) Williams, ANMM *Julia Ann* Reference Files.

278. Andrew Jensen, "Eldredge, John Sunderlin" *LDS Biographical Encyclopedia* vol 4 (Salt Lake City: Western Epics, 1971), 700.

279. AMMH, March 30, 1853. Culled from a typescript which stated, "Chapter Nine John Sunderlin Eldredge. . ." comp. Welma (Hoggard) Williams, ANMM *Julia Ann* Reference Files.

280. See "Steerage Passengers on Bark Francis Palmer," Series 82, box 2, "Passenger Arrivals and Departures, 1856 out," Hawaii State Archives, Honolulu, Hawaii.

281. "John Sunderlin Eldredge," www.findagrave.com, accessed July 26, 2013. The date of Eldredge's death is disputed. Andrew Jensen in the

LDS Biographical Encyclopedia records his death as May 7, 1873; see Andrew Jensen, "Eldredge, John Sunderlin" *LDS Biographical Encyclopedia* vol. 4 (Salt Lake City: Western Epics, 1971), 700. Welma Williams in her compilation of information on John Eldredge noted his death on May 5, 1874; see "Chapter Nine John Sunderlin Eldredge. . ." comp. Welma (Hoggard) Williams, ANMM *Julia Ann* Reference Files. However, his gravestone says May 5, 1871.

282. Culled from a typescript which stated, "Chapter Nine John Sunderlin Eldredge. . ." comp. Welma (Hoggard) Williams, ANMM *Julia Ann* Reference Files.

283. "Ships articles and crew lists, 1854–1856, 1861–1862, 1883, 1886, 1892" U.S. Custom List, San Francisco, microfilm # 0,976,995; See also July 24, 1855 crew manifest from San Francisco to Sydney, ANMM *Julia Ann* Reference Files, copy in author's possession.

284. Andrew Jensen, "Farnham, Augustus" *LDS Biographical Encyclopedia* vol 4 (Salt Lake City: Western Epics, 1971), 307.

285. *East of Antelope Island* 4 ed. (Salt Lake City: Publishers Press, 1971), 282.

286. Allen D. Roberts, "Pioneer Architects" *Sunstone* 1, no. 3 (1976), 51.

287. Andrew Jensen, "Farnham, Augustus" *LDS Biographical Encyclopedia* vol 4 (Salt Lake City: Western Epics, 1971), 307.

288. AMMH, 1.

289. "Quarterly Conference," *Zion's Watchman* 1, nos. 8–9 (January 28, 1854), 57.

290. "Minutes of the half-yearly Conference . . . September 30th 1855," *Zion's Watchman* 1 [2], no. 4 (October 27, 1855), 60–63.

291. "Annual Conference of the Australasian Mission . . . April 6th 1856," *Zion's Watchman* 5, no. 2 (May 24, 1856), 72.

292. AMMH, 1.

293. Andrew Jensen, *History of Las Vegas Missions* (Salt Lake City, 1926), CHL.

294. "Tanner Family History," http://wc.rootsweb.ancestry.com, accessed July 24, 2013.

295. "Burr Frost," www.findagrave.com, accessed June 6, 2013

296. "Burr Frost—Blacksmith," *Our Pioneer Heritage*, 2:554–555.

297. Andrew Jensen, "Frost, Burr" *LDS Biographical Encyclopedia*, vol. 4 (Salt Lake City: Western Epics, 1971), 703–4.

298. "Minutes of the Annual Conference of the Australasian Mission, . . .

April 2nd, 1854," *Zion's Watchman* 1, nos. 12–13 (May 6, 1854), 90.

299. Andrew Jensen, "Frost, Burr" *LDS Biographical Encyclopedia*, vol. 4 (Salt Lake City: Western Epics, 1971), 703–4.

300. "James Graham (1804–1857)," www.geni.com, accessed May 6, 2013.

301. "James Graham," www.findagrave.com, accessed May 6, 2013.

302. "Quarterly Conference," *Zion's Watchman* vol. 1, nos. 26–27 (January 15, 1855), 201.

303. See "Steerage Passengers on Bark Francis Palmer," Series 82, box 2, "Passenger Arrivals and Departures, 1856 out," Hawaii State Archives, Honolulu, Hawaii.

304. Journal of James Graham, "Graham Family Notebook," 1, (CHL).

305. Andrew Jensen, *History of Las Vegas Missions* (Salt Lake City, 1926), CHL.

306. "James Graham," www.findagrave.com, accessed May 6, 2013.

307. "Register Book of the Names and Particulars of Distressed Subjects of Great Britain," Tahiti British Consulate Papers, Mitchell Library, Sydney, Australia, copy in author's possession, courtesy of Paul Hundley.

308. "Lucas," http://mormonmigration.lib.byu.edu, accessed July 30, 2013.

309. See "Harris, Eliza," in "Australian Mission List of 19th Century Members," comp. Marjorie Newton.

310. Leslie Albrecht Huber, "Kerstina Nilsdotter: A Story of the Swedish Saints," *Journal of Mormon History* 31, no. 2 (2005), 258–259.

311. John Devitry-Smith, "The Wreck of the *Julia Ann*" *BYU Studies* 29, no 2 (1989), 255

312. Leslie Albrecht Huber, "Kerstina Nilsdotter: A Story of the Swedish Saints," *Journal of Mormon History* 31, no. 2 (2005), 258–259.

313. "Sydney to San Pedro on the *Lucas*," www.mormonmigration.com, accessed July 25, 2013.

314. "Register Book of the Names and Particulars of Distressed Subjects of Great Britain," Tahiti British Consulate Papers, Mitchell Library, Sydney, Australia, copy in author's possession, courtesy of Paul Hundley.

315. Marjorie Newton, "'Seduced Away': Early Mormon Documents in Australia" *BYU Studies* 35, no 3 (1995–6), 149–154.

316. "Sydney to Unknown on the *Julia Ann*: Humphreys, Martha Maria," www.mormonmigration.byu.edu, accessed June 7, 2013.

317. Marjorie Newton, "'Seduced Away': Early Mormon Documents in Australia" *BYU Studies* 35, no 3 (1995–6), 149–154.

318. "William Hyde," www.geni.com, accessed July 1, 2013.

319. "Quarterly Conference . . . ," *Zion's Watchman* 1, nos. 8–9 (January 28, 1854), 57.

320. Letter of William Hyde to Augustus Farnham in *Zion's Watchman* vol. 1, nos. 10–11 (March 4, 1854), 73.

321. Andrew Jenson, "Hyde Park," *Encyclopedic History of the Church of Jesus Christ of Latter-day Saints* (Salt Lake City: *Deseret News* Publishing Company, 1941), 349.

322. "William Hyde," www.geni.com, accessed July 1, 2013.

323. Journal of William Hyde, February 2, 1853. "On the Death of Joseph and Hyrum Smith," *Zion's Watchman* 1, nos. 10–11 (March 4, 1854), 88.

324. "William Hyde," www.geni.com, accessed July 1, 2013.

325. See "Jones, John," in "Australian Mission List of 19th Century Members," comp. Marjorie Newton.

326. Passenger list of *Agnes Ewing*, Liverpool to Sydney, http://srwww.records.nsw.gov.au, accessed July 30, 2013.

327. John Jones, "A Sketch of the History of the Work of the Lord in the Australasian Colonies," *Zion's Watchman* 1, nos. 32–33 (April 12, 1855), 260; AMMH, November 2, 1851.

328. John Jones, "A Sketch of the History of the Work of the Lord in the Australasian Colonies," *Zion's Watchman* 1, nos. 32–33 (April 12, 1855), 262; AMMH, July 5, 1852.

329. Augustus Farnham, "Preface," *Zion's Watchman* 1, no. 1 (August 13, 1853), no page number given.

330. John Jones, "Consistency Against the S. M. Herald," *Zion's Watchman* 1, no. 1 (August 13, 1853), 7–8; "To the Australian Public," Quarterly Conference . . . ," *Zion's Watchman* 1, nos. 8–9 (January 28, 1854), 63, in which Jones refers to the literary "trash and abuse," of the *Sydney Morning Herald*. A thoughtful address to the Saints given in Sydney on August 20, 1854 is evidenced in "A Discourse," *Zion's Watchman* 1, nos. 18–19 (September 16, 1854), 139–144, and a good defense of Mormonism to the Reverend S. C. Kent in "The Substance of Elder J. Jones' First Lecture . . . on Mormonism, Delivered in Sydney, on Sunday, August 12th," in *Zion's Watchman* 1 [2], no. 4 (October 27, 1855), 51–60.

331. John Jones, "Where Shall I Bury My Dead," written December 7, 1854, and published in the *Sydney Morning Herald* and the *Empire* on December 9, 1854. Also later published in "Original Correspondence," *Zion's Watchman* 1, nos. 24–25 (December 15, 1854), 199.

332. "General Intelligence," *Zion's Watchman* 1, nos. 18–19 (September 16, 1854), 152.

333. "A Sketch of the History of the Work of the Lord in the Australasian Colonies." *Zion's Watchman* 1, nos. 32–33 (April 12, 1855): 260–265.

334. "Quarterly Conference . . . ," *Zion's Watchman* 1, nos. 8–9 (January 28, 1854), 57, 62–63; "Quarterly Conference . . ." *Zion's Watchman*, vol. 1, nos. 26–27 (January 15, 1855), 201;

335. "Editorial and General Intelligence," *Zion's Watchman* 2, no. 1 (May 15, 1855), 12.

336. Marjorie Newton, *Southern Cross Saints*, 225.

337. Letter of John S. Eldredge in *Deseret News* [Weekly] 6, no. 17 (July 2, 1856).

338. See letter of Alex Chisholm, British Consul on Raiatea, to Captain Pond, "Papers of Captain B. F. Pond," Nov 23, 1855, in possession of Pond's great-granddaughter Meg Rasmussen.

339. Consular record showing payment, papers in possession of Pond's great-grandaughter Meg Rasmussen.

340. "The Wrecked Passenger of the *Julia Ann*," Tahiti, Jan. 6, 1856, to the Editor of the *San Francisco Herald*, by Thomas Magee and others. Article from the papers of Captain Benjamin F. Pond in possession of Meg Rasmussen, though the *San Francisco Herald* is not dated.

341. "Register Book of the Names and Particulars of Distressed Subjects of Great Britain," Tahiti British Consulate Papers, Mitchell Library, Sydney, Australia, copy in author's possession, courtesy of Paul Hundley.

342. Paul Hundley personal papers, copy in author's possession.

343. "Total Loss of the American Barque *Julia Ann*" *Sydney Morning Herald*, April 2, 1856, 6.

344. "They were Pioneers," maintained by Lee Drew 2007, www.famhist.us, accessed November 12, 2012.

345. Marjorie Newton, "Rosa Clara Friedlander Logie (1837–1913)" *Women of Faith* eds. Richard E. Turley, Jr. and Brittany Chapman, vol. 2, 1.

346. AMMH, October 3, 1853.

347. "Shipwrecked in the South Pacific," maintained by Lee Drew 2007, http://www.famhist.us, accessed September 17, 2012.

348. Marjorie Newton, "Rosa Clara Friedlander Logie (1837–1913)," in *Women of Faith* eds. Richard E. Turley, Jr. and Brittany Chapman, 13–14.

349. "Death of Mrs. Rosa Logie," *American Fork Citizen*, June 21, 1913, 1.

350. Marjorie Newton, "Rosa Clara Friedlander Logie (1837–1913)," eds.

Richard E. Turley, Jr. and Brittany A. Chapman *Women of Faith* vol. 2 (Salt Lake City: Deseret Book, 2012), 196.

351. "Death of Mrs. Rosa Logie," *American Fork Citizen*, June 21, 1913, 1.

352. "Sketch of the Life of Annie Augusta Logie Clark," www.ancestry.com, accessed August 26, 2011.

353. "Register Book of the Names and Particulars of Distressed Subjects of Great Britain," Tahiti British Consulate Papers, Mitchell Library, Sydney, Australia, copy in author's possession, courtesy of Paul Hundley. The author is grateful for additional documentation on Thomas and Eliza Magee provided by Diane Benedetti, a great-granddaughter of Thomas and Eliza Magee; and Susan Clemons, a great, great-grand-daugter of Thomas and Eliza Magee.

354. "The Wrecked Passenger of the *Julia Ann*," Tahiti, Jan. 6, 1856, to the Editor of the *San Francisco Herald*, by Thomas Magee and others. Article from the papers of Captain Benjamin F. Pond in possession of Meg Rasmussen, Pond's great-grandaughter, though the *San Francisco Herald* is not dated.

355. "Total Loss of the American Barque *Julia Ann*" *Sydney Morning Herald*, April 2, 1856, 6.

356. Stella B. Neilson *History of John McCarthy* 1–32, CHL

357. Andrew Jenson, "Murdock, John" *LDS Biographical Encyclopedia* vol 2 (Salt Lake City: Western Epics, 1971), 362–4; Reed Murdock, *John Murdock: His Life and His Legacy* (Layton, Utah: Summerwood Publishers, 2000), 255–262.

358. "Ships articles and crew lists, 1854–1856, 1861–1862, 1883, 1886, 1892" U.S. Custom List, San Francisco, microfilm # 0,976,995 ; Personal Files of Paul Hundley.

359. Autobiography of Captain B. F. Pond, 202.

360. Autobiography of Captain B. F. Pond, 219.

361. Autobiography of Captain B. F. Pond, 230.

362. "Christmas Island history," www.janeresture.com/kiribati_line/christmas_island.htm, accessed on June 6, 2013.

363. Pegg Family Group Record-13, NSW Early Church Records, vol 10 #68, St Johns, Parramata, courtesy of Marjorie Newton.

364. Email to author from Marjorie Newton, March 5, 2013

365. *Sydney Morning Herald*, January 10, 1859, 4

366. "LDS Passengers on *Julia Ann*" Paul Hundley personal papers, copy in author's possession.

367. "NSW Death Registration Transcription" ref no 1866/5905, email to author from Marjorie Newton, March 5, 2013

368. *Saints' Herald Obituaries*, 1885, 143; *Early Members of the Reorganized Church* 4:777.

369. "Register Book of the Names and Particulars of Distressed Subjects of Great Britain," Tahiti British Consulate Papers, Mitchell Library, Sydney, Australia, copy in author's possession, courtesy of Paul Hundley.

370. "Elizabeth Thompson," www.ancestry.com, accessed July 30, 2013.

371. Passenger list of *Palmyra*, Liverpool to Sydney, http://srwww.records.nsw.gov.au, accessed July 30, 2013.

372. "John Penfold: Passenger list of the September 1855 voyage of the *Julia Ann*," http://mormonmigration.lib.byu.edu, accessed June 7, 2013.

373. "Quarterly Conference of the Australasian Mission ," *Zion's Watchman* 2, no. 3 (June 18, 1855), 40.

374. Andrew Jenson, "The *Julia Ann* Wreck," *Deseret Weekly News* (May 14, 1898), 697.

375. "Register Book of the Names and Particulars of Distressed Subjects of Great Britain," Tahiti British Consulate Papers, Mitchell Library, Sydney, Australia, copy in author's possession, courtesy of Paul Hundley.

376. "1860 United States Federal Census: John Penfold,"ancestry.com, accessed March 19, 2013.

377. *Early Members of the Reorganized Church* 4:777.

378. "Register Book of the Names and Particulars of Distressed Subjects of Great Britain," Tahiti British Consulate Papers, Mitchell Library, Sydney, Australia, copy in author's possession, courtesy of Paul Hundley.

379. "1870 United States Federal Census: Peter Penfold," ancestry.com, accessed May 17, 2013.

380. *Early Members of the Reorganized Church* 4:778.

381. "Register Book of the Names and Particulars of Distressed Subjects of Great Britain," Tahiti British Consulate Papers, Mitchell Library, Sydney, Australia, copy in author's possession, courtesy of Paul Hundley.

382. *Early Members of the Reorganized Church* 4:778.

383. "1880 United States Federal Census: Peter Penfold," ancestry.com, accessed May 17, 2013.

384. "1910 United States Federal Census: Stephen Penfold," ancestry.com, accessed May 17, 2013.

385. "Stephen Penfold," ancestry.com, accessed May 17, 2013

386. "Ships articles and crew lists, 1854–1856, 1861–1862, 1883, 1886, 1892" U.S. Custom List, San Francisco, microfilm # 0,976,995; See also July 24, 1855 crew manifest from San Francisco to Sydney, ANMM *Julia Ann* Reference Files, copy in author's possession.

387. Jane Benson, "History of John Perkins and His Wife," 1–3, Harold B. Lee Library, L. Tom Perry Special Collections, Provo, Utah.

388. *Zion's Watchman* 2, no. 3 (June 18, 1855), 45.

389. "Minutes of the half-yearly Conference . . ." *Zion's Watchman* 1 [2], no. 4 (October 27, 1855), 50.

390. Jane Benson, "History of John Perkins and His Wife," Harold B. Lee Library, L. Tom Perry Special Collections, Provo, Utah.

391. *Autobiography of B. F. Pond*, introductory page (not numbered), 21

392. *Autobiography of B. F. Pond*, 7. Herein, (pp. 19–21), Pond now at the age of nineteen, suddenly did not have joint pain any longer, but gave up school as he felt so far behind in his studies.

393. *Autobiography of B. F. Pond*, 22.

394. *Autobiography of B. F. Pond*, 35–37, 82, 125–130, 191, 247, 249.

395. *Autobiography of B. F. Pond*, 82.

396. *Autobiography of B. F. Pond*, 135–136.

397. *Autobiography of B. F. Pond*, 2.

398. *Autobiography of B. F. Pond*, 249, 258.

399. *Autobiography of B. F. Pond*, 258.

400. *Hackensack Republic*, January 1938; *Autobiography of B. F. Pond*, 257, 260.

401. *The New York Times*, September 23, 1884 "Rubber Factory Burned in Tenafly"

402. *The World* "Nominated Thomas L. James" February 24, 1895.

403. *The New York Times*, January 28, 1901.

404. Andrew Jenson, "Pratt, Parley Parker" *LDS Biographical Encyclopedia* vol 1 (Salt Lake City: Western Epics, 1971), 83–85.

405. Davis Bitton, *Guide to Mormon Diaries and Autobiographies*, (Provo, UT: BYU Press), 282.

406. Andrew Jenson, "Pratt, Parley Parker" *LDS Biographical Encyclopedia* vol 1 (Salt Lake City: Western Epics, 1971), 83–85.

407. *The Mormon Vanguard Brigade of 1847: Norton Jacob's Record*, ed. Ronald O. Barney (Logan, UT: Utah State University Press, 2005), 354–355.

408. Andrew Jenson, "Pratt, Parley Parker" *LDS Biographical Encyclopedia*

vol 1 (Salt Lake City: Western Epics, 1971), 83–85.

409. "Ships articles and crew lists, 1854–1856, 1861–1862, 1883, 1886, 1892" U.S. Custom List, San Francisco, microfilm # 0,976,995; See also July 24, 1855 crew manifest from San Francisco to Sydney, ANMM *Julia Ann* Reference Files, copy in author's possession.

410. "Arrivals," *Sydney Morning Herald*, August 17, 1855, 4.

411. "Lola Montez and Her Company," *Sydney Morning Herald*, Sept 11, 1855.

412. Autobiography of Captain B. F. Pond, 230

413. Paul Hundley Passenger List, copy in author's possession.

414. "Esther M. Spangenberg," ancestry.com, accessed July 30, 2013.

415. "1860 United States Federal Census: Esther Spangenberg," ancestry. com, accessed July 30, 2013.

416. "Ships articles and crew lists, 1854–1856, 1861–1862, 1883, 1886, 1892" U.S. Custom List, San Francisco, microfilm # 0,976,995; See also July 24, 1855 crew manifest from San Francisco to Sydney, ANMM *Julia Ann* Reference Files, copy in author's possession.

417. Inez Smith, "Biography of Charles Wesley Wandell," *Journal of History* vol. 3 (October 1910):456. For a more comprehensive biography of Wandell, see Marjorie Newton, *Hero or Traitor: A Biographical Study of Charles Wesley Wandell* (Independence, MO: Independence Press, 1992).

418. Andrew Jenson, "Wandell, Charles Wesley," *Latter-day Saint Biographical Encyclopedia* 4 vols. (Salt Lake City: Andrew Jenson History Company, 1920), 3:551–52.

419. Inez Smith, "Biography of Charles Wesley Wandell," *Journal of History* vol. 3 (October 1910):465.

420. *The Saint's Herald* vol 22, p 344 (also in History of the Reorganized Church, vol 4, p 95)

421. *The Deseret News*, December 20, 1906, 7.

422. Family Tree of Glade Nelson, in author's possession.

423. Diane R. Parkinson, "The Maiden Voyage of the '*Julia Ann*,'" 1–2, unpublished paper in possession of the author.

424. *The Deseret News*, December 20, 1906, 7.

425. "Beaver Ward" compiled by Andrew Jensen, *Beaver Ward Manuscript History* Church History Library.

426. *The Deseret News*, December 20, 1906, 7.

427. Lee Drew, "Shipwrecked in the South Pacific," www.famhist.us, accessed June 6, 2013.

428. "Bully Williams," *Irish American Weekly*, November 8, 1879, 4

429. "Register Book of the Names and Particulars of Distressed Subjects of Great Britain," Tahiti British Consulate Papers, Mitchell Library, Sydney, Australia, copy in author's possession, courtesy of Paul Hundley.

430. Paul Hundley personal papers, copy in author's possession.

431. "The Wrecked Passenger of the *Julia Ann*," Tahiti, Jan. 6, 1856, to the Editor of the *San Francisco Herald*, by Thomas Magee and others. Article from the papers of Captain Benjamin F. Pond in possession of Meg Rasmussen, though the *San Francisco Herald* is not dated.

432. Paul Hundley personal papers, copy in author's possession.

433. Evidence that Captain Pond wanted to make his protest well-known is attested by the fact that this document was published both in a "Letter Addressed by Captain Pond to the United States Consul at Tahiti," *New York Herald* (March 17, 1856), 2; as well as Pond's *Narrative of the Wreck of the Barque "Julia Ann"* (New York: Francis & Loutrel, 1858), 33–36. Notwithstanding the protest, in a letter written in French by the British consul to the consul in Papeete, dated December 27, 1855, from Papeete, the British consul notes that the American consul has informed him that Captain Pond "submitted himself completely to the laws of the United States" (translation by Christian Frandsen).

BIBLIOGRAPHY

1860 US Census.

1880 US Federal Census. *Ancestry.com*, accessed May 17, 2013.

1910 Federal US Census. *Ancestry.com*, accessed May 17, 2013.

"Abroad." *Times and Seasons* 6, no. 13 (July 15, 1845): 975.

"Account on *Julia Ann* 1855," *Mormon Migration*, http://mormonmigration.lib.byu.edu/Search/searchAll/keywords:Account+on+Julia+Ann+1855, accessed June 6, 2013.

Adams, Corlyn Holbrook. *The Jose Family: Utah by Way of Australia*. Wolfe City, TX: Hennington Publishing, 1995.

Allen Hackworth Family Histories, http://allenhackworth.com/McCarthy/johnstory.htm, accessed June 6, 2013.

Allen, James B., and Glen M. Leonard. *The Story of the Latter-day Saints*. 2nd ed. Salt Lake City: Deseret Book, 1992.

Allen, James B., and Malcolm R. Thorp. "The Mission of the Twelve to England, 1840–41: Mormon Apostles and the Working Class." *BYU Studies* 15, no. 4 (Summer 1975): 499–526.

Allen, James B., Ronald K. Esplin, and David J. Whittaker. *Men With a Mission 1837–1841: The Quorum of the Twelve Apostles in the British Isles*. Salt Lake City: Deseret Book, 1992.

Ancestry.com, http://boards.ancestry.com/surnames.spangenburg/7/mb.ashx, accessed June 6, 2013.

Ancestry.com, http://search.ancestryinstitution.com/cgi-bin/sse.dll?rank=1&new=l&MSAV=1&msT=1&gss=angs, accessed June 4, 2013.

Ancestry.com, http://tree.ancestryinstitution.com/tree/21495271/person/1092780457, accessed May 17, 2013.

Anderson Family Group Record, courtesy of Marjorie Newton, copy in possession of the author.

Anderson, Andrew. Letter quoted in "Still Later From England." *Times and Seasons* 6, no. 14 (August 1, 1845): 988–90.

———. Letter to Augustus Farnham, February 22, 1856. *Zion's Watchman* 2, no. 5 (May 24, 1856): 75–77.

"An Epistle of the Presidency of the Australian Mission." *Zion's Watchman* 1, nos. 20–21 (October 14, 1854): 153–54.

"Annual Conference of the Australasian Mission . . . April 6th, 1856." *Zion's Watchman* 2, no. 5 (May 24, 1856): 72–79.

Arrington, Leonard J. *Great Basin Kingdom: An Economic History of the Latter-day Saints 1830–1890*. Lincoln: University of Nebraska Press, 1958.

"Arrival of Mormonites from Australia." Reprinted from the *Los Angeles Star*. *Zion's Watchman* 1, nos. 20–21 (October 14, 1854): 167–68.

"Arrivals." *Messenger de Tahiti*, December 23, 1855.

"Augustus Farnham Immigrating Company Journal, 1856 May-August," Church History Library, Salt Lake City.

"Australia.—Death of Elder John Hyde." *Millennial Star* 16, no. 10 (March 11, 1854): 155.

Australian Mission Manuscript History, Church History Library, Salt Lake City.

Autobiography of Captain B. H. Pond, Written at the Request of his Wife and Children. 1895. Typescript, Eliza Goodman, National Archives, Washington D. C.

Barney, Ronald O., ed. *The Mormon Vanguard Brigade of 1847: Jacob Norton's Record*. Logan, UT: 2005.

Barrows, H. D. "Don David W. Alexander." *Annual Publication of the Historical Society of Southern California* 4, no. 1 (1897): 43–45.

Beattie, George William and Helen Pruitt Beattie. *Heritage of the Valley: San Bernardino's First Century*. Pasadena, CA: San Pasqual Press, 1939.

"Beaver Ward." Compiled by Andrew Jensen, *Beaver Ward Manuscript History,* Church History Library, Salt Lake City.

Benson, Jane. "History of John Perkins and His Wife," 1–3, L. Tom Perry Special Collections, Harold B. Lee Library, Provo, Utah.

Bitton, Davis. *Guide to Mormon Diaries & Autobiographies.* Provo, UT: Brigham Young University Press, 1977.

Black, Harvey. *Early Members of the Reorganized church of Jesus Christ of Latter-day Saints.* 6 vols. Provo, UT: Infobase, 1996.

Black, Susan Easton. *Early Members of the Reorganized Church of Jesus Christ of Latter-Day Saints.* 5 vols. Provo, UT: BYU Religious Studies Center, 1993.

Blainey, Geoffrey. *The Tyranny of Distance: How Distance Shaped Australia's History.* Melbourne: Sun Books, 1966.

Britsch, R. Lanier. *Unto the Islands of the Sea: A History of the Latter-day Saints in the Pacific.* Salt Lake City: Deseret Book, 1986.

Brown, Matthew B. *Exploring the Connection Between Mormons and Masons.* American Fork, UT: Covenant Communications, 2009.

Buerger, David John. "The Development of the Mormon Temple Endowment Ceremony." *Dialogue: A Journal of Mormon Thought* 20, no. 4 (Winter 1987): 33–76.

"Burr Frost," *Find a Grave,* http://www.findagrave.com/cgi-bin/fg.cgi?page=gr&GRid=15025278, accessed June 6, 2013.

Burr Frost Journal, October 1852–1854. Church History Library, Salt Lake City.

Bushman, Richard L. "Mormon History Inside Out." *Fides et Historia* 43, no. 2 (Summer/Fall 2011): 2–8.

Cannon, M. Hamlin. "Migration of English Mormons to America." *American Historical Review* 52, no. 3 (April 1947): 436–55.

Charlwood, Don. *The Long Farewell.* Victoria: Allen Lane, a division of Penguin Books, 1981.

"Christmas Islands," *Jane Resture,* http://www.janeresture.com/kiribati_line/christmas_island.htm, accessed on June 6, 2013.

Clark, James R., ed. *Messages of the First Presidency of the Church of Jesus Christ of Latter-day Saints*. Vol. 2. Salt Lake City: Bookcraft, 1965.

Clement, Russell T. "The Shipwreck of the *Julia Ann*." Paper presented at the Mormon Historical Association Conference, Provo, UT, May 1984.

Colton, Alonzo. *Alonzo Colton Diary*, 1855 October and 1856 May–August. Church History Library, Salt Lake City.

Cordon, Alfred. "Reminiscences and Journal, 1839–68." *Millennial Star*. Church History Library, Salt Lake City.

"Correspondence." *The Saint's Herald* 22, no. 11 (June 1, 1875): 344.

Crawley, Peter. "The First Australian Mormon Imprints." *Gradalis Review* 2 (Fall 1973): 38–51.

"David W. Alexander," Wikipedia, http://en.wikipedia.org/wiki/David_W._Alexander, accessed June 4, 2013.

"Death of Mrs. Rosa Logie." *Lehi Banner*, June 21, 1913.

Deseret News 1997–98 Church Almanac. Salt Lake City: *Deseret News*, 1998.

Deseret News. December 20, 1906.

Devitry-Smith, John. "The Wreck of the *Julia Ann*." BYU Studies 29, no. 2 (Spring 1989): 5–29.

———. "The Wreck of the *Julia Ann*." *In Coming to Zion*, edited by James B. Allen, and John W. Welch, 225–60. Provo: BYU Studies, 1997.

———. "William James Barratt: The First Mormon 'Down Under.'" *BYU Studies* 28, no. 3 (Summer, 1988): 53–66.

Doctrine and Covenants of the Church of Jesus Christ of Latter-day Saints. Salt Lake City: The Church of Jesus Christ of Latter-day Saints, 1981.

Dowdle, Absalom P. "Foreign Correspondence. New South Wales." Letter to Franklin D. Richards, July 7, 1856. *Millennial Star* 18, no. 44 (November 1, 1856): 702.

"Early Members of the Reorganized Church of Jesus Christ of Latter-day Saints about Andrew Anderson," *Ancestry.com*, accessed May 30, 2013.

"Early Members of the RLDS John Penfold." *Ancestry.com*, accessed March 19, 2013.

"Editorial and General Intelligence." *Zion's Watchman* 2, no. 1 (May 15, 1855): 11–14.

"Editorial and General Intelligence." *Zion's Watchman* 2, no. 5 (May 24, 1856): 82–83.

"Editorial." *Zion's Watchman* 1 [2], no. 4 (October 27, 1855): 63–64.

"Elders from Zion who have Labored in the Australasian Mission." *Australasian Mission Manuscript History*, Church History Library, Salt Lake City.

E.M. Spangenberg household, 1860 US Census, San Francisco City 6th District, San Francisco County, California, dwelling 309, family 290, p 436 [FHL film 0, 803,067], Family History Library, Salt Lake City.

Edgartown, MA, Town and Vital Records, 28; http://interactive.ancestry.com/2495/40369_264875__0008-00022/10953767?backurl=http%3a%2f%2fsearch.ancestry.com%2fcgi-bin%2fsse.dll%3fgst%3d-6&ssrc=&backlabel=ReturnSearchResults, accessed June 7, 2013.

Eldredge, John S. Letter to George Q. Cannon, San Francisco, April 28, 1856. Reprinted from the *Western Standard*. *Deseret News*, July 2, 1856.

Ennis, Helen. *In a New Light: Australian Photography 1850s–1930s*. Canberra, Australia: National Library of Australia, 2003.

Family Group Record-13, NSW Early Church Records, Vol. 10 #68, St Johns, Parramata.

Family Tree of Glade Nelson, copy in author's possession.

Farnham, Augustus, and Josiah W. Fleming. "Second Epistle of the Presidency of the Australasian Mission." *Zion's Watchman* 2, no. 3 (June [July] 18, 1855): 30–39.

Farnham, Augustus. "Australian Mission." Letter to President S. W. Richards, July 25, 1853. *Millennial Star* 15, no. 47 (November 19, 1853): 766–67.

———. "Foreign Correspondence, Australia." Letter to President Franklin D. Richards, January 26, 1855. *Millennial Star* 17, no. 18 (May 5, 1855): 283–84.

———. "Foreign Correspondence, New South Wales." Letter to President Franklin D. Richards, May 31, 1855. *Millennial Star* 17, no. 37 (September 15, 1855): 590–92.

———. "Foreign Correspondence. Australia." Letter to Franklin D. Richards, January 26, 1855. *Millennial Star* 17, no. 18 (May 5, 1855): 183–84.

———. "Foreign Correspondence. Australia." Letter to Franklin D. Richards, September 18, 1854. *Millennial Star* 16, no. 50 (December 16, 1854): 798–99.

———. *Augustus A. Farnham Journals*, 1852–1856, Church History Library, Salt Lake City.

———. Preface to *Zion's Watchman* Vol. 1 (August 1853–April 1855).

Fleming, J. [Josiah] W. "Foreign Correspondence, Australia." Letter to President Richards, June 16, 1854. *Millennial Star* 17, no. 1 (January 6, 1855): 11–12.

"Foreign Intelligence—Australia." *Millennial Star* 16, no. 16 (April 22, 1854): 249.

"Foreign Intelligence. Australia." *Millennial Star* 16, no. 23 (July 15, 1854): 441.

Freemasons Nauvoo Lodge. "Freemasons minutebook, 1841 October–1846 February." Church History Library, Salt Lake City.

Frost, Burr. "Original Correspondence." Letter to President Augustus Farnham, April 26, 1855. *Zion's Watchman* 2, no. 1 (May 15, 1855): 10–11.

Garr, Arnold K., Donald Q. Cannon, and Richard O. Cowan,

eds. *Encyclopedia of Latter-day Saint History*. Salt Lake City: Deseret Book, 2000.

"General Intelligence." *Zion's Watchman* 1, nos. 10–11 (March 4, 1854): 85–86.

"General Intelligence." *Zion's Watchman* 1, nos. 18–19 (September 16, 1854): 151–52.

Gérald Tulasne, Interview in French (with interpreter) by Fred E. Woods, January 26, 2013, Papeete, Tahiti.

Goodman, David. Gold Seeking: Victoria and California in the 1850s. Stanford, CA: Stanford University Press, 1994.

"Graham Family Notebook." Church History Library, Salt Lake City.

Hackensack Republic. January 1938.

Haines, Robin. *Life and Death in the Age of Sail: The Passage to Australia*. Sydney: University of New South Wales Press Ltd., 2003.

Hassam, Andrew. *Sailing to Australia: Shipboard Diaries by Nineteenth-Century British Emigrants*. Manchester: Manchester University Press, 1994.

Hawaii Honolulu Mission Manuscript History and Historical Reports, 1850–1967. Church History Library, Salt Lake City.

Hedlock, Reuben. "Still Later from England." Letter from Reuben Hedlock to Brother Pratt, Liverpool, May 8, 1845. Reprinted from *New York Messenger*. *Times and Seasons* 6, no. 14 (August 1, 1845): 988–90.

Hindley, Jane Charters Robinson. "Journals 1855–1905" vol. 1, Church History Library, Salt Lake City.

"History of John McCarthy, comp. Stella B. Nielson." Church History Library, Salt Lake City.

History of the Reorganized Church of Jesus Christ of Latter-day Saints. 8 vols. Independence, Missouri: Herald House, 1977.

Hogan, Mervin B. "The Milieu of Mormonism and Freemasonry at Nauvoo: An Interpretation." Transactions of the American

Lodge of Research for Free and Accepted Masons 13, no. 2 (1976): 188–202.

Huber, Leslie Albrecht. "Kerstina Nilsdottir: A Story of the Swedish Saints." *Journal of Mormon History* 31, no. 3 (Fall 2005): 241–63.

Hundley, Paul. "Captain Coffin and the *Julia Ann*." *Signals: The Quarterly Magazine of the Australian National Maritime Museum*, no. 35 (June–August, 1996), 9.

———. "USA Gallery Update." *Signals: The Quarterly Magazine of the Australian National Maritime Museum*, no. 52 (September-November, 2000): 20–22.

Hunter, Milton R. "The Mormon Corridor." *Pacific Historical Review* 8, no. 2 (June 1939): 179–200.

Hyde, William. "On the Death of Joseph and Hyram Smith." *Zion's Watchman* 1, nos. 10–11 (March 4, 1854): 88.

———. "Original Correspondence." Letter to Augustus Farnham, San Bernardino, July 1, 1854. *Zion's Watchman* 1, nos. 22–23 (November 15, 1854): 184.

———. "Original Correspondence." Letter to Augustus Farnham, San Pedro, June 12, 1854. *Zion's Watchman* 1, nos. 20–21 (October 14, 1854): 157–58.

———. "The Australian Mission." Letter to President S. [Stephen] W. Richards, November 7, 1853. *Millennial Star* 16, no. 9 (March 4, 1854): 141–42.

———. Letter to President Augustus Farnham, February 15, 1854. *Zion's Watchman* 1, no. 4 (March 4, 1854): 73–75.

———. Letter to President Augustus Farnham, Sydney, February 15, 1854. *Zion's Watchman* 1, nos. 10–11 (March 4, 1854): 73–75.

———. *The Private Journal of William Hyde.* L. Tom Perry Special Collections, Harold B. Lee Library, Provo, Utah.

"Individual Report for Charles Joseph Gordon Logie." http://www.famhist.us/genealogy, accessed June 6, 2013.

"Jenny Ford," *Mormon Migration*, http://mormonmigration.lib. byu.edu/Search/searchAll/keywords:Jenny+Ford+1856+, accessed June 6, 2013.

Jenson, Andrew. "Australian Mission." *Encyclopedic History of the Church of Jesus Christ of Latter-day Saints*, 35–37. Salt Lake City: *Deseret News* Publishing, 1941.

———. "Church Emigration." *Contributor* 12, no. 12 (October 1891): 441–450.

———. "The *Julia Ann* Wreck." *Deseret Weekly News*, May 14, ———. "Zion's Watchman." *Encyclopedic History of the Church of Jesus Christ of Latter-day Saints*, 976. Salt Lake City: *Deseret News* Publishing, 1941.

———. *Australasian Manuscript History*, Church History Library, Salt Lake City.

———. L.D.S. *Biographical Encyclopedia*, 4 vols. Salt Lake City: Andrew Jenson History Company, 1901. Reprint, Salt Lake City: Western Epics, 1971.

John Murdock to First Presidency of the Church, January 22, 1852. In *Journal of John Murdock*, Church History Library, Salt Lake City.

"John Penfold," *WikiTree*, http://www.wikitree.com/wiki/Penfold-348, accessed March 25, 2013.

Jones, John. "A Discourse." An address given to the Saints in Sydney on August 20, 1854. *Zion's Watchman* 1, nos. 18–19 (September 16, 1856): 139–44.

———. "A Sketch of the History of the Work of the Lord in the Australasian Colonies." *Zion's Watchman* 1, Nos. 32–33 (April 12, 1855): 260–65.

———. "Consistency Against the S. M. Herald." *Zion's Watchman* 1, no. 1 (August 13, 1853): 7–8.

———. "Original Correspondence." Letter entitled "Where Shall I Bury My Dead" written to the Editor of the *Sydney Morning Herald*, December 7, 1854. Reprinted from *Sydney Morning*

Herald. Zion's Watchman 1, nos. 24–25 (December 15, 1854): 199.

———. "To the Australian Public." *Zion's Watchman* 1, nos. 8–9 (January 28, 1854): 63.

Joseph Smith Papers, http://josephsmithpapers.org/site/second-volume-of-histories-series-now-available, accessed May 10, 2013.

Journal History of the Church, Church History Library, Salt Lake City.

Journal of John Murdock, Church History Library, Salt Lake City.

"Julia Ann 1854," *Mormon Migration,* http://mormonmigration.lib.byu.edu/Search/searchAll/keywords:Julia+Ann+1854, accessed June 6, 2013.

"Julia Ann Found on Coral Bed." *Signals: The Quarterly Magazine of the Australian National Maritime Museum,* no. 38 (March-May, 1997): 7

Krythe, Maymie. *Port Admiral: Phineas Banning.* San Francisco: California Historical Society, 1957.

"LDS Passengers on *Julia Ann.*" From Paul Hundley personal papers, copy in author's possession.

Letter of Martha Humphreys to her Mother, December 8, 1853. Mitchell Library, Sydney, Australia.

"List of Letters." *New York Herald,* August 15, 1856.

List of passengers, biographical information, and other notes compiled by Paul Hundley; copy in author's possession.

Logie, Charles. "Local and Other Matters." *Deseret Weekly,* April 23, 1898.

Lyman, Amasa, and Charles C. Rich. "Letters from Elders A. Lyman and C. C. Rich." *Millennial Star* 14, no. 5 (March 1, 1852): 75–76.

Lyman, Edward Leo. *San Bernardino: The Rise and Fall of a California Community.* Salt Lake City: Signature Books, 1996.

Macintyre, Stuart. *A Concise History of Australia*. Cambridge, UK: Cambridge University Press, 2004.

Manuscript History and Historical Reports of the Australasian Mission, Church History Library, Salt Lake City.

"Married." *Nantucket Inquirer* 38, no. 309 (September 23, 1826): 3.

McCarthy, John. "Quarterly Conference of the Australasian Mission of the Church of Jesus Christ of Latter-day Saints, Held in Sydney, July 1st, 2nd, 3rd, and 4th, 1855." *Zion's Watchman* 2, no. 3 (June [July] 18, 1855): 39–46.

———. Letter to George Q. Cannon, San Francisco, April 25, 1856. Reprinted from the *Western Standard*. *Deseret News*, July 2, 1856.

Merkley, Arid G., ed. *Monuments to Courage: A History of Beaver County*. Salt Lake City: The Beaver County Chapter of the Daughters of Utah Pioneers, 1948.

"Minutes of the Annual Conference of the Australasian Mission . . . April 2nd, 1854." *Zion's Watchman* 1, nos. 12–13 (May 6, 1854): 90–95.

"Minutes of the Half-Yearly Conference of the Australasian Mission . . . September 30th, 1855." *Zion's Watchman* 2, no. 4 (October 27, 1855): 49–51.

Mormon Migration, http://mormonmigration.lib.byu.edu, accessed June 6, 2013.

Murdock, S. Reed. *John Murdock: His Life and His Legacy*. Layton, UT: Summerwood Publishers, 2000.

Neilson, Reid L., and Laurie F. Maffly-Kipp. "Nineteenth-Century Mormonism and the Pacific Basin Frontier." *Proclamation to the People: Nineteenth-Century Mormonism and the Pacific Basin Frontier*. Edited by Laurie F. Maffly-Kipp and Reid L. Neilson. Salt Lake City: University of Utah Press, 2008.

New Bedford Mercury 40, no. 16 (November 20, 1846): 3.

New York Times, January 28, 1901.

Newton, Marjorie. *Hero or Traitor: A Biographical Study of Charles*

Wesley Wandell. Independence, Missouri: Independence Press, 1992.

———. "Pioneering the Gospel in Australia," *Ensign*, October 1986, 32–41.

———. "Rosa Clara Friedlander Logie (1837–1913)," eds. Richard E. Turley and Brittany A. Chapman, *Women of Faith* vol. 2. Salt Lake City: Deseret Book, 2012, 196–209.

———. "'Seduced Away': Early Mormon Documents in Australia." *BYU Studies* 35, no. 3 (1995–96): 149–65.

———. *Southern Cross Saints: The Mormons in Australia*. Laie, Hawaii: The Institute of Polynesian Studies, Brigham Young University Hawaii, 1991.

———. "The Gathering of the Australian Saints in the 1850s." *Proclamation to the People: Nineteenth-Century Mormonism and the Pacific Basin Frontier*. Edited by Laurie F. Maffly-Kipp and Reid L. Neilson. Salt Lake City: University of Utah Press, 2008.

"Nominated Thomas L. James." *The World*, February 24, 1895.

"Notice." *New Bedford Mercury* 33, no. 14 (September 27, 1839): 3.

"NSW Death Registration Transcription" ref no. 1866/5905.

"Original Correspondence." *Zion's Watchman* 1, nos. 20–21 (October 14, 1854): 157–161.

"Orson Pratt," *Wikisource*, http://en.wikisource.org/wiki/Author:Orson_Pratt, accessed June 6, 2013.

"Orson Spencer," *Wikipedia*, http://en.wikipedia.org/wiki/Orson_Spencer, accessed June 6, 2013.

Our Family Info, http://ourfamilyinfo.org/genealogyd/getperson.php?personID=I0316&tree=AndersonKitchen, accessed June 7, 2013.

Our Pioneer Heritage. 20 vols. Salt Lake City: Daughters of the Utah Pioneers, 1958.

"Pacific Ocean," *Encyclopedia of Australian Shipwrecks*, http://oceans1.customer.netspace.net.au/pacific-wrecks.html, accessed June 6, 2013.

"Papers of Captain B. F. Pond." In possession of his great-granddaughter, Meg Rasmussen.

Parkinson, Diane. "The Maiden Voyage of the *Julia Ann*." Unpublished document, copy in author's possession.

Parrish, Alan K. "Beginnings of the *Millennial Star*: Journal of the Mission to Great Britain." *Regional Studies in LDS Church History: British Isles*, 135–39. Edited by Donald Q. Cannon. Provo, UT: Department of Church History and Doctrine, Brigham Young University, 1990.

"Passenger list of the September 1855 voyage of the *Julia Ann*," Found at: http://mormonmigration.lib.byu.edu/Search/show-Details/db:MM_MII/t:passenger/id:74047/keywords:Julia+Ann+September+1855, accessed June 7, 2013.

"Passenger List" for the *Tarquinia*, April 27, 1855, Outward Passenger Lists (January–May 1855), Microfilm: VPRS 3506, reel 10, Victoria Archives Center, Melbourne.

Paul Hundley personal papers, in possession of author.

Peel, Mark, and Christina Twomey. *A History of Australia*. New York: Palgrave Macmillan, 2011.

Penfold, John. Letter to President Augustus Farnham, Tahiti, March 21, 1856. *Zion's Watchman* 2, no. 5 (May 24, 1856): 70–71.

Penfold, Peter. Letter to Charles Penfold, Tahiti, February 17, 1856. *Zion's Watchman* 2, no. 5 (May 24, 1856): 77–78.

Perkins, John. John Perkins Diary, 1853 December–1854 November, Church History Library, Salt Lake City.

———. *John Perkins Journal*, 1855–1857, Church History Library, Salt Lake City.

Phelps, William W. "The Gallant Ship Is under Weigh." Sacred Hymns and Spiritual Songs for the Church of Jesus Christ of Latter-day Saints, no. 220. Salt Lake City: *Deseret News*, 1891.

"Phineas Banning," *Wikipedia*, http://en.wikipedia.org/wiki/Phineas_Banning, accessed June 4, 2012.

Pond, Benjamin F. *Narrative of the Wreck of the Barque "Julia Ann."* New York: Francis & Loutrel, 1858.

Pratt, Belinda Martin. "Defense of Polygamy. By a Lady of Utah, in a Letter to her Sister in New Hampshire." Reprinted from the *Millennial Star*. *Zion's Watchman* 1, nos. 22–23 (November 15, 1854): 171–80.

Pratt, Orson. "A Sermon on Plurality of Wives." Address delivered in the Salt Lake Tabernacle on August 29, 1852. *Zion's Watchman* 1, nos. 2–3 (September 24, 1853): 9–22.

———. "Celestial Marriage." 12 parts. *The Seer* 1, nos. 1–12 (January to December, 1853).

———. "Celestial Marriage." Discourse delivered on August 29, 1852.

———. *Account of Several Remarkable Visions and the Late Discovery of Ancient American Records*. 3rd American edition. New York: Joseph W. Harrison, Printer, 1842.

Pratt, Parley P. "Address of P. P. Pratt on the Occasion of Laying the Foundation Stones of the Temple, April 6, 1853." *Zion's Watchman* 2, no. 2 (June 15, 1855): 20–25.

———. *A Voice of Warning*. New York: W. Sandford, 1837.

———. *Autobiography of Parley P. Pratt*, 3rd ed. Salt Lake City: Deseret Book, 1938.

———. "Proclamation! To the People of the Coasts and Islands of the Pacific; of Every Nation, Kindred and Tongue." Pts. 1 and 2. *Millennial Star* 14, no. 30 (September 18, 1852): 465–70; 14, no. 31 (September 25, 1852): 481–85.

"Profitable Farming." *Zion's Watchman* 2, no. 1 (May 15, 1855): 15. Register Book of the Names and Particulars of Distressed Subjects of Great Britain. *Tahiti British Consulate Papers*. Mitchell Library, Sydney, Australia.

"Quarterly Conference of the Australasian Mission . . . January 7th, 1855." *Zion's Watchman* 1, nos. 26–27 (January 15, 1855): 201–205.

"Quarterly Conference of the Church of Jesus Christ of Latter-day Saints . . . January 1st, 1854." *Zion's Watchman* 1, nos. 8–9 (January 28, 1854): 57–62.

"Redlands California Temple," *LDS Church Temples*, http://ldschurchtemples.com/redlands, accessed June 6, 2013.

"Religious Wants of the Colonies." *Colonial Magazine* 2, no. 6 (July 1840): 195–206.

"Remain in Homelands, Members Counseled." *Church News*, December 11, 1999.

"Report of my mission to Australia, addressed to the Conference held in G. S. L. City April 1853." In *Journal of John Murdock*, Church History Library, Salt Lake City. Roberts, Allen D. "More of Utah's Unknown Pioneer Architects: Their Lives and Works." *Sunstone* 1, no. 3 (Summer 1976): 42–56.

Roberts, B. H. Comprehensive History of the Church. 6 vols. Salt Lake City: *Deseret News* Press, 1930.

"Rubber Factory Burned in Tenafly." *New York Times*, September 23, 1884.

Saints' Herald Obituaries, 1885, 143, Early Reorganized Minutes, 1872–1905, Book G.

"San Bernardino, California," *Wikipedia*, http://en.wikipedia.org/wiki/SanBernardino_California, accessed June 6, 2013.

"Shipwrecked in the South Pacific," *Family Histories*, http://www.famhist.us/genealogy/chasrosalogiehistory.php, accessed June 6, 2013.

"Shipwrecked in the South Pacific." *Lee Drew 2007*, http://famhist.us/genealogy/chsrosalogiehistory.php, accessed June 6, 2013.

Silverwood, Jean, and John Silverwood. *Black Wave: A Family's Adventure at Sea and the Disaster that Saved Them.* New York: Random House, 2008.

"Sketch of the Life of Annie Augusta Logie Clark." *Ancestry.com*, accessed August 26, 2011. Smith, George A. "My Journal,"

Instructor 82, no. 9 (September 1947): 415–17.

Smith, Inez. "Biography of Charles Wesley Wandell." *Journal of History*, Vol. 3 (October 1910): 453–71.

Smith, Joseph, Jr. "The Articles of Faith of the Church of Jesus Christ of Latter-day Saints." The Pearl of Great Price. Salt Lake City: The Church of Jesus Christ of Latter-day Saints, 1981.

Smith, Joseph, Jr. *History of the Church of Jesus Christ of Latter-day Saints*. Edited by B. H. Roberts, 7 vols., 4th ed. Salt Lake City: Deseret Book, 1965.

Smith, Joseph, Jr. *Teachings of the Prophet Joseph Smith*. Edited by Joseph Fielding Smith. Salt Lake City: Deseret Book, 1972.

Smyth, Richard. "Israel, Israel God is Calling." *Hymns of the Church of Jesus Christ of Latter-day Saints*, no. 7. Salt Lake City: The Church of Jesus Christ of Latter-day Saints, 1985.

"Society Islands," *Wikipedia*, http://en.wikipedia.org/wiki/Manuae_(Society_Islands), accessed May 11, 2013.

Sonne, Conway B. *Saints on the Seas: A Maritime History of Mormon Migration 1830–1890*. Salt Lake City: University of Utah Press, 1983.

Sonne, Conway B. Saints, *Ships, and Mariners: A Maritime Encyclopedia of Mormon Migration 1830–1890*. Salt Lake City: University of Utah Press, 1987.

"South Australia." *The Argus* (Melbourne, Aus.), July 18, 1855.

Spangenberg, Esther. "Particulars of the Wreck of the Bark *Julia Ann*." The *San Francisco Daily Herald*, March 11, 1856.

"Special Conference of the Australasian Mission . . . May 4th 1856." *Zion's Watchman* 2, no. 5 (May 24, 1856): 81.

Special to the *New York Times*, January 18, 1938.

Spencer, Orson. Letters Exhibiting the Most Prominent Doctrines of the Church of Jesus Christ of Latter–day Saints by Orson Spencer . . . in Reply to the Rev. William Crowell. Liverpool: Orson Spencer, 1848. Accessed online at: http://

ia700404.us.archive.org/21/items/lettersexhibitin03spen/let-tersexhibitin03spen.pdf, June 6, 2013.

Stammers, Michael K. *The Passage Makers*. Brighton, Sussex: Teredo Books Ltd., 1978.

Stayner, Thomas C. "Original Correspondence." Letter to Josiah Fleming, June 18, 1854. *Zion's Watchman* 1, nos. 16–17 (August 5, 1854): 124–125.

"Steerage Passengers on Bark Francis Palmer," Series 82, box 2, "Passenger Arrivals and Departures, 1856 out," Hawaii State Archives, Honolulu, Hawaii.

Stegner, Wallace. *The Gathering of Zion: The Story of the Mormon Trail*. New York: McGraw Hill Book Company, 1964.

Sydney Morning Herald. August 17, 1855. zpub.com/sf/history/lola/Bc1855.doc, accessed June 6, 2013.

Sydney Morning Herald. January 10, 1859.

Sydney Morning Herald. September 11, 1855.

"Sydney to San Pedro on the *Jenny Ford*," *Mormon Migration*, http://mormonmigration.lib.byu.edu/Search/showDe-tails/db:MM_MII/t:voyage/id:189/keywords:jenny+ford+, accessed June 4, 2013.

"Sydney to San Pedro on the *Lucas*," *Mormon Migration*, http://mormonmigration.lib.byu.edu/Search/showDetails/db:MM_MII/t:voyage/id:216, accessed June 6, 2013.

Taylor, P. A. M. *Expectations Westward: The Mormons and the Emigration of British Converts in the Nineteenth Century*. Ithaca, NY: Cornell University Press, 1966.

"The Flight of the Mormons." *The Argus* (Melbourne, Aus.), April 27, 1855.

"The Mormons in San Bernardino." Reprinted from the *Daily Alta California*. *Zion's Watchman* 1, nos. 18–19 (September 16, 1854): 150–151.

"The Substance of Elder J. Jones' First Lecture in Reply to the Rev. S. C. Kent's Lecture on Mormonism, Delivered in Sydney, on

Sunday, August 12th." *Zion's Watchman* 2, no. 4 (October 27, 1855): 51–60.

"The Wreck of the American Bark *Julia Ann.*" *New York Herald*, March 17, 1856.

"The Wrecked Passenger of the *Julia Ann.*" Letter to the Editor of the *San Francisco Herald* by Thomas Magee and others, Tahiti, January 6, 1856. In papers of Captain Benjamin F. Pond in possession of Meg Rasmussen.

"They Were Pioneers." Website maintained by Lee Drew, www.famhist.us, accessed June 6, 2013.

Timpson, Laura Clara Logie. "A Brief History of the Lives of Charles Joseph Gordon Logie & Rosa Clara Friedlander Logie," 1965, typescript in private possession of the author.

"Total Loss of the American Barque *Julia Ann.*" *Sydney Morning Herald*, April 2, 1856.

Tulasne, Gérald. "Un siècle de franc-maçonnerie à Tahiti. 1842–1940: Implantation, chroniques et portraits." *Mémoire de maîtris*, Université de Polynésie française, 2004.

Underwood, Grant. *The Millenarian World of Early Mormonism.* Urbana: University of Illinois, 1993.

Wandell, Charles W. "Mission to Australia." Letter to President Franklin D. Richards, August 30, 1851. *Millennial Star* 13, no. 22 (November 15, 1851): 349–50.

———. *History of the Persecutions!! Endured by the Church of Jesus Christ of Latter-day Saints In America.* Sydney: Albert Mason, Printer, n. d., ca. 1850.

———. Letter to President S. [Stephen] W. Richards, December 20, 1852. *Millennial Star* 15, no. 14 (April 2, 1853): 220–21.

Warby, James. "Extract of a Letter from James Warby, Formerly of the Williams River Branch." *Zion's Watchman* 2, no. 2 (June 15, 1855): 31–32.

West, Barbara A., and Frances T. Murphy. *A Brief History of Australia.* New York: Checkmark Books, 2010.

Western Standard, March 15, 1856.

Wheelock, Cyrus H. "Ye Elders of Israel." *Hymns of the Church of Jesus Christ of Latter-day Saints*, no. 319. Salt Lake City: The Church of Jesus Christ of Latter-day Saints, 1985.

Whitney, Orson F., *Life of Heber C. Kimball*. Salt Lake City: Bookcraft, 1978.

Williams, Welma Hoggard. "Chapter Nine John Sunderlin Eldredge . . ." Typescript. Private papers of Paul Hundley, Australian National Maritime Museum, Sydney.

Wilmington's Irish Roots, http://www.lalley.com/, accessed May 6, 2013.

Woods, Fred E. *A Gamble in the Desert: the Mormon Mission in Las Vegas (1855–1857)*. Salt Lake City: Mormon Historic Sites Foundation, 2005.

———. *Gathering to Nauvoo*. American Fork, UT: Covenant Communications, Inc., 2002.

———. *Water and Storm Polemics against Baalism in the Deuteronomic History*. American University Studies: Series 7, Theology and Religion, vol. 150. New York: Peter Lang Publications, 1994.

Family Search, www.new.familysearch.org, accessed June 4, 2013.

X. Y. Z. [pseud.] "To The Editor . . ." *The Argus* (Melbourne, Australia), April 20, 1855.

Young, Brigham, Heber C. Kimball, and Jedediah M. Grant. "Fifth General Epistle . . ." *Millennial Star* 13, no. 14 (July 15, 1851): 209–216.

Young, Brigham, Heber C. Kimball, and Willard Richards. "Eleventh General Epistle of the Presidency of the Church of Jesus Christ of Latter-day Saints." *Zion's Watchman* 1, nos. 24–25 (December 15, 1854): 185–91.

———. "Sixth General Epistle of the Presidency of the Church of Jesus Christ of Latter-day Saints." *Millennial Star* 14, no. 2 (January 15, 1852): 17–25.

Young, Brigham. "Letter from President B. Young." Letter to Augustus Farnham, October 31, 1853. *Zion's Watchman* 1, nos. 12–13 (May 6, 1854): 89–90.

————. Letter to Augustus Farnham, August 19, 1854. *Zion's Watchman* 1, nos. 28–29 (February 15, 1855): 217–18.

————. Letter to Augustus Farnham, January 31, 1855. *Zion's Watchman* 2, no. 3 (June [July] 18, 1855): 43.

INDEX

ABOUT THE AUTHOR

DR. FRED E. WOODS completed a BS degree in Psychology (1981) and a MS degree in International Relations (1985) from Brigham Young University. In 1991 he earned a PhD in Middle East Studies from the University of Utah with an emphasis in Hebrew Bible. He is a professor at Brigham Young University in the department of Church History & Doctrine. Professor Woods has lectured at many universities in America and internationally and is a bridge builder among peoples of varied cultures and faiths. He held the Richard L. Evans Chair of Religious Understanding (2005–2010).

Professor Woods has produced several documentaries, including *The Soul of Kalaupapa*, and *That Promised Day: The Coming Forth of the LDS Scriptures*. He was also the historical consultant for *Fires of Faith*, a three-hour documentary on the history of the English Bible. His most recent publications include *Mormon Yankees: Giants On and Off the Court*, and *Finding Refuge in El Paso: The 1912 Mormon Exodus from Mexico*, which include a DVD documentary, each of which was published by Cedar Fort in 2012. Dr. Woods is the compiler and editor of the Mormon Migration website http://mormonmigration.lib.byu.edu/ and has authored dozens of articles and several works on Mormon migration. He has a specialty in Mormon maritime immigration to America in the nineteenth century, which has prepared him to carefully analyze the story of the *Julia Ann*. He is married to JoAnna Merrill and they are the parents of five children and five granddaughters.